Craig Weber has done it again. Following up on his first book, *Conversational Capacity*, Weber reminds us that conversation is perhaps the most powerful tool we have at our disposal in creating positive relationships and productive teams. Too often we take talk for granted, and we do not pay attention to what we are creating together. *Influence in Action* offers concrete steps that empower us to be mindful in our relationships and teams so that we can make a meaningful difference when and where it counts.

> —**Frank J. Barrett, PhD,** Professor of Management
> and Organizational Behavior, Global Public Policy,
> Naval Postgraduate School, and author of *Yes to the
> Mess: Surprising Leadership Lessons from Jazz*

Craig Weber makes a convincing case that the most important skill we can cultivate as leaders—the most game-changing, life-changing, world-changing thing we can learn—is the ability to have better conversations in difficult circumstances. Then he shows us how to do it. *Influence in Action* is a practical guide for turning dialogue into a discipline, a map for finding the sweet spot where unspoken biases, hidden agendas, and entrenched positions yield to healthy, productive collaboration. I can't imagine a more essential read for complex times.

> —**Chris Koch,** Chief Marketing Officer, Banyan Communications

I've known Craig for years through our work developing engineering leaders. His ideas and skills for having effective leadership conversations in challenging circumstances were a central part of engineering leadership development. If you're looking to gear up your ability to work well with others under pressure, have greater influence when it counts, and make a big difference in your team or organization, you must read this book!

> —**Dr. John J. Tracy,** retired Chief Technology
> Officer and SVP of Engineering, Operations,
> and Technology, The Boeing Company

I count myself among those who loved *Conversational Capacity* and, after rereading it a few times, was looking for more. Craig delivers it in this book. He expands our understanding of the sweet spot and provides us with invaluable tools for taking our conversational capacity and our ability to be a positive influence in the lives of others to new heights.

> —**Leo Bottary,** coauthor of *The Power of Peers*
> and author of *What Anyone Can Do*

The lack of self-awareness and purposeful communication can ruin any business. Craig established himself as the foremost thought leader on these issues in his seminal book, *Conversational Capacity*. In his new book, *Influence in Action*, Craig ups the ante with additional tools that empower leaders to transcend productive conversations to inspirational leadership. A personal game-changer, *Influence in Action* is a must-read for any current, or aspiring, leader.

—**Drew Fortin,** SVP of Sales and Marketing, The Predictive Index

Since reading *Conversational Capacity*, I have applied the concepts of candor and curiosity in my professional and personal life over the past five years and have seen the positive difference it has made. In *Influence in Action,* Weber illuminates the reality that progress and success depend as much on effective collaboration and communication as on resources and strategy. These truths inspire a renewed commitment to intentional leadership, focusing on what is possible, thoughtfully bringing your team on the journey, and remembering to have some fun along the way.

—**Maya H. Pack, MS, MPA,** Associate Executive Director,
South Carolina Institute of Medicine and Public Health

Everyone wants to make a difference. *Influence in Action* will help you build the skills you need to make a difference that matters.

—**Karina Forrest-Perkins,** CEO, People's Center Clinic & Services

Influence in Action provides a simple, practical, yet incredibly powerful methodology for building your conversational capacity while making a profound difference in your teams, organization, or community. This book will transform the way you think about leadership and how to build a strong, adaptive, sustainable, visionary, high-performance organization.

—**Andy Restivo,** President and CEO, Creative Channel Services

Business leaders can fall in love with strategic planning and flavor-of-the-month leadership approaches. Yet, without active communication, the best intentions can stall and team dysfunction often takes root. *Influence in Action* provides CEOs and key executives the tools and a pathway to become leaders of engaged teams.

—**John Surge,** President, The A|E|C Agency, and Chair,
Think Tank Roundtable

Influence in Action delivers. As a practitioner who not only uses *Conversational Capacity* in my work but also teaches it, this new book is exactly what I've needed. It's not one of those follow-up books that simply repackages content from the first: *Influence in Action* provides both deeper insight into the basic discipline as well as foundational how-to practices to help you build and strengthen your conversational capacity. The insights and skills you'll learn will make you more effective in all your relationships, and you might just find the motivation and confidence to work on those difficult, important issues you've been avoiding.

> **—Chris Soderquist,** President, Pontifex Consulting,
> and creator of SysQ (Systemic Intelligence)

Craig's first book, *Conversational Capacity,* helped me to better understand myself and improve my interactions with others to such a degree that I recommend it as the singular most important text for institutional leadership of any kind. *Influence in Action* takes the ideas and skills he shared in *Conversational Capacity* a step further by providing action steps and opportunities for practice. Weber's work is deeply impactful on an individual level, but more important, it has the ability to transform institutions into places where growth and learning are cherished, and which yield better outcomes for all parties involved. The work isn't easy, but it's worth it!

> **—Krista L. Taylor,** 2015 Educator of the Year for Cincinnati
> Public Schools and coauthor of *Angels and Superheroes:*
> *Compassionate Educators in an Era of School Accountability*

Communication is the cornerstone of culture. I spend over 1,000 hours a year with CEOs in private conversations. The top issue in almost every case is the avoidance of the most important conversation. *Influence in Action* is like a highlighter for *Conversational Capacity*. This book opens doors to successful relationships, enhanced effectiveness, and leadership growth using clear, real-world techniques.

> **—Tom Cuthbert,** Vistage® Chair and CEO Coach, San Antonio, TX

Influence in Action is a critical next step into the sweet spot of conversational capacity. In this new book, Craig details the mental software necessary to eliminate dysfunctional interpersonal behaviors and to bring out the best in each individual. I recommend *Influence in Action* to everyone willing to embrace the daily leadership opportunities that await them and who would like to take their seat as part of a high-performance team.

> **—Tom Van Dorpe,** President and CEO, VCA Consultants, Inc.

This book applies to all aspects of your life, professionally and personally. In fact, once you start practicing Craig Weber's *Conversational Capacity* model, you'll become more effective in all your relationships. It's work—real introspection and growth always is—but you have nothing to lose (except your dysfunctional need to be "right") and everything to gain!

> **—Lynn Marmer,** retired Group Vice President for Corporate
> Affairs, Kroger Co., and former Executive Director,
> The Child Poverty Collaborative of Cincinnati

For the past 30 years my mission has been to help build leadership capacity in line leaders and executives, helping them to create environments where people and their organizations can flourish. Somewhere during the last few years, I lost sight of my purpose. Exercising leadership has been replaced with learned silence. *Influence in Action* has helped me reframe my thinking and reexamine my skill set by providing a structured guide for doing meaningful work and making a powerful difference. This book has given me the desire, courage, and specific actions needed to expand my ability to stay in the sweet spot and get myself back in the game! Thank you, Craig, for such a motivational and practical guide!

> **—Dr. Tony Herrera,** Chief Learning Officer and SVP
> of Learning and Development, LPL Financial

When we launched the Child Poverty Collaborative, we knew we needed to have deep, meaningful community conversations about an often controversial, even divisive subject: the causes and solutions of poverty. Craig Weber taught our 40-person Steering Council how to develop our conversational capacity. Craig's content was so strong and his style so inviting that I asked him to train our entire 120-person United Way staff team in several sessions. Diving into Craig's new book, *Influence in Action*, I was reminded of how important Craig's trinity of awareness, mindset, and skills are to the development of conversational capacity, while I picked up some great new tips for continuing to develop my conversational skills. If you can't have Craig guide you in person, reading and using *Influence in Action* is the next best thing. Better yet, do both!

> **—Rob Reifsnyder,** President, RCR Philanthropic Solutions, LLC,
> and retired President, United Way of Greater Cincinnati

Craig has written another masterpiece that addresses what I believe to be one of the most critical and important leadership/human functions: to communicate clearly, collaboratively, and effectively and influence others to do the same! Since most issues seem to revolve around human beings interacting with one another, the communication concepts and best practices that Craig has so expertly covered will make anyone willing to apply these have more success in their relationships, business, and life!

—**Bob Dabic,** Vistage Master Chair for Orange County
and Best Practice Chair for Los Angeles

Success in today's complex world requires agile and resilient teams. Craig Weber's work on conversational capacity provides practical tools to develop and empower people to meet these adaptive challenges. It's an immensely powerful framework for leaders building collaborative teams and organizations. *Influence in Action* takes the tool sets from his first book several steps further, equipping leaders and teams with additional skills and skill-building to shift their thinking and their behavior to better meet the messiness of tomorrow's challenges.

—**Lee Davis,** General Manager, Rheinmetall Defence Australia

Finally, it's here! As a student of conversational capacity for the past five years, I have been hungry for more ways to learn and practice. *Influence in Action* is just that—a practitioner's guide to sharpening your conversational capacity and getting the most out of your interactions in work and in life. I appreciate all the practice exercises, especially the personal plan worksheet, that help me get clear on the skills I want to improve by creating a focused road map—and accountability tool—to improve my thinking and my actions.

—**Rachel Ferencik, MPA,** health policy professional

Once again, Craig continues to write in a manner that is accessible to all readers, presenting ideas that are extremely practical. If you want to learn methodologies that you can employ to help you develop your teams, then this book will provide many of the tools that will help facilitate this process. Based on excellent research and relevant to current leaders, this book will help you build the conversational capacity of your team, ensuring future success in their performance.

—**Brendan Newell,** General Manager Competency Training,
Logicamms Australia

How to Build Your
Conversational Capacity,
Do Meaningful Work, and
Make a Powerful Difference

INFLUENCE IN ACTION

CRAIG WEBER

Mc
Graw
Hill

New York   Chicago   San Francisco   Athens   London   Madrid
Mexico City   Milan   New Delhi   Singapore   Sydney   Toronto

1 2 3 4 5 6 7 8 9   LCR   24 23 22 21 20 19

ISBN   978-1-260-45256-3
MHID   1-260-45256-5

e-ISBN 978-1-260-45257-0
e-MHID   1-260-45257-3

The views and opinions expressed in this publication are those of the author and do not necessarily reflect the views or opinions of Federated Investors, Inc., or its affiliates.

Library of Congress Cataloging-in-Publication Data

Weber, Craig, author.
Influence in action : how to build your conversational capacity, do meaningful work, and make a powerful difference / Craig Weber.
Description: 1 Edition. | New York : McGraw-Hill, [2019] | Summary: "The author of Conversational Capacity shows professionals how to achieve greater effectiveness—and deeper purpose and meaning—by building their ability to engage in open, constructive, learning-focused dialogue when it counts"—Provided by publisher.
Identifiers: LCCN 2019012597 (print) | LCCN 2019981147 (ebook) | ISBN 1260452565 | ISBN 9781260452563 | ISBN 9781260452570 (ebook other) | ISBN 1260452573 (ebook other)
Subjects: LCSH: Business communication. | Influence (Psychology)
Classification: LCC HF5718 .W4163 2019 (print) | LCC HF5718 (ebook) | DDC 650.101/4—dc23
LC record available at https://lccn.loc.gov/2019012597
LC ebook record available at https://lccn.loc.gov/2019981147

McGraw-Hill Education books are available at special quantity discounts to use as premiums and sales promotions or for use in corporate training programs. To contact a representative, please visit the Contact Us pages at www.mhprofessional.com.

To Renee

and to everyone striving to make the
world around them a better place

CONTENTS

PART III
SKILLS

PART IV
MOVING FORWARD

PREFACE

I grew up terrified of two things: going to *war* and going to *work*. The funny thing is that between the two, going to work scared me the most. I know that doesn't seem logical, but the way I looked at it, going to war was possible, but going to work was *inevitable*.

It all started at my family dinner table. Evening after evening my parents would roll the television into the kitchen and we'd watch George Putnam deliver the news while we ate. As I watched the battle footage from Vietnam I fretted over the question, "Will I be forced to do that when I turn 18?"

At that same table I'd also listen to my dad review his workday at the postal service, often with stories about inept managers, annoying coworkers, and bureaucratic incompetence. I loved my dad, so listening to his stories upset me, but they also filled me with a genuine sense of dread. I knew I'd eventually have to get a job, and from everything I was hearing it seemed like a miserable, soul-sucking way to spend time.

Fast-forward several decades and I still feel the familiar mix of irritation and anger when I hear family members, friends, colleagues, or clients describe the unfair, incompetent, or inhumane nonsense they experience in the workplace. It's frustrating because it's unnecessary, it's counterproductive, and it's just plain stupid.

But at least now I can do something about it. Building on my formal education in organizational development and organizational psychology, I'm on a mission to help people create more engaged, healthy, and adaptive workplaces:

- *Engaged.* I help people do more meaningful work that contributes to their organization's success while developing skills that serve them well beyond the workplace.

- *Healthy.* I help people build and lead organizations that are good for people, good for business, and good for the community.

- *Adaptive.* I help people and teams *shift their thinking to fit a new problem* rather than interpret a new problem to fit their old thinking.

I strive to empower those noble souls trying to do good work, make constructive change, stand up for what's competent and just, and make the world around them a better place. How do I do this? I show them how to improve their performance by treating dialogue as a discipline.

I refer to this discipline as *Conversational Capacity*—the ability to engage in constructive, learning-focused dialogue about difficult subjects, in challenging circumstances, and across tough boundaries. It's being used to bolster the performance of surgical units, flight crews, management cohorts, professional sports organizations, CEOs and their executives, school faculties, CDC emergency response teams, boards of directors, military organizations, community workers, nonprofit organizations, and all manner of work groups. In more than a dozen U.S. states, it is even helping Republican and Democratic legislators work together more effectively as they craft public policy.

But since my first book, *Conversational Capacity*, came out, hundreds of people have made comments and asked questions that can all be summed up by one question: *How do I get better at this?*

- *Can you help? I'm a really curious person until someone disagrees with me—then it's all candor.*

- *I love* Conversational Capacity *but it's harder than it looks. How do I build it?*

- *I'm too nice so I have a hard time with the candor side of things. How can I improve my ability to speak up?*

- *How do I stay in the sweet spot when I often don't even recognize I've left it?*

- *I understand the mindset. I want to think that way. But how do I learn to really mean it?*

This book is my response. I hope it inspires you to build your capacity to influence, and to put that expanded ability into action to make the world around you a better place.

ACKNOWLEDGMENTS

My name is on the cover, but writing a book is a team effort. So I'd like to thank a range of people who've been part of my "team" on this project (and beyond). Thanks first to my family—Renee, Claire, Jason, Bethany, Aly, and Maisie (and our dog Harley)—for their support and patience. They had to put up with a husband, father, father-in-law, and grandfather (and trail-running partner), who was regularly absent or distracted throughout the process of putting this book together.

A lifetime of gratitude goes to Dean Williams, to whom I dedicated my first book and who has been a pivotal influence in my life and my work. I must also acknowledge the late Chris Argyris, with whom I had the good fortune to work and whose research provides a major platform on which this work sits.

Chris Soderquist and Frank Barrett—two close friends and colleagues with whom I've worked for years—continually inspire (and provoke) me to higher levels of thinking and performance. Chris's work on systemic intelligence (*SysQ*) and Frank's work on jazz performance and leadership competence (*Yes to the Mess*) are two additional "enabling competencies" that integrate with *Conversational Capacity* in a practical, powerful, and mutually reinforcing way.

I also have a set of great friends and colleagues who have shared their ideas, criticisms, advice, enthusiasm, and encouragement—many of them for years—and who suffered regularly as I droned on about this project ad nauseam. This group includes Chris and Shelly Ball, Maria and Jim Kostas, Tony Herrera, Mel Booker, Tre' Balfour, Shakiyla Smith, Jennifer Wyatt Kaminski, Kim Armstrong, Bob Noel, Beth Bratkovic, Brendan Croucher, Greg Whicker (who also helped with the diagrams in the book), and Colin Baird.

I'm particularly indebted (the drinks are on me) to Chris Ball, Colin Baird, Chris Soderquist, and, most of all, Randy Weber (my editorial consigliere), for the sharp and ruthlessly compassionate editorial assistance they provided with large portions of the manuscript.

I also owe a bucketload of thanks to the countless people with whom I've interacted in workshops, speeches, and presentations in a wide variety of organizations—especially those individuals who've shared their success stories, their epic failures, their adaptive challenges, their zeal, and, most important, their great questions. They've been a continual source of energy, ideas, and inspiration, and they provide a testament to the power of building your conversational capacity and then using it to address the issues that matter most. This includes the thousands of Vistage members and chairs with whom I've worked over the past two decades; my colleagues at the Boeing Leadership Center where, among other things, I facilitated the Engineering Leadership Program for 15 years; and all my friends at Boeing Defence, Australia, who have taken a dedicated interest in building their conversational capacity and that of the organization. I also appreciate my friends in the "CDC Conversational Capacity Network" at the Centers for Disease Control and Prevention for their enthusiasm and support.

Over the past few years I've also been honored to work with legislators from a range of U.S. states. For the invitation and opportunity to do this work I thank my friends and associates at three institutions: the Georgia Health Policy Center at the Andrew Young School of Public Health at Georgia State University; the Health Policy Fellows Program of the South Carolina Institute of Medicine & Public Health; and the Center for the Advancement of Leadership Skills of the Southern Office of The Council of State Governments. These organizations each provide a forum for demonstrating that it is possible for legislators with radically different political orientations to work together in a more constructive, learning-focused way as they craft policy for the people they represent.

Finally, I want to thank my ever-supportive literary agent, Lorin Rees, at The Rees Literary Agency, as well as my editor, Casey Ebro, and her brilliant team at McGraw-Hill.

Power is about making a difference in the world. . . .
We make a difference in the world by influencing other people.
—**DACHER KELTNER**

INTRODUCTION

The World Needs People Willing to Stand Up, Speak Out, and Make a Difference

> *... insist on taking part in what is healthy, generous, and responsible. Stand up, speak out, and when necessary fight back. Get down off the fence and lend a hand, grab a-hold, be a citizen—not a subject.*
>
> **—EDWARD ABBEY**

Inspiring and leading constructive change is never easy. Due to the organizational equivalent of Sir Isaac Newton's first law of motion, the status quo is preserved unless acted on by an *intervening* force. Put differently, when it comes to our teams, organizations, and communities, little progress is possible unless people stand up, speak out, and make a difference.

There is a growing need for people willing to do this. The soaring rate of technological, climatic, economic, social, ideological, and political turbulence makes the ability to foster constructive change more vital than ever. There is a surging need, in other words, for people willing to exercise leadership.

But let me be clear. By leadership I don't mean someone with all the right answers who steps in and takes charge. Real leadership isn't about position, expertise, or authority. *It's about the kind of work you're doing.* As Dean Williams puts it, someone exercising real leadership is working to "expand boundaries, cross divides, and build bridges to address shared challenges."[1] Seen this way, leadership is about helping people and groups solve tough problems by spurring adaptive learning. It's less about answers and more about questions. It's less about building silos and more about breaking them down. It's less about stroking your ego and more about stoking change.

This work may sound appealing, but there are a couple of sobering factors to consider. First, inspiring and leading such work is *difficult*. To facilitate meaningful change, you must get groups who tend to pull apart to start working together, raise issues others would prefer to avoid, and encourage people to think and act in new and unfamiliar ways. As you do all this you must also deal with defensive people standing in the way of change because their egos—and often their livelihoods—are tied to the status quo. Real leadership, therefore, is awkward, stressful, and scary. It puts you in situations where your good intentions are easily overwhelmed by your need to *minimize* or *"win."** It's challenging work.

But this work is not just difficult—it's *dangerous*. The sad reality is that the people trying to make the biggest difference often pay the steepest price.

The people trying to make the biggest difference often pay the steepest price.

Try to spark adaptive learning and meaningful change, for instance, and you risk being labeled a poor team player, a troublemaker, or a heretic. When the status quo fights back, you're often demeaned, demoted, demonized, or worse. Threaten a sacred cow, and the villagers pick up their pitchforks.

Threaten a sacred cow, and the villagers pick up their pitchforks.

So our world needs more than people with noble intentions willing to exercise leadership; it needs people who can do so with mental and social dexterity, people able to provoke more learning than defensiveness, more head-nodding than eye-rolling, more focusing on the problem and less killing of the messenger. It needs people who can keep their behavior and their intentions aligned under pressure.

This book will help you build that competence. As you work through the chapters, you'll learn to strengthen your mental, emotional, and social

---

* There is nothing wrong with winning. If you are playing tennis or chess, competing to win is what makes it fun. But in a conversation, the need to *"win"*—to be right, to get your way, to get people to adopt your point of view—is often counterproductive. It turns the conversation into a zero-sum contest that cripples learning. So, when I talk about the *"win"* tendency I always use quotation marks.

agility so that when you choose to exercise leadership—whether from a position of authority or not—you'll be less defensive, mercurial, and scatterbrained and more open, purposeful, and clearheaded. You'll learn to strengthen your conversational capacity so you're better equipped to deal with those prickly villagers and their pointed pitchforks.

What You'll Get Out of This Book

In the famous "marshmallow tests" conducted by the late Nobel Prize–winning psychologist Walter Mischel, a child was provided a choice between one treat right away—a marshmallow, cookie, or some other tasty snack—or two treats if the child waited 15 minutes or so. The tester then left the child alone in a plain room with a single treat sitting on the table in front of him or her. Many kids wolfed down the single tasty tidbit, while others mustered the self-control to wait for an additional goody. Simple enough.

But here's what's interesting. Longitudinal research found that the kids who set aside immediate gratification in pursuit of the greater reward (the second marshmallow) had significantly better SAT scores, higher levels of education, greater physical fitness, and lower rates of divorce. It turns out that people with greater self-discipline—who can set aside short-term gratification to achieve loftier objectives—*lead better lives.*

This is an important point to consider as you dive into this book. Every conversation about an important issue is, in essence, a "marshmallow test." It provides you the choice to indulge your immediate desire to *minimize* or *"win"*—the ego-satisfying equivalents of the first marshmallow—or to exercise restraint and focus on balancing candor and curiosity—the purpose-driven and learning-focused equivalent of the second marshmallow.

By working through the pages that follow you'll build the discipline to wait for that second marshmallow in the conversations that matter to you. More specifically, I have two main goals for this book:

- First, to help you build your *personal* conversational capacity—your ability to remain smart, steady, and purposeful under pressure—so that you're increasingly adept at exercising real leadership when it counts.

- Second, to show you how to do all of this as you work to build a healthier and more productive workplace.

Your Personal Work

I've never met anyone who enjoys incompetence, relishes mediocrity, or dreams of lacking influence. Nor have I met anyone who revels in being manipulated, seeks out opportunities to react defensively, or delights in seeing their behavior and their intentions part ways. But while no sane person seeks these experiences, everyone falls prey to them from time to time (often more frequently than that). One big reason: They're all consequences of low conversational capacity.

This book will help you avoid these unpleasant experiences by strengthening your ability to keep your intentions and behavior aligned when it counts. And, unlike many books on the market, it'll take you beyond good ideas to provide clear and tangible skills for putting those ideas to use.

Whenever you choose to exercise leadership your conversational capacity is a pivotal variable that determines whether you make a constructive difference or a bigger mess.

Treating Work as Your Dojo

Like any competence worth acquiring—whether it's playing the piano, performing brain surgery, or flying a plane—building this discipline takes practice. Fortunately, if you know where to look, then places to practice are easy to find. Your workplace is full of them. Do you see policies that subvert your organization's strategy or decrease your team's effectiveness? Do you see a manager behaving in a way that makes their team dumber when their job is to make the team smarter? Is there an opportunity for improvement that is being missed or ignored? Are your meetings unproductive? Are there "baton passes" between people and groups where the baton keeps getting dropped? Are there interpersonal or intergroup relationships in need of repair? Is the decision-making in your team unclear and inconsistent? Are major problems continually downplayed or avoided? Is your organization facing hard new realities that people refuse to confront? Are people clinging to the status quo when major change is required? Are there festering conflicts that generate lots of heat and dysfunction but little light and progress?

If you answered *yes* to any of these questions, congratulations; you've got a place to practice, learn, and grow. By rolling up your sleeves and addressing these kinds of issues, you'll learn to do the following:

- Make any meeting, team, project, or conversation *smarter* than it would be without you.

- Exert greater *influence* and help good ideas get the traction they deserve.

- Boost your *competence* and *confidence* for dealing with tough issues and stressful circumstances.

- Remain *levelheaded* and *learning-focused* in frenzied circumstances that cause most people to shut down or go ballistic.

- Strengthen your *emotional* and *social intelligence.*

- Increase your *mental toughness.*

- Participate in your teams, projects, and organizations in a way that *cultivates the higher aspects of your humanity*—candor, curiosity, courage, humility, conviction, and compassion.

- Transform your workplace into a *dojo* by treating problems as precious opportunities for practice.

- Earn far more than just an income from your work by developing skills you can use in every aspect of your life.

How to Use This Book

This book will help you think differently, acquire new skills, and take more effective action, even when circumstances conspire against you. But it's a two-way street. For this book to help you, *you've got to work with me.* To that end, here are a few suggestions for how you and I can work together to make this the most useful experience possible.

Read My First Book

For starters, please read my first book, *Conversational Capacity: The Secret to Building Successful Teams That Perform When the Pressure Is On.* If you have read it, but it's been a while, I'd strongly suggest a thorough review.

Partner Up

I suggest teaming up with at least one other person who is interested in building their own competence. Then help each other along by sharing insights and goals, holding each other accountable, and keeping each other focused on moving forward.

Pace Yourself

Like a smart new runner, don't try to cover too much distance at once. Focus on a couple of high-leverage practices to bring more balance to your *current* behavioral patterns and then slowly adopt more practices. This is important, for in the same way that novice runners can burn themselves out by pushing too hard too fast, you can limit your long-term learning by trying to do too much in a hurry. It's best to build up your conversational capacity slowly, steadily, and resolutely.

Get Curious When You Fail

Face it. You're going to trip up. You're going to fumble the ball. Sometimes you'll drop candor when you should speak up and take a stand. Other times you'll ditch curiosity when you ought to keep quiet and listen. It's going to happen. Just admit it. When you do slip, the important thing is not to waste the experience by getting overly self-critical and beating yourself up about it. It's better to treat the experience as an opportunity to learn by getting curious and exploring it. "How interesting? In our meeting today I triggered into *'win'* mode and called the sales guy a 'hypo-frontal halfwit.' What triggered me? And what would be a better way to manage my reaction next time I find myself in a similar situation?" Treat your lapses and slipups as opportunities to learn rather than occasions for self-flagellation.

Be Patient

Accept that progress will be deliberate and cumulative, not effortless and instant. You'll do a brilliant job in a meeting in the morning, only to lose discipline and snap back to old habits that same afternoon. Don't worry about it. Adopt the long perspective and focus on the trend over time.

Be Persistent

"Permanence, perseverance and persistence in spite of all obstacles," said Thomas Carlyle, "distinguishes the strong soul from the weak." The ability to remain candid and curious under pressure is a discipline that takes practice to achieve. You must have the mental toughness to stick with it.

Practicing for a week before giving up will yield the same result as practicing tennis for a week and then putting down your racket or practicing the piano for a week and then never again touching the keys.

Use Your Context

You don't learn these skills in a vacuum, so look for opportunities to improve a process or relationship and use them as practice. At the very least, you'll build your skills. At best, you'll also inspire meaningful progress on an issue that matters.

Maintain "Structural Tension"

In his book, *The Path of Least Resistance*, the composer Robert Fritz suggests that creative energy comes from focusing on two things at once: Your *current reality* and a *clear vision* of where you want to go. Both are essential. So be brutally honest with yourself about your tendencies and your current ability to manage them well, while at the same time keeping a sharp focus on the conversational competence you want to achieve.

Take Your Ego to the Mat

To use it to its full advantage, take your ego to the mat and read the book in a humble, curious, compassionate way.* Focus on stretching the boundaries of your conversational competence and on how much you are learning, rather than inflating your sense of self-importance or how much you think you know.

Look in the Mirror

This is as much a *warning* as it is a suggestion: Beware of the urge to use the frameworks for blaming or shaming. Avoid the temptation to critically assess the behavior of *others*, and, instead, look in the mirror and critically assess your own. Yes, you need the ability to recognize when others are out of balance, but *only so you can respond in a balanced way*, not to judge them, mock them, or feel superior. Remember, as you build your conversational capacity, a sure sign of progress is that *your humility is going up and your arrogance is going down*.

---

* For a short refresher on the concept of "taking your ego to the mat," see *Conversational Capacity,* pages 118–120.

As you build your conversational capacity, a sure sign of progress is your humility is going up and your arrogance is going down.

Have Fun

Adopt a serious yet playful attitude as you work through the pages. Then apply what you learned.

Make It Your Own

Experiment. Read other related material. Share what you're doing and learning with others. Be creative. Use this book well and by the time you reach the last page it will be as much yours as it is mine.

Where We Go from Here

You cannot get through a single day without having an impact on the world around you. What you do makes a difference, and you have to decide what kind of difference you want to make.
—JANE GOODALL

To build the discipline to remain in the sweet spot—both candid and curious—in an important conversation, you'll need to strengthen your competence in three interrelated areas: disciplined *awareness*, a guiding *mindset,* and a practical *skill set*. This book will help you cultivate all three areas.

To kick things off, in the next chapter I'll share a story that will set up the rest of the book by reviewing a few basic concepts from *Conversational Capacity* and introducing you to a few new ones. From there, I'll move into the three main parts of the book in which you'll explore ways to sharpen your *awareness*, transform your *mindset*, and build your *skill set*.

Awareness (Chapters 2–5)

This section will focus on the relationship between conversational capacity and three kinds of awareness:

1. *Disciplined awareness.* The ability to direct your attention and hold it on the object of your choice.

2. *Personal awareness.* The ability to train your mindful awareness on your internal state so you quickly recognize when you're at risk of being triggered. This ability, you'll see, is the key to three mental activities: *catching, naming,* and *taming.*

3. *Situational awareness.* You'll also learn to focus on people, patterns, and purpose; on what your team or organization is trying to accomplish; and whether behavior—yours and that of others—supports or subverts that goal.

Mindset (Chapters 6–9)

The mindset is the key to building your conversational capacity because it *refocuses* your attention on clear values and goals that you *choose* to make more important than feeling comfy or being right. In this book, I'll not just show you how to remain more learning-focused under pressure, I'll introduce an expanded set of characteristics that bring more power and concentration to your conversational North Star.

Skills (Chapters 10–14)

The skill set consists of four basic behaviors for making the conversational capacity mindset active, skills that help you keep your actions and your intentions aligned under pressure. To be clear, these behaviors won't rid you of your knee-jerk emotional reactions. They'll just help you act more deliberately and effectively despite them. Put differently, you'll be less a victim of your habitual defensive reactions because you'll be able to *replace* them with the proper skills for staying balanced. I'll therefore help you dramatically improve your understanding of these skills, as well as your ability to employ them.

You'll also explore a variety of ways to turn your workplace into a space for regular practice, a dojo for practicing these behaviors while you're doing meaningful work. Finally, to wrap it all up, I'll help you put together a personal plan for making the learning stick.

One Last Thing

I'm not writing this book as the perfect master of my tendencies, but as a practitioner repeatedly humbled by the power of his *min* and *"win"* reactions to subvert his good intentions. I offer this book as someone who works hard at better managing my emotions every day of my life, and I'm encouraging you to do the same. It requires serious effort, but it's worth it. Why, you ask? I'll give you five reasons:

- First, learning these skills is easier than not learning them. When you lack the ability to stay balanced and non-reactive under pressure, the world is a far more intimidating and frustrating place.

- Second, by learning these skills you'll bring more meaning to your work. You spend a tremendous amount of time in the workplace to earn a living. Wouldn't it be nice to get far more out of your time than just a paycheck?

- Third, even if the organization never improves you'll still bolster your personal effectiveness. In this sense, the workplace becomes your own personal gymnasium for building your conversational capacity; it is something you'll take with you everywhere in life—to your home, friends, community, new roles, or future places of employment.

- Fourth, as you grow more socially intelligent and emotionally disciplined you'll set a constructive example that sets you apart from your more volatile, less disciplined associates.

- Fifth, when you think about it, what else are you going to do with your time at work? I mean, really. If you have to work, you might as well get more out of it than just remuneration, a cynical attitude, a facial tic or an ulcer, and the depressing sense that you're wasting a big chunk of your life. It is better to put in the additional effort to build your ability to converse in the sweet spot, and, in the process, increase your strength, balance, and resilience. You have nothing to lose and everything to gain.

My main point is this: While it's possible to avoid the work of building your conversational capacity, *it's impossible to avoid the consequences of not building it.*

THE CASE OF STEVE

The Key to Conversational Leadership Lies in Your Capacity to Influence

Communication is the real work of leadership.
—NITIN NOHRIA

Giving feedback to a boss is never easy. But it's particularly difficult when the feedback is about your boss's menacing reactions to negative information. You risk falling victim to the very problem you're trying to solve.

In this chapter, I'll set the stage for the rest of the book by sharing a story of someone addressing this very issue. The story chronicles the experience of Steve, a manager who used the conversational capacity skills to raise a challenging issue with his new boss—a risky conversation his colleagues urged him to avoid. But, despite these hurdles, Steve, low-key and studious by nature, and not someone you'd expect to adopt this forbidding challenge, initiated a powerful conversation that sparked a surprising and powerful lesson—for both his boss and the team.

I first met Steve, the new director of operations, at a workshop I conducted as part of the leadership development curriculum at his firm in Silicon Valley. To prepare, participants were asked to identify a leadership challenge that they wanted to tackle and identify a specific conversation required to address it. The problem was to be difficult and nontrivial—something that would have a big impact on the business but tough to address.

Steve chose to address the gap between the espoused values of his new boss, Phil, and Phil's actual behavior. But when Steve shared this goal, the other members of Phil's executive team reacted with alarm. Yes, they agreed that it was an important issue, but they disagreed with Steve's goal of approaching Phil about it.

"Pick something else," one said.

"That's a bonehead move," snapped another.

Another colleague declared that raising the issue with Phil would be "career suicide."

A Little Background

The problem Steve wanted to solve is as commonplace as it is corrosive. Phil was a stickler for accurate, timely information, and he insisted his people talk to him *straight* whenever there was a problem. And this wasn't just lip service. Phil consistently hired and promoted people who would tell it to him like it is. It was Steve's down-to-earth but straightforward style, in fact, that won him the job.

"You were by far the most straightforward person we talked to," Phil told him after he was hired. "Everyone who interviewed you thought you were the person for the role. There wasn't even a close second." Steve was thrilled to land the position.

But as he settled into his new job Steve began to see a disturbing gap between what Phil *said* and how Phil actually *behaved*. His rhetoric notwithstanding, Phil made it difficult for others to talk openly with him. On several occasions Steve witnessed Phil snap in a meeting—rolling his eyes, raising his voice, and firing off a string of sharp, biting questions.

Worse yet, this reaction usually occurred when someone was sharing bad news. Steve recently spent nearly 30 minutes trying to calm down a traumatized project manager whom Phil had grilled in a meeting. Steve learned that there was even a new nickname for Phil's behavior: "The Gestapo Interrogation."

The problem was that Phil's reactions were being widely discussed around the division and people were more and more reluctant to give Phil critical news for fear of incurring his wrath. (Steve actually had someone looking into a rumor that several managers were withholding information about a delay in a critical project for fear of Phil's response.) Steve's primary concern was that important information would be increasingly covered up or distorted if Phil's behavior continued, and that the impact on the business would be dire.

Despite the stern warnings from his colleagues, Steve stuck with his plan, and my workshop afforded him the opportunity to prepare for this important but difficult intervention. "We all know it's a big problem, and we're all talking about it behind Phil's back," Steve said, "so I'm willing to bring it up with him. But it makes me nervous. I know it won't be easy."

The Fork in the Road

Steve's choice reflects the two primary options everyone faces when they see a problem: Sit back and do nothing or take action and try to solve it. While his teammates advocated the passive approach, Steve chose the active one. His willingness to take action was fueled by the attitude: "This problem won't go away if I don't give it a go." The exercise of real leadership always begins with an affirmative stance.

But Steve's no dummy. He's facing a 10/10 conversation and he knows that he's in over his head.* To be effective, he realizes, he'll need more than good intentions; he'll need practice. So, despite all his misgivings, Steve declared his intention to address the issue as well as his eagerness for assistance.

"I'll minimize like crazy if I don't get some help," he admitted.

Developing a Game Plan

In his upcoming conversation with Phil, Steve faces an intentional conflict† of formidable proportions: He wants to *solve the problem* but at the same time he doesn't want to commit *"career suicide."* He also knows that to achieve the former and avoid the latter he'll need practice. But what does he need to practice? Skills that increase his conversational capacity—the ability to remain candid and courageous, yet curious and humble—even under withering pressure.

When I asked the participants in my workshop to break into small groups for practice, Steve chose the two colleagues who were most convinced he *shouldn't* make the attempt. In an impressive, Lincolnesque

---

* On page 107 in *Conversational Capacity,* I provided a simple chart that shows where a conversation sits on a quadrant; on one axis there's a scale of difficulty and on the other axis there's a scale for importance. This conversation ranks a 10 on both difficulty and importance, making it a "10/10."
† See Chapter 2 in *Conversational Capacity* for more on "Intentional Conflict."

move, he picked his own little team of rivals. Who better, after all, to help him prepare for this tough conversation than the two people who are most adamant he shouldn't do it? They'll be his most ruthlessly compassionate partners; the cops to his architect; the coaching sand in his conversational oyster.*

I asked Steve and his cohorts to work through a simple process to develop a conversational game plan. (I'll share this process with you in Chapter 15.) Not only did they practice during the workshop, Steve later told me that he and his colleagues got together for more practice after the workshop ended. He was determined to go into this conversation highly prepared.

The Conversation with Phil

A few days later Steve went in for his talk with Phil. After some brief small talk, he got right to the point: "I've got something I'd like to bring up with you and it's not going to be easy for me to say, and I'm pretty sure it's not going to be easy for you to hear. Please keep in mind that I'm really trying to help."

Phil sat up and nodded, so Steve led off with his *position*: "Phil, I've never worked for someone who's more open about his need for timely and accurate information as you, and I applaud that. But despite your good intentions I think you act in ways that make it really difficult for people to do what you're asking." (This is a clear position expressed in just two sentences.)

Steve then shared the underlying *thinking* that informed his position: "That's very hard for me to say to you, and I'm sure you're not happy to hear it, so let me explain what I've been seeing around here that makes me think we've got a problem, and then I'd like to get your thoughts on it all." He went on to describe the hallway conversations, the reactions in meetings, the coaching he provided to the shell-shocked project manager. Steve even shared the new nickname people had for their meetings with Phil: "They call it 'The Gestapo Interrogation.'"

Steve then added another powerful example. "I was told by several of my colleagues that I shouldn't even bring this up with you," he said. "One person said I'd be committing 'career suicide.' That's how bad it's getting."

---

* For a review of the "cop and the architect" analogy, see Chapter 6 in *Conversational Capacity*.

"My biggest concern," Steve continued, "is that if this behavior continues you'll get less and less information about what's really going on in the business and the consequences could be severe. Again, I know this can't be easy to hear." Steve then employed an empathetic test that was suggested by one of his colleagues in their practice sessions: "Push back on me here," he said, "especially if you think I'm being unfair."

The Reaction

Steve started the conversation much the way he planned. He stated a clear position, provided a lucid account of his thinking, and then tied a bow around it all with a strong test. So far, so good.

So how do you think Phil responded? Steve was using the skills well, so Phil surely responded positively, right? Perhaps by saying, in essence: "Wow, thanks for the feedback. Obviously, I need to change my leadership behavior immediately."

Not even close.

Phil leaned forward and said: "Look, I appreciate that you're willing to bring this up, but I think you're making a mountain out of a molehill."

Is Phil dismissing the feedback, or is he merely expressing a different point of view? Is he being defensive, or does he know something Steve doesn't know? It's easy to assume the worst, but there is no way to really know unless Steve understands Phil's reasoning. To do this, he needs to curiously *inquire* into Phil's clear position. The driving questions running through Steve's mind should be these:

- *What leads Phil to think I'm making a mountain out of a molehill?*

- *What's he seeing that I'm not?*

- *How does the situation look from his perspective?*

There was only one problem. These were not the only questions running through Steve's mind. There were also these:

- *Were my colleagues right?*

- *Am I about to get my ass handed to me on a silver platter?*

- *Did I just commit career suicide?*

With every fiber in Steve's being telling him to smile, minimize, and get out of the room, it took clear focus and mental strength to avoid blurting out: "That's great news, boss. Glad to hear it. I gotta go."

But to Steve's credit (and to the credit of his colleagues who coached him so well) he set aside his *minimizing reaction* and *inquired* into Phil's point of view: "I don't think I'm making a mountain out of a molehill, but maybe I'm missing something. What makes you say that? What are you seeing that I'm not?"

"I've got a steady stream of people coming into my office day-in and day-out with all sorts of problems," said Phil. "You're saying people are afraid to come into my office with bad news. I'll be honest, some days I wish that were true."

A Pivotal Point

This is a critical point in the conversation. Phil's perspective—the way he's climbed the Ladder of Inference*—contradicts Steve's view of the situation. This "cop and the architect" moment presents Steve with a choice about how to respond:

1. He can *minimize*. ("Gotcha. Thanks Phil. Glad we cleared that up. I'll be on my way.")

2. He can snap into *"win"* mode and argue back. ("You are obviously not listening to me, Phil. So, I'll explain it to you one more time.")

3. He can get curious and *inquire* further into Phil's contrasting view.

Steve chose the third option. He set aside his defensive reactions to explore how the situation looked from Phil's standpoint. He worked hard, in other words, to pull Phil's "ladder" into the conversation.

"You obviously see this differently than I do," Steve said. "Can you give me a couple of examples? Who is coming into your office, and what kind of stuff are they bringing up?"

As he listened to Phil share a couple of examples, Steve's view of the problem began to shift. "As I listen to what you're saying, I realize that you might be right. Perhaps this isn't as big a problem as I've made it out to be. But to be honest, I think it's going to become a bigger problem if we don't

---

* See Chapter 6 in *Conversational Capacity* for a review of the Ladder of Inference.

deal with it. Let me explain what I mean and then push back if you still think I'm making a mountain out of a molehill."

The Situation Goes Sideways

Steve and Phil went back and forth, exploring the issue. It was tense, but the conversation seemed to be going well ... right up to the point when Phil snapped. "I'm going to stop you right now," he said. "I'm really getting frustrated here. I feel like you're just putting me between a rock and a hard spot."

Like an electrician touching a live wire, Phil's charged response shocked Steve. But his practice paid off and, despite his knee-jerk desire to retreat, he inquired into Phil's reaction.

"I'll leave right now if you like. But can you at least tell me how I'm putting you between a rock and a hard spot? That's not what I came in here to do."

As clearheaded as it is courageous, that's a great inquiry. And it yielded an unexpected response. Phil paused, set his glasses on his desk, and said, in a more subdued tone: "Alright, look. I'm going to share something with you, but I don't want it to leave this room." Now Steve leaned in.

"Before you came on board my new boss [an executive who came from a firm famous for its aggressive, performance-focused culture] conducted a survey, which included feedback and recommendations for each of his direct reports," said Phil. "I got high scores for the morale in my division. That's good. But I got low scores for holding people accountable for performance. So, my new boss thinks I'm soft on the business, and told me that I need to demonstrate that I can be tougher with my team. Now you're saying that people are afraid to talk to me. That's just great. I can't win."

Double-Loop

Phil's confession triggered a double-loop aha moment for Steve.* The entire problem suddenly *looked* different. Steve, along with everyone else on Phil's team, had erroneously assumed it was a routine, one-dimensional issue: If Phil would just tone down his behavior, the problem would be solved. But

---

* For a review of the concept of Double-Loop Learning refer to Chapter 7 in *Conversational Capacity.*

now Steve realized the situation was not that simple. Phil was in a real bind. If he meets his team's expectations, then he disappoints his boss. This is bad for Phil. But if he meets his boss's expectations, then he alienates his team. Again, this is bad for Phil. The situation, it turns out, was far more adaptive* than it first appeared.

At this point, Steve could have responded with: "Well, good luck with that," or, "Man, you're screwed." But he didn't. He sat there for a few seconds, absorbing what he'd learned, and then he offered a suggestion:

> I think you should bring this up with the rest of the team. Everyone has the wrong impression. They don't see you as stuck between a rock and a hard spot; they just see you saying one thing and doing another. And if you don't tell them what you just told me then things are going to get nothing but worse. What's your reaction to that idea?

To Steve's surprise, Phil simply said, "I think you're probably right."

Taking the Problem to the Team

Phil decided to share his dilemma with the entire team at a quarterly off-site. By this time Phil and every member of his team had attended one of my workshops so they shared a framework for engaging in the conversation that was to follow.

Phil kick-started the day by telling them about his predicament, going so far as to hand out copies of the report with the feedback he'd received from his new boss. He then told his team about his new mandate to run a more rigorous, disciplined business by holding people more accountable for their performance.

> So, I'm in a tough spot here. I really do want people to be open with me, but I also have to show I'm holding people accountable. Steve explained that people are scared to talk with me, especially when it's about bad news. So now I feel like I'm in a lose-lose situation.

---

* For a review of the important distinction between Routine Problems and Adaptive Challenges, revisit pages 7–8 and 182–187 of *Conversational Capacity*, or read the article "Leaning into Difference—The Key to Solving Tough Problems" at https://www.weberconsultinggroup.net/leaning-into-difference-the-key-to-solving-tough-problems/.

The team was taken aback by Phil's candid admission. The IT director openly sympathized with Phil, admitting that she was having the same problem with her own team. (She'd recently discovered people were covering up information about a disastrous IT project because they feared *her* reactions.)

Phil's revelation now sparked a double-loop shift in how the *team* was making sense of the predicament. And it was a problem with which they could all identify. Everyone in a position of authority, in fact, faces the same basic dilemma: You need to hold people accountable for performance and yet you need them to tell it to you like it is. Yet these two important factors can, if not handled deftly, work directly against one another.

The Search for Solutions

It was now the team's turn to feel stuck. They understood the problem in a new way, but finding a solution proved difficult. I was in the room to help facilitate the session, and I chose to intervene. "Can I ask a question of the team on Phil's behalf?" People looked me in the eye and nodded in a "Please, yes," way. "The basic question this team needs to answer is this: 'How can Phil meet his boss's expectations with flying colors, but do it in a way that keeps each one of you coming into his office with all the information he needs to run this business with his eyes wide open?' So, to find an answer to that question, let me ask you another one: To help him do a better job of striking that important balance, *what would you like more of and less of from Phil?*"

The room went silent as the team struggled to come up with an answer. "That's a good question. I don't know," someone finally said.

I suggested we break into separate groups to explore the question (and to do so while practicing the skills for balancing candor and curiosity). The team pulled their chairs together in the meeting room, while Phil and I set up camp at a coffee bar in the hotel lobby.

An hour later we gathered back in the main room. There were two requests to solve the problem. The first came from the team:

> Phil, we don't mind when you are tough with us. We expect it. It's your job. But when you're holding our feet to the fire it'd be easier to take if you used more testing and inquiry. It'd feel more like a conversation than an interrogation. That's all we ask. What's your take on this idea?

To the relief of everyone in the room, Phil agreed with the request. "That makes sense. I do a poor job of that," Phil admitted. "I will try to do better, but in the heat of the moment I know I'll forget, so we need to figure out a way you can remind me."

After a little discussion the team agreed on a hand signal. It was a "T" with two hands, like a "time-out" sign, but that meant, in essence: "Get curious, please, and *test* your view."

The second request came from Phil. It sparked the second big aha for the day.

"Here's how you can help me," Phil said to his team:

> From now on, when you bring a problem to my attention, please bring in more than just your *position* on the issue. Give me more background. Don't make me hunt for it because when I get worked up and start asking hard questions, I get accused of attacking the messenger.

He followed up his request with two recent examples before saying: "Does this make any sense at all? What do you all think?"

Like George Clooney walking into a room full of paparazzi, the light bulbs went off. Up to this point, the team members could see how *Phil's behavior* contributed to the problem, but they were blind to how *their own behavior* contributed to it. But in a flash of double-loop insight they recognized that by bringing a position to Phil without clarifying the thinking behind it ("We've got a problem on the production floor") they often triggered the very interrogation they feared. What people viewed as an interrogation was in essence Phil's *inquiry* into the problem. His aggressive questioning was in pursuit of something people often failed to provide: more information.

Imagine instead, that when a manager raised an issue with Phil, she stated a clear position, *shared the underlying information behind it*, and then *tested her assessment* of the issue with him. She'd be far less likely to provoke an interrogation because Phil wouldn't be forced to ask so many questions to hunt for information. This approach is more likely to produce just what the team was requesting: less interrogation and more *conversation*.

Aha Moments

This situation is a great example of how easily things can go wrong when you act from a blind spot. Phil assumed his behavior was an appropriate way to deal with the situation he was facing. He didn't realize his behavior was creating another problem of equal weight. His team, on the other hand, assumed Phil wasn't serious about creating an open environment. The team didn't realize that Phil was also in a bind, and that simply toning down his behavior could easily create an even bigger problem.

Up to this point no one was taking any responsibility for the issue. Everyone viewed someone else as the source of the trouble. "Phil needs to tone it down," complained the team. "The team needs to toughen up," thought Phil. No one was able to expand or improve their limited view of the problem because no one dared to raise the subject. No one, that is, except Steve. And in the candid and curious dialogue only he was willing to initiate, both he and Phil learned there was far more to the problem than anyone realized. The conversation sparked two big aha moments that shifted not just how the team was *dealing with the situation*, but how the team was *framing* it. Everyone now realized they needed to adjust their own behavior to solve the problem: Phil by cranking up his curiosity; the team members by ratcheting up their candor.

Essential Points

Before we move on, here are a few important points to consider:

- Learning to balance candor and curiosity didn't eradicate the team's business problems, the *minimizing* and *winning* tendencies of its members, or the divergent personalities, perspectives, and roles in the team. It just improved how they *handled* it all. It enabled them to better surface and engage difficult issues and to then get more traction and progress out of their conversations.

- It wasn't easy. One thing about the conversation that Steve wasn't prepared for, he later told me, was how much he perspired. "I was drenched in sweat."

- Steve didn't go it alone. He enlisted the help of tough partners who were critical to his success. Without the coaching and practice provided by his colleagues, it is very unlikely his conversation with Phil would have been so productive because Steve's minimizing tendency would have pulled him out of the sweet spot long before they reached their transformative aha moments.

- Steve's actions were driven not by the need to be comfortable or to be right, but the pursuit of smart, informed, effective choices. He set aside his ego-protective tendencies in the service of adaptive learning and progress.

- Steve's intervention was an act of *courage*: Raising this issue with Phil was neither easy nor risk-free. But it was also an exercise in *humility*: Appreciating he was not up to the task, Steve reached out for help to prepare for the conversation. Then, in the conversation, he held his views about Phil's behavior as hypotheses to test rather than truths to sell.

- It was a skilled use of *candor*: Steve put his views on the table and clearly explained them. But it was also a skilled use of *curiosity*: Steve worked just as hard to get Phil's view of the situation on the table and to understand it.

- An issue that at first appeared one-dimensional and routine turned out to be far more complex and *adaptive*. Rather than "Phil needs to tone it down" or "The team needs to toughen up," the more challenging frame was: "We all need to get on the same page and improve how we work with one another."

- *Steve exercised real leadership*: His willingness to tackle a tough issue, even when his colleagues advised against it, is impressive. No significant progress would have been possible if Steve hadn't been willing to stand up, speak out, and make a difference.

- *Building and applying the skills for working in the sweet spot was the key to doing all this well.*

Before We Move On

Situations like this rarely improve without an intervening agent, someone with the courage to take a risk. But in addition to courage, tackling important challenges also requires skill. It does no good to blunder into a conversation armed with the best of intentions if you lack the capacity to competently act on them.

It does no good to blunder into a conversation armed with the best of intentions if you lack the capacity to competently act on them.

The chapters that follow will help you build your ability to remain smart, steady, and purpose-focused under pressure so that you're able to spark pivotal learning around the big issues facing *your* team, organization, or community. As I mentioned in the Introduction, to build this discipline, you'll focus on three activities: increasing your *awareness,* cultivating a new *mindset,* and honing your behavioral *skills.* So, if you're ready to dive in, consider these application questions, turn the page, and let's go:

- *What are the issues you and your team need to be addressing?*

- *How can you play a role—like Steve did—in helping your team, organization, or community pull together to address those issues?*

Keep these questions in mind as you work through the book because in Chapter 16 I'll help you craft a *personal plan* for building your conversational capacity while doing work that makes a meaningful difference.

PART

I

AWARENESS

For leaders to get results they need all three kinds of focus. Inner focus attunes us to our intuitions, guiding values, and better decisions. Other focus smooths our connections to the people in our lives. And outer focus lets us navigate in the larger world. A leader tuned out of his internal world will be rudderless; one blind to the world of others will be clueless; those indifferent to the larger systems within which they operate will be blindsided.

—DANIEL GOLEMAN

DISCIPLINED AWARENESS

Learning to Control Your Beam of Attention

Though it matters enormously for how we navigate life, attention in all its varieties represents a little-noticed and underrated mental asset.
—DANIEL GOLEMAN

If, like Steve, you want to take action, have influence, and make a difference, there's a foundational ability you need to cultivate. Nurses use it to lessen anxiety and enhance their coping skills. Patients use it to reduce the impact of chronic pain and to maintain a positive state of mind during treatment. Pilots use it to improve their communication and decision making in a crisis. Soldiers use it to boost their energy and reaction time in combat, and to guard against post-traumatic stress disorder. Police officers use it to remain clearheaded in high-pressure situations. Teachers use it to more effectively deal with difficult students, parents, administrators, and faculty. Firefighters use it to build their resilience and reduce stress and anxiety. Athletes use it to reach peak performance. *You* can use it to make your mind more focused and resilient, to reduce pain and stress, and to build your conversational capacity.

What wields such impressive power? *Mindful awareness.*

It's clear that mindful awareness isn't screwball, foo-foo nonsense. It's being used to improve the performance of people in a variety of high-stress roles. Mindful awareness is mainstream.

But what is it? *Mindful awareness* is often explained as the ability to notice what's happening in the moment—both around you and within you—but it's more than that. When you're mindfully aware, you're not just noticing stuff— you're noticing that you're noticing. As one researcher puts it, it's "the intentional use of attention."[1] You're not just aware, you're consciously *attending to* and *directing* your awareness. You're paying attention, in other words, to how you're paying attention.

When you're mindfully aware, you're not just noticing stuff—

you're noticing that you're noticing.

In this chapter, we'll explore the importance of building your mindful awareness—the ability to willfully direct and concentrate your attention on the subject of your choosing—a bedrock skill that provides a base for all the other competencies you'll be cultivating. With high mindful awareness, you have the mental discipline to choose the subject of your attention and to hold that focus until you choose to focus elsewhere. The important concepts here are *discipline* and *choice*. You are making conscious, deliberate decisions about *where* to focus your attention and *how long* to hold it there.

With high mindful awareness, you have the mental

discipline to choose the subject of your attention and to

hold that focus until you choose to focus elsewhere.

This seems like an obvious and easy thing to do, but to appreciate how deceptively difficult it is, try this simple experiment: After setting a timer for two minutes, focus on a single spot in front of you—a doorknob, a light switch, the number 6 on a clock—and hold your focus on that spot with full concentration without letting your mind wander. If your attention drifts (and trust me, it will) to your thoughts, an itch, or noises, simply notice your attention has drifted and refocus on your object. It's only two minutes, right? How hard can it be?

It turns out that for most beginners, this task is extremely challenging. I've heard people refer to it as *painful* or *torturous*. Even in this brief two-minute exercise it becomes obvious your mind doesn't like being told what to do. Rather than remain focused on one spot, it prefers—like a spider monkey on crystal meth—to bounce from thought to thought, and from object to object, in madcap and erratic ways.

Mindful awareness, then, is the ability to *choose* what you focus on, and to *stay* focused on it. It's an important skill. If you lack this ability, your "monkey mind" jumps around wildly as your untethered thoughts leap from branch to branch on the tree of awareness, never resting long in one place. You may *want* to focus on an object, but your simian awareness has other ideas, and it's used to doing as it damned well pleases.

> *I cannot keep my subject still. It goes along befuddled*
> *and staggering, with a natural drunkenness.*
> —MICHEL DE MONTAIGNE

Once you begin paying attention to how hard it is to pay attention, you quickly realize you're up against a formidable challenge. You're trying to focus on a financial report to prepare for your weekly Friday meeting, but your mind wants to think about the upcoming weekend. You want to focus on what your friend is talking about at lunch, but your mind prefers the game on the television behind the bar. You need to be focused on the busy road on which you're cycling, but your mind insists on considering the busy day ahead.

It gets worse. You're so accustomed to it, you usually don't even recognize that your mind is running around like a five-year-old in a toy store. It just seems normal. A door slams, someone bursts into laughter, or the smell of tacos from the restaurant across the street hits your nose, and boom, your attention flies off the object on which you were previously focused. The harsh reality is that you rarely make deliberate choices about where your mind focuses because, quite frankly, your mind has a mind of its own.[2] It's no wonder that learning to halt all this mental drifting takes a lot of practice.

Your Beam of Attention

Here's a big part of the problem. You can't pay attention to everything going on around you because you have such a narrow *beam* of conscious awareness. We all experience life through the perceptual equivalent of a paper towel tube. Take, for example, your focus on these words. You are noticing the page, the font, the contrast between the letters and the paper. Now move your beam of focus and place it on one of your fingernails for a few seconds. Done? Now move it to something across the room—a cup sitting on a table or a doorknob—and, as you do, pay attention to the *act* of intentionally moving your beam.

Did you "see" it move? Did you sense that narrow area of focus you're able to consciously direct? That is the key: learning to notice, direct, and hold this beam of awareness at will. Your ability to do this is the measure of your mindful awareness.[3]

Now try something different. Shift your focus to your breathing and hold it there for a minute. Notice the air moving in and out, in and out, in and out. Don't feel frustrated or discouraged if other thoughts intrude—it's natural; just notice them as quickly and neutrally as you can and refocus on your breathing.

As you do this, observe how the things that fall outside of your beam of focus disappear into your peripheral vision (peripheral *experience* is a more accurate term). Said differently, anything outside of your beam is, by definition, out of focus.

Done? Okay, now redirect your beam to a sound—a bird chirping in the yard or the hum of the dishwasher. Keep your beam locked onto the noise, and, when it drifts to other objects or uninvited thoughts, calmly notice the drift and return your beam to the sound.

> . . . *the faculty of bringing back a wandering attention, over and over again, is the root of judgment, character, and will. No one is [a master of himself] if he has it not.*
> —**WILLIAM JAMES**

Internal Focus

There's yet another nifty aspect of your beam: *You can direct it inward.* Try it. Take your beam and move it *internally.* What are you feeling? Are you tired? Alert? A little stressed? Annoyed that I'm asking you to do all this?

Now as you notice all these things, also notice that you're noticing. You're aware of your *beam of consciousness* and you're directing it deliberately. This, again, is the big difference between *awareness* and *mindful awareness.* I can be vaguely aware of the smell of pizza wafting in from the kitchen, but not be aware of my awareness. I smell it, but I'm not *focused* on the smell. "That pizza smells good," says a friend, and then, suddenly, I'm not just aware of the smell. I'm aware I'm aware. The smell of pizza suddenly snaps into focus as my beam locks onto it.

Disciplined Awareness

Given that people with high mindful awareness are able to make more deliberate choices about where to focus their beam, and then to sustain that focus despite internal and external distractions, *disciplined awareness* is a more accurate term. With disciplined awareness you're able to tame your "monkey mind" and stay locked onto an issue in a more deliberate and sustained way. With *undisciplined awareness*, on the other hand, your beam of attention bounces around willy-nilly, from one thing to another.

MINDFUL AWARENESS	MINDLESS AWARENESS
Disciplined	Undisciplined
Conscious	Unconscious
Deliberate	Fleeting
Focused	Unfocused
Stable	Drifting

Why Is It so Important?

The ability to direct your beam at will is a powerful competence for several reasons.

It's Transformational

Mindful awareness transforms your experience. This stands out in one of my passions in life: trail running. When I run *without* a mindful focus (most easily accomplished by listening to music), my immediate experience largely disappears. I'm out of touch with my breathing, my heart rate, my pace, and my energy level. At the same time, the outside world fades away as I focus on what I need to do after the run, my next trip, an upcoming call with my editor, or a thousand other monkey-mind thoughts. The trail becomes such a hazy, abstract thing that after my run I can't remember entire sections of my route. But that really shouldn't be a surprise. I really wasn't there. My mind wasn't on the trail much at all.

I no longer listen to music when I run. Instead, I've adopted the practice of *meditative running*.[4] Learning to remain mindful transforms my experience of the trail. My worlds, both inner and outer, suddenly snap into sharper focus. I'm keenly aware of my breathing, the feel of my feet

on the uneven ground, the cool·wind on my face, the smell of the bloom-
ing sage, the cirrus clouds in the sky, the color of the rocks on the trail, the
call of a meadowlark, and the joyous meanderings of my dog, Harley, as she
runs ahead of me up the hill. What's more, when the run is over, I feel more
refreshed, clear-headed, and upbeat.

I experience this same contrast in meetings. When I'm mindless, I
retreat into my head—drifting along aimlessly in a steady stream of chaotic thoughts—and the meeting dissolves away. After the meeting I can't
recall much of what was discussed or decided because, physically present
but mentally absent, *I really wasn't there.* But with a mindful focus the conversations snap into sharp relief. I see more clearly both my own behavior
and the behavior of others. *Fully* in the meeting, I'm better at recognizing
when the way we're talking together and the reason we're talking together
are out of alignment, so I'm able to participate in a more intentional and
constructive way.

It Elevates Your Self-Awareness

You're able to observe your behavior from an elevated place of awareness as
if you're up on the balcony. You're also able to watch your own thoughts and
actions as if they are actors down on a stage. In their book, *The Mind & The
Brain*, Jeffrey Schwartz and Sharon Begley write that "... through mindful
awareness, you can stand outside your own mind as if you were watching
what is happening to another rather than experiencing it yourself." Someone with high mindful awareness, they continue, "views his thoughts,
feelings, and expectations much as a scientist views experimental data—
that is, as natural phenomenon to be noted, investigated, reflected on, and
learned from. Viewing one's own inner experience as data allows the med-
itator to become in essence his own experimental subject."[5]

It Exercises Your "Cold Brain"

Disciplined awareness also helps you build your conversational capacity because it exercises your "cold brain." What does that mean? It turns
out that there are two parts of your brain: the "hot brain" and the "cold
brain." The emotional *hot* part is the older, deeper, more reactive part of
the brain from which your potent emotional fight-or-flight responses ema-
nate. The more rational *cold* part of your brain, newer and centered in your
neocortex, is where your goal-oriented, self-disciplined behavior springs.
When these two parts of the brain work *against* each other, they render

you dumber and more incompetent. Why? When your emotional *hot* brain overrides your *cold* brain, your behavior and your intentions swiftly part ways. This explains Daniel Goleman's observation that "out of control emotions can make smart people stupid."[6]

It was the clash of the hot and cold regions of my brain, in fact, that produced the intentional conflict I described at the beginning of my first book *Conversational Capacity*.* When I saw my friend on the playground, in the grips of a seizure and being abused by a group of older kids, my strategic *cold* brain told me to "help out and speak up." But the defensive *hot* part of my brain told me to "watch out and shut up." Because the *hot* brain is older, faster, and more emotionally charged—and I lacked the awareness to catch the conflict— "watch out" won out. I didn't help my friend.

The problem is that your *hot* brain is older and faster, so it enjoys an unfair advantage in affecting your behavior—and it always wants to scarf down the first marshmallow. But you can level the playing field, so to speak, and give your *cold* brain a greater advantage, by building your disciplined awareness. The greater your ability to recognize and resolve the conflict between your *hot* and *cold* brains, the easier it is to align your behavior and your intentions under pressure. As you build your awareness you're strengthening the part of your brain that is willing to wait for the second marshmallow. By so doing, you gain more self-control because your higher level of awareness gives you more choices about how to respond. (You'll learn more about this topic in the next chapter.)

A Foundational Competence

Disciplined awareness is a foundational competence if you're to remain balanced under pressure. Your capacity to control your beam of attention determines whether you keep your *cold* brain in the driver's seat when your *hot* brain tries to take the wheel, and it determines your ability to focus on what *matters* in a conversation. Moreover, to build your conversational capacity you must cultivate disciplined awareness and apply it on two fronts:

1. **Personal Awareness.** The ability to remain poised under stress by monitoring your internal state and refusing to allow your emotional reactions to hijack your good intentions. (This is the subject of the next chapter.)

---

* See *Conversational Capacity*: Chapter 2: "Intentional Conflict: Why Good Intentions Are Never Enough," pages 33–59.

2. **Situational Awareness.** The ability to notice what's happening in the here and now and then compare that with the overarching goals in the situation. With high situational awareness, you're able to assess your context and keep your beam of attention focused on what matters in the moment. You're closely monitoring the fit between the *purpose* of the conversation and the *patterns* of the conversation. (This is the subject of Chapter 4.)

In the next two chapters, you'll see that building your ability to focus more deliberately—on your *self* and on your *context*—results in a presence of mind that allows you to stay grounded, focused, and intentional in situations in which everyone else is caving in or wigging out.

PERSONAL AWARENESS

The First Step in Getting Out of Your Own Way

Self-awareness is the meta-skill of the twenty-first century.
—**TASHA EURICH**

received a phone call one evening from a client I'd been coaching. "Do you have a minute?" he asked. "I'm feeling really frustrated right now. In my afternoon meeting, today, I shot my finance guy in the face."

"Like Dick Cheney?" I asked.

"No. Of course not. He just said something I didn't like, and I didn't listen, I didn't inquire. I just shot him down and moved on. But that's not why I'm calling. What frustrates me is that I didn't *realize* what I'd done until I was driving home. How the hell am I supposed to stay in the sweet spot if I don't even recognize when I'm leaving it?"

That's a good question. You have little hope of staying balanced, after all, if you don't even notice when you're losing it. So how do you get better at catching it when you start to slide?

In the last chapter, we explored your beam of attention and the power you gain in learning to control it. In this chapter, I'll show you how to focus this beam internally, on what you're thinking and feeling in a situation. I'll show you how building your *personal awareness* will increase your conversational capacity by empowering you to monitor and manage your reactions to what's going on in the moment.

What Is Personal Awareness?

Personal awareness is the ability to pay attention to the workings of your inner world—your thoughts, tendencies, and emotions—in real time. If you want to be more disciplined and deliberate when things get difficult—and less a hostage to your knee-jerk reactions—learning to focus your beam internally is the first step.

Strengthening your personal awareness is key to staying in the sweet spot for a very simple reason: *You can't solve a problem you can't see.* Without the ability to control and focus your attention, you're blind to when your intentions and your behavior part ways. In a tough conversation, trying to stay in a learning-focused state of mind without personal awareness is like trying to navigate a mountain road in a car without windows. It's unlikely you'll reach your intended destination.

Mindsight

The ability to focus your beam on your internal world is a skill that the author and psychiatrist Dan Siegel refers to as "mindsight," which he describes as "a kind of focused attention that allows us to see the internal workings of our own minds."[1] This is an important ability. *High conversational capacity*, remember, can be defined as the ability to keep your intentions and your behavior aligned under pressure. The ability to focus your beam of attention on what's happening *inside* you allows you to see when this alignment is at risk and gives you more choices about how to act in the moment. Self-awareness "isn't just navel-gazing," Siegel says. "It's the presence of mind to actually be flexible in how you respond."[2]

To increase your ability to respond more flexibly you must strengthen your focus on four things:

- Your *emotional* reactions
- Your *cognitive* reactions
- Your *bodily* sensations
- Your *predilections, tendencies,* and *habits*

Awareness of Your Emotional Reactions

Remaining candid and curious under pressure is simple in concept but difficult in practice because the emotions that throw you off-kilter are intense and instinctive. Recall, for instance, situations in which you were triggered out of the sweet spot. There are probably times when you noticed it as it was happening. But there are many more times when you caught it only after you were highly triggered, at which point regaining balance was far more difficult—if not impossible. Increasing your ability to monitor your emotional reactions, therefore, is the first step in learning to manage them more effectively.

Space to Choose

"Between stimulus and response there is a space," it's been said. "In that space is our power to choose our response." When your personal awareness is low you tend to react in more undisciplined and impulsive ways because there's little or no space between a stimulus and your response. High awareness increases this gap, giving you more time to choose how to act. "Mindsight helps us to be aware of our mental processes without being swept away by them, enables us to get ourselves off the autopilot of ingrained behaviors and habitual responses, and moves us beyond the reactive emotional loops we all have a tendency to get trapped in," says Siegel.[3] With clear awareness of your emotions, you're better at monitoring and managing your reactions in the moment—particularly your powerful *min* and *"win"* tendencies.

It's hard to overstate how important this is. Your *min* and *"win"* reactions have a scary ability to separate your behavior from your intentions. But because they're your emotional factory settings, so to speak, they're exceptionally hard to recognize and rein in. Without a strong ability to monitor your emotions, you're going to continually experience disturbing disconnects between how you *want* to behave and how you *actually* behave—especially in challenging circumstances.

Going back to my earlier book, for example, I intended to help my friend on the playground but instead I just stood there, watching him suffer. That's a big disconnect. As a U.S. Air Force officer and future NASA astronaut, Mike Mullane intended to land on a runway in his F-111, but instead he floated below a parachute as his aircraft crashed to the ground. Here's another big disconnect. I've talked to nurses who intended to speak up when they noticed a surgeon opening the wrong leg on a patient, but they stood there silently until the surgeon figured it out. In this book, I discussed how Phil wanted his executives to open up to him and tell it like it is, but his aggressive behavior encouraged people to do the opposite.

The more aware we are, the less likely any trigger, even in the most mundane circumstances, will prompt hasty unthinking behavior that leads to undesirable consequences. Rather than operate on autopilot, we'll slow down time to think it over and make a more considered choice.

—MARSHALL GOLDSMITH

These examples all highlight the same problem: When you combine low personal awareness and a triggering event, you're in big trouble. Your blindness makes you reactive, weak, and incompetent. Poorly managed emotions make smart people *act* stupid.

With high personal awareness, however, you can monitor what's going on in your mind. This gives you what psychologists refer to as *cognitive control,* which results in greater mental strength and behavioral competence. The ability to recognize and manage emotions helps smart people *act* smart.

The ability to recognize and manage emotions helps smart people act smart.

Operationalized Emotional Intelligence

When it comes to keeping your actions and your intentions in sync, this ability to focus your beam of attention on your emotional reactions separates the wheat from the chaff. Contrast the executive who only noticed his *"win"* reaction on the drive home after his afternoon meeting, for instance, with Steve in his conversation with Phil. When Phil challenged him, Steve *felt* like running away, but his higher personal awareness allowed him to catch this defensive reaction and behave more consistently with his intentions.

Low personal awareness renders you chronically incompetent because you never recognize when or how you're getting in your own way. You're little more than a conversational crash test dummy repeatedly smashing into emotional walls of your own making. This explains why conversational capacity has been described as *operationalized emotional intelligence*. Noticing a feeling as it wells up, and then intentionally managing it, is a primary skill of someone with high emotional quotient (EQ). Conversational capacity, therefore, can be defined in another way:

It is the ability to recognize and manage your emotional reactions under pressure.

The key to all this is cultivating your "observer self," the part of your mind that is up on your mental balcony observing the part of your mind that is down on the dance floor doing its thing. The ability to focus your beam internally allows you to recognize when you're leaving the sweet spot *before* you react like a conversational puppet, with your behavioral strings pulled by your defensive tendencies. With low personal awareness, you're little more than a marionette behaving at the mercy of your puppet-master emotions.

―――――――→ ● ←―――――――

With low personal awareness, you're little more than a marionette behaving at the mercy of your puppet-master emotions.

―――――――→ ● ←―――――――

Zoom In, Zoom Out

In her book, *Insight*, Tasha Eurich describes her experience of identifying an emotional reaction before she acted on it. She was dealing with an airline gate agent, Bob, after a frustrating day trying to get to Hong Kong. For hours, the airline kept boarding and deplaning the passengers until the flight was finally canceled. Furious, Tasha approached Bob, who had been catching flak from many of the flight's unhappy passengers. She was ready to lay into him.

"Luckily I'd recently learned about a tool developed by psychologist Richard Weissbourd called 'Zoom In, Zoom Out,'" she writes. "To successfully take others' perspectives in highly charged situations, Weissbourd advises we should start by 'zooming in' on our perspective to better understand it. So, I zoomed in: *I'm hungry, tired, and furious at the airline for its mechanical ineptitude.* Next, we should 'zoom out' and consider the perspective of the other person. When I imagined what Bob was experiencing, I thought, *Poor Bob. I wonder what his day has been like.*" She then reflects on how she reacted:

> "Were you scheduled to work this evening?" I asked. "No, ma'am," he instantly responded, pointing to his colleagues, "All four of us were heading home for the evening but were called back in. I was supposed to pick up my kids from school because my wife is out of town. I'll probably be here until ten p.m." I'd been feeling pretty sorry for myself, but now I felt even worse for Bob.[4]

Tasha's story is a perfect example of high emotional awareness—the power of having enough space between stimulus and response to choose your actions rather than letting your emotions make the choice for you.

Awareness of Your Cognitive Reactions

With high personal awareness you're not just noticing your emotional reactions in the moment, you're also scrutinizing your *cognitive reactions*—how you're making sense of what's going on around you. This is important for two reasons:

- First, recognizing you are jumping to a conclusion makes it easier to hold your views of "reality" hypothetically, to question and test them, and to inquire into the views of others. Being conscious of the leaps of logic that your mind is making increases your intellectual agility and humility.

- Second, your cognitive and emotional reactions are interrelated. How you frame affects how you emote.

Take for example, Stephen R. Covey's experience one morning on a New York City subway:

People were sitting quietly—some reading newspapers, some lost in thought, some resting with their eyes closed. It was a calm, peaceful scene.

Then suddenly, a man and his children entered the subway car. The children were so loud and rambunctious that instantly the whole climate changed.

The man sat down next to me and closed his eyes, apparently oblivious to the situation. The children were yelling back and forth, throwing things, even grabbing people's papers. It was very disturbing. And yet, the man sitting next to me did nothing.

It was difficult not to feel irritated. I could not believe that he could be so insensitive as to let his children run wild like that and do nothing about it, taking no responsibility at all. It was easy to see that everyone else on the subway felt irritated, too. So finally, with what I felt like was unusual patience and restraint, I turned to him and said, "Sir, your children are really disturbing a lot of people. I wonder if you couldn't control them a little more?"

The man lifted his gaze as if to come to a consciousness of the situation for the first time and said softly, "Oh, you're right. I guess I should do something about it. We just came from the hospital where their mother died about an hour ago. I don't know what to think, and I guess they don't know how to handle it either."

Can you imagine what I felt at that moment? My paradigm shifted. Suddenly I saw things differently, and because I saw differently, I thought differently, I felt differently, I behaved differently. My irritation vanished. I didn't have to worry about controlling my attitude or my behavior; my heart was filled with the man's pain. Feelings of sympathy and compassion flowed freely. "Your wife just died? Oh I'm so sorry! Can you tell me about it? What can I do to help?" Everything changed in an instant.[5]

Covey's initial emotional reactions, irritation and anger, were the product of his cognitive reactions—how he was *interpreting* the situation: "This is an irresponsible father who obviously doesn't care if his kids are bothering other people on the train." But after his paradigm shift, his response changed to compassion and concern. His story is a great example of the classic observation by Epictetus: "People are not disturbed by things, but by the view they take of them."

Framing also played a key role in Steve's willingness to engage Phil. Steve framed the predicament, as risky, but he believed he could make a difference. This encouraged him to speak out. His colleagues, however, interpreted the same predicament very differently. They saw Steve's willingness to engage the issue as "career suicide."

With all this in mind, when you catch an emotional reaction, ask yourself this question: "What is it about the way I'm framing the situation that may be leading me to react this way?"

Awareness of Your Bodily Sensations

With high personal awareness, you're also conscious of your physical condition. "Our first five senses allow us to perceive the outside world—to hear a bird's song or a snake's warning rattle, to make our way down a busy street or smell the warming earth of spring," says Dan Siegel. "What has been called our sixth sense allows us to perceive our internal bodily states—the quickly beating heart that signals fear or excitement, the sensation of butterflies in our stomach, the pain that demands our attention."[6] When your sixth sense is strong you notice when you are hungry, weary, stressed, jet-lagged, tense, nauseous, or in pain. So you can take responsibility for mindfully managing these states rather than letting them mindlessly manage you.

What You Bring to the Table

You're also taking into account the general predilections and habits you bring to any situation or conversation. So you're able to manage them responsibly. These include:

- *Your personality traits.* Are you generally pessimistic or optimistic? Open to new and conflicting ideas? Or do you prefer the familiar? ("I'm low on openness to new experience, and pessimistic, so I need to monitor my negative reactions to different ideas. . . ." Or, "I'm a strong introvert so speaking up candidly is something on which I need to focus.")

- *Your habitual behaviors.* You're aware of your behavioral tendencies. ("I tend to acquiesce when someone disagrees with me." Or, "I tend to get hostile when someone challenges my view.")

- *Your filters.* You recognize how such factors as your training, education, or experience create a unique lens through which you tend to see the world. ("I'm a finance person so I tend to see decisions through a narrow finance lens." Or, "I went through a calamitous merger once and that experience may cloud my judgment about this one." Or "Trained as an engineer, I tend to bring a strongly risk-averse disposition to most problems and decisions.")

- *Key triggers.* You're conscious of the issues and situations that often provoke your *min* or "*win*" reactions. ("I hate to feel stupid, so I tend to react sharply when someone suggests I don't know what I'm talking about.")

The Basic Discipline:
Catching, Naming, and Taming

Self-awareness, according to Tasha Eurich, the author of *Insight*, "is the meta-skill of the twenty-first century."[7] It's certainly a meta-skill when it comes to staying in the sweet spot because it's the key to the first three steps in the basic discipline of conversational capacity: catching, naming, and taming.

Catching

We have to beware the trapdoors of the self.
—WAYNE SHORTER

Catching your *min* and *"win"* reactions before they dictate how you think and how you act is the first step. You want to cultivate this ability because of a point I failed to stress in my first book: The *distance* from the sweet spot represents the intensity of the reaction. The further you get from the sweet spot, the more severely you've been triggered. So, the ability to catch a reaction quickly gives you greater control over your response. It's easier to regain balance when you've just barely been triggered than when the sweet spot is a mere speck in the distance.

Catching it early is also vital because of what psychologists refer to as "emotional flooding." When you're emotionally flooded, your *rational mind*—based in the neocortex and the source of your good intentions—is inundated by intense feelings generated in a deeper and older part of your brain. "The difference between flooding and more manageable experiences of our emotions is one of magnitude," says Stephanie Manes at the Gottman Institute. "You reach the point when your thinking brain . . . is shut out."[8]

There's little power in making the observation, "Well, it appears I've been triggered," as you're shrieking at your colleague across the conference table. You have far more power, on the other hand, when you're able to catch the reaction quickly: "I can feel my *'win'* tendency starting to tug at me. I need to keep an eye on that or I risk slipping out of the sweet spot."

*Emotional reactivity starts as a tightening. There's the familiar tug
and before we know it, we're pulled along. In just a few seconds, we go
from being slightly miffed to completely out of control. Nevertheless, we
have the inherent wisdom and ability to halt this chain reaction early
on. To the degree that we're attentive, we can nip the addictive urge
while it's still manageable. Just as we're about to step into the trap, we
can at least pause and take some deep breaths before proceeding.*

—PEMA CHÖDRÖN

Here is why all of this matters. With high internal awareness you're con-sciously monitoring your emotional state so you quickly *recognize* when your defensive, anti-learning tendencies are triggered and you're in danger of losing balance. This is simple to state but hard to do. These reactions are so automatic, and you're so used to them, that you often don't realize you've been triggered until it's too late. Chris Argyris referred to this problem—where your habitual, practiced, automatic behaviors work against your genuine intentions—as "skilled incompetence."[9] Increasing your personal awareness, therefore, is the first step in moving from skillfully incompe-tent reactions to skillfully competent actions. Your goal is to *catch it* when you're barely out of balance, or better still, to notice when you're at risk of losing balance.

Naming and Taming

Noticing is only the first step. Once you *catch* the emotional cues that a tendency is being triggered, the next step is to label it, to give the reaction a *name*:

"Ah, there's my need to *minimize* trying to shut me down," or "There's my craving to *'win'* telling me what to do."

This seemingly minor step yields major results. Research shows that labeling your tendency generates *more* self-control. That's right, simply giv-ing your reaction a name gives you more power over it. Psychologists refer to this as "naming and taming."

*We are not primitive sea slugs responding with twitchy movements
whenever we're poked with a needle. We have brain cells. We can think.*

—MARSHALL GOLDSMITH

The increase in self-discipline you gain from labeling your emotions comes from a specific part of your brain, which Dr. Matthew Lieberman, a neuroscientist at UCLA, describes as the "brain's braking system."[10] He explains why *affect labeling*—giving your emotional reactions a name— helps you manage them more effectively.

"In the same way you hit the brake when you're driving when you see a yellow light," Lieberman says, "when you put feelings into words, you seem to be hitting the brakes on your emotional responses." Labeling a reaction activates your brain's braking system, giving you more emotional control. "Putting feelings into words," says Lieberman, "is a form of emotion regulation."

The brain's braking system—based in the right ventrolateral prefrontal cortex—helps you remain on track in pursuit of a goal even when you're tempted to stray off-path. It's a critical discipline. "Self-control allows us to persist in the face of other appealing options," Lieberman explains, "and to adapt rather than being slaves to our impulses."

This is not a big secret. "Parents and teachers have long told children to 'use your words' because it is assumed to help calm the children down when they are overly emotional or over-aroused. It turns out this is surprisingly good advice," Lieberman argues, ". . . putting feelings into words serves as an unexpected gateway into the brain's braking system, setting self-control processes in motion without the individual intentionally trying to engage in self-control."

Your braking system is responsible for all aspects of self–control, from eating the carrot sticks rather than the glazed donut, to running on a cold morning rather than staying in your warm bed, to listening to someone with a view that clashes with your own view rather than arguing with them, to reining in your emotional reactions when you feel like letting them loose. Your emotional reactions work like an accelerator. Without brakes, you're going to careen out of control. It is your brain's braking system that enables you to wait for that second marshmallow in tough conversations.

Your emotional reactions work like an accelerator.

Without brakes, you're going to careen out of control.

There's yet another reason that *naming and taming* helps you stay out of your own way: Labeling your emotional reactions actually makes them less intense.[11] It turns out that naming an emotional reaction has a dampening effect, which makes the reaction easier to control, and control is the essence of discipline. This explains why mindfulness is so essential; you won't know to hit the brakes if you can't see the need. And without the ability to brake when appropriate your emotional reactions will continue to accelerate and drive you further away from your effectiveness.

Here's even more good news. Just by building your *disciplined awareness* you bolster your ability to brake. It appears, says Lieberman, that you can "strengthen the impact of putting feelings into words through mindful meditative practice." How does this work? "Mindfulness involves a non-judgmental awareness of what one is thinking, feeling, and experiencing, which bears some strong resemblances to affect labeling."[12]

This is particularly true with your *min* and *"win"* reactions because, due to their limbic, fight-or-flight origins, they're extra hard to restrain. "When we are in the grip of craving or fury, . . . or recoiling in dread," says Daniel Goleman, it is the limbic system that has us in its grip."[13] So it's best to brake early—by *catching, naming,* and *taming*—before your limbic reactions hijack your good intentions.

How Catching, Naming, and Taming All Work Together

Imagine that you are in a meeting at the end of a long, stressful week, when a colleague attacks your idea in a snide and pompous way. If you lack the ability to focus your beam internally, your mind shifts into a reactive gear. Insulted and incensed, you adopt a venomous, victim-minded focus on the injustice.

"Who does this guy think he is? That was totally out of line. What a jerk," you say to yourself. "He did this three weeks ago to Hiromi, too. Cretins like this should be fired. And why doesn't our spineless manager step in and say something? I'm so sick of this nonsense I could just explode."

With each thought, a tsunami of negative sentiment grows, moving you from a deliberate and focused state of mind to a highly reactive and ego-driven state. You're increasingly out of control. You lose power. (Remember the old Lexus commercial: "The ultimate expression of power is control.") Simply stated, you don't have your emotions; your emotions have you.

Finally, it all comes bursting out in a stream of ugliness. "You self-centered jerk! Keep your bonehead opinions to yourself. No one on this team gives a flying fox what you think."

But now imagine you've built up your ability to focus your beam of attention on your inner world. The comment and your initial reaction are the same, but you *respond* differently. First, you *catch* your initial reaction—that burst of negative feelings after the comment telling you to attack back. You then *name* the reaction you're having—"There's my *'win'* tendency telling me to attack this guy." The mere process of seeing and labeling eases the tension you're feeling, and as the tension dissipates, you're able to *refocus* on your real objective: participating productively in the meeting. As your emotional reactions accelerate, your mind sees the crash coming and pumps the brakes.

This is how *catching*, *naming*, and *taming* all work together. You don't allow your thoughts and behaviors to take off down the track like a runaway train on a downhill slope, hauling your effectiveness off with it. By exercising your ability to pull back to your deliberate focus of attention, you're expressing the power to recognize and control your emotional reactions. You have your emotions; your emotions don't have you.

Proactive Trigger Scanning

It gets better. With clear mindsight, you're not only more conscious of your tendencies, you're better at spotting the situations, people, issues, and behaviors that set them off in the first place. Like a trail runner scanning for roots, rocks, and rattlesnakes on the unfolding trail ahead, you're better equipped to recognize and avoid your defensive triggers and ego traps *before* you trip over them. You're proactively scanning for potential pitfalls because you can only avoid an obstacle if you can first see it. This means that while *proactive* trigger scanning requires high personal awareness, it also requires high situational awareness, something we'll talk about in the next chapter.

The Why

Learning to focus your beam of attention on your internal world is hard work that many people would rather avoid. "For most people, it's easier to choose self-delusion—the antithesis of self-awareness—over the cold, hard truth," says Tasha Eurich. But she goes on to explain why it's worth the effort:

> There is strong scientific evidence that people who know themselves and how others see them are happier. They make smarter

decisions. They have better personal and professional relationships. They raise more mature children. They're smarter, superior students who choose better careers. They're more creative, more confident, and better communicators. They're less aggressive and less likely to lie, cheat, and steal. They're better performers at work who get more promotions. They're more effective leaders with more enthusiastic employees. They even lead more profitable companies.[14]

They also have higher conversational capacity. So, if you want to build your ability to stay in the sweet spot—and then use that ability to wield greater influence and make a bigger difference—you'll need to make the deliberate choice of self-awareness over self-delusion.

SITUATIONAL AWARENESS

Paying Attention to People, Patterns, and Purpose

Situational Awareness is the ability to identify, process, and comprehend the critical elements of information about what is happening to the team with regards to the mission. More simply, it's knowing what is going on around you.
—**U.S. COAST GUARD TRAINING MANUAL**

In the last two chapters, we explored the importance of *disciplined* awareness and *personal* awareness. But if you're to act effectively under pressure you must also cultivate your *situational* awareness, the ability to direct your beam of attention on what's happening around you. You're not improving your conversational capacity just for the fun of it, after all. You're building it to expand your ability to respond to difficult people, issues, and circumstances in a more disciplined, learning-focused way. To do this well, you not only need to be focused on your own internal machinations; you also need to be aware of the behavior of others and the larger context in which it's all unfolding.

To show why this matters, let me repeat the brilliant line from the jazz percussionist Airto Moreira that I shared in my first book: when it comes to playing jazz, he said, "I listen to what's being played, and then I play what's missing."[1] When you are trying to make a constructive difference in a meeting or conversation, you're doing the same thing—watching what's being played and playing what's missing. And there's no way to do this well if you're not sure of what's going on in the first place.

—————— ● ⬅——————

"I listen to what's being played, and then I play what's missing."

—————— ● ⬅——————

Becoming more contextually conscious requires that you learn to focus on two things:

1. **People.** Focus on how others are participating (or not participating) in a conversation—on their behavior, goals, concerns, thoughts, and feelings.

2. **The fit between *patterns* and *purpose*.** Focus on the alignment (or the lack of it) between the patterns of behavior in a situation and the purpose of that situation.

For a commanding example of the importance of paying attention to people, patterns, and purpose, consider the story of Lt. Col. Chris Hughes:

In April 2003, Lt. Col. Hughes led soldiers from the 101st Airborne toward Najaf, one of the holy cities in Iraq, to secure the town and protect two things: the Ali Shrine, the purported burial site for Noah and Adam; and the Grand Ayatollah Sistani, a Shia cleric who had been put under house arrest by Saddam Hussein.

As he and 200 of his men approached the ayatollah's home, conditions were perfect. The ayatollah knew they were coming, and the crowd was friendly.

But suddenly everything changed. Unknown to him, Baathist agitators had begun to circulate the claim that the Americans weren't there to protect their religious leader; they there were there to invade the mosque. In a matter of seconds, the friendly crowd became angry, shouting, "In city 'yes.' In city 'OK.' Mosque 'NO!' "

More people gathered. The crowd began to surge toward the troops. Rocks began to fly. Hughes's troops, who hadn't slept in two or three days, were tense and armed to the teeth. A bloodbath seemed imminent.

Everyone knew that Hughes's response would color the way the Iraqis would view the American forces from that day on.

It's hard to imagine a situation with graver stakes and higher stress than this. It could turn deadly in a flash. With such an elevated level of misunderstanding and agitation, in fact, there was probably a greater likelihood of violence than not. But in this intense, high-stakes moment, Lt. Col. Hughes responded in a remarkable way:

In the midst of all the agitation, he raised his rifle upside down, to indicate that he had no intention of firing it.

Then, he told his men to take a knee. They must have wondered what in the world he was doing, but they trusted him. And 200 soldiers took a knee.

Then he told them to lower their weapons and SMILE. And they did. The crowd quieted, and some began to smile back.

Finally, he told his warriors to back up, turn around, and walk away. As a last gesture, he placed his flat hand against his heart in the traditional Islamic gesture meaning "peace be with you." He said, "Have a nice day," and walked away . . .

Later on, once the confusion was cleared up and the agitators were removed, they entered Najaf peacefully. Mission accomplished.[2]

The actions of Lt. Col. Hughes provide a stellar example of why situational awareness is so essential. Even under withering pressure Lt. Col. Hughes focused his beam of attention on how both the villagers and his troops were responding to the situation—their behavior, tone, and mood—and, at the same time, on the goals of the overall mission. The ability to see the relationship among people, patterns, and purpose allowed him to think smarter and act faster in an explosive setting.

The ability to see the relationship among people, patterns, and purpose allows you to think smarter and act faster in an explosive setting.

This example also illustrates how *personal awareness* and *situational awareness* are interrelated. While Lt. Col. Hughes was focused on context, he was also managing his own reactions carefully to ensure that they fit the purpose of the situation. Imagine if Lt. Col. Hughes had cowered. His display of weakness might have encouraged more aggression. Or imagine if he'd been triggered to *"win"* and asserted his dominance to demonstrate he was in charge. Or what if he just wasn't paying attention to the situation and assumed that the villagers would acquiesce to the presence of his troops. In each case, he could have thrown gasoline on the fire by reinforcing the fears of the crowd.

But instead of letting his primal reactions take charge, he remained in control of his actions and tightly focused on the mission. Even under extreme pressure, Lt. Col. Hughes was able to focus on a number of important factors:

- His own *internal state*. (His cognitive and emotional reactions to the predicament.)

- The state of his *troops*. (They're tired, stressed out, and in a more reactionary state of mind.)

- The thoughts, feelings, and behaviors of the *crowd*. (People were primed to assume the worst about the motives of U.S. troops and were increasingly angry and aggressive.)

- The *purpose* of the situation. (Their mission, remember, was to connect with the local imam to help *protect* the mosque and the community.)

- The *lack of fit* between patterns and purpose. (The troops were entering the town to help make the community more stable, but the reaction of the crowd was having the opposite effect.)

Lt. Col. Hughes and Steve

Lt. Col. Hughes's predicament in Iraq and Steve's situation with his boss are both instructive examples of the value of disciplined awareness and the ability to focus it on your internal and external circumstances in tough moments. The situation in Iraq is more dangerous, but the situation in Phil's office is more common. (You are probably less likely to lead troops into a hostile environment than you are to give tough feedback to someone who is difficult to approach.) But while their situations differ, the response of both is similar. Both men maintain a sharp focus on their own reactions, the reactions of others, and the purpose of the encounter, and then respond accordingly.

Even in a life-threatening situation, Lt. Col. Hughes was able to look *inward* to monitor his own reactions, look *outward* at his soldiers and the people of Najaf, and at the same time keep an eye on the overall *mission*: to coordinate with local leaders and protect the villagers. In a similar way, Steve juggled multiple subjects of focus in his conversation with Phil—Steve's own tendencies and behavior; the issue he's trying to address with Phil; how he wants to frame it; and Phil's reactions—while remaining focused on the overarching *purpose* of the encounter: to improve how Phil and his management team work together when the pressure is on.

Learning to deliberately focus your beam of attention on people, patterns, and purpose will keep you in tune with what's going on in the moment on multiple fronts. This will help you make better choices about how to participate in a meeting or conversation where something important is at stake. You'll be better equipped, in other words, to listen to what's being played and to play what's missing.

Focus on People

You're paying close, curious attention to other people in multiple ways. You're employing *cognitive empathy*—"the ability to understand another person's ways of seeing and thinking."[3] You're curious about how others have gone up the ladder of inference, their *point of view*, their goals and agendas, and how they're making sense of an issue or problem. You're not doing this in the quest for agreement, but for learning. You want to see what their views might teach you about the issue you're facing.

You're exercising *emotional empathy*—the ability to notice how others are feeling. You're dialed into the emotional reactions they're having to the issue or the situation. Do they feel strongly about what they're saying or tentative? Do they seem apathetic? Worried? Angry? Excited? Confused? Hesitant?[4]

At the same time, you're attuned to the *behavior* of other people—their volume, body language, tone of voice, and the words they're saying. You take note when others are interrupting, shutting down, rolling their eyes, grinning, sighing, and glancing at others across the table. What's more, you're not just noticing the behavior of others, you're evaluating it. You're constantly assessing behaviors in the meeting—your own and those of others—and asking whether they align with or work against the purpose of the meeting.

You're constantly assessing behaviors in the meeting—

your own and those of others—and asking whether they

align with or work against the purpose of the meeting.

Does the behavior, for example, encourage balanced dialogue, or deter it? Does it help people get their views into the conversation, or hinder it?

Are people managing their emotional reactions effectively or poorly? Given the purpose of the meeting or conversation, is their behavior constructive or destructive? Helpful or hurtful?

Focus on Patterns and Purpose

As if focusing on *self* and *others* isn't challenging enough, to be effective in important conversations you must also direct your beam to the *fit* between patterns and purpose. What does this mean?

- First, you're mindful of the *purpose* of the conversation or meeting. What is the goal of the encounter? What are you trying to accomplish? Is it to reach a decision? Is it to resolve a conflict? Is it to solve a problem? Is it to clear up a misunderstanding? Is it to improve a relationship?

- Second, you're paying attention to what's happening in the conversation—the patterns of behavior—and whether they support or subvert the purpose of the conversation. If the purpose of a meeting is to brainstorm, for example, but no one is sharing ideas, there's a poor fit between the patterns and the purpose. If the goal of the conversation is to make a collaborative decision but everyone is arguing, there's a bad fit. If the objective of the encounter is to provide useful feedback to a colleague, but people are watering down their points and withholding information to spare the colleague's feelings, there's another lousy fit.

With high situational awareness, you're constantly monitoring the degree of fit between what's happening in the moment and the goals for the moment. And the patterns matter. If Lt. Col Hughes had only seen one or two upset people in that big crowd in Najaf, it wouldn't have been such a big deal. But when he notices the entire town is angry, it's a major problem.

This is important because the level of *fit* determines the health of the conversation. A lack of fit between patterns and purpose is unhealthy, unproductive, or even destructive, while a tight fit is healthy, productive, and constructive.* This is critical. It's hard to close a gap between patterns and purpose if you don't even see it. So, to assess the fitness of a conversation or meeting, ask yourself these two sets of questions:

---

* Assuming, of course, that the purpose is constructive to begin with—an issue we'll explore in depth in a later chapter is about the "The Leadership Mindset."

1. *What is the purpose of this conversation or meeting? What are we try-*
ing to accomplish? What is the problem we're trying to solve? What is
the learning that needs to occur if we're to make meaningful progress?

2. *Do the patterns of discourse line up with that purpose? Do the behav-*
iors on display—mine and those of others—align with those objectives?
Given what we're up to, what is the smartest way we could all be work-
ing and communicating together? Is the way we're conversing with one
another in alignment with that way? And, if there's a gap, how can I
"play what's missing"?

Why Awareness Is so Important

If an organization is a community of discourse, and leadership is about
shaping the nature of the discourse, then conversational leadership is
about increasing the fit between the patterns and purpose of the conversation. To do this well you must sharpen your abilities on three interrelated
fronts: disciplined awareness, internal awareness, and awareness of the
overall context:

1. **High disciplined awareness.** The ability to direct and hold your
beam of attention at will.

2. **High self-awareness.** The ability to focus your beam internally, so
you recognize both what you're bringing to a conversation and how
you're reacting in the moment.

3. **High situational awareness.** A clear view of what other people
are bringing to the conversation, and the fit between patterns and
purpose.

The good news is that you have little reason to sit in a boring meeting
again. If you're mindfully aware, there's a plethora of factors on which to
focus. But remember, your motivation isn't to be entertained, or to passively
record what you're seeing, like Jane Goodall documenting the behavior of
the bonobos. Concerned about the conversational welfare of others, and
the effectiveness of the encounter, you're listening to what's being played
so you can play what's missing. If there's a lack of candor or curiosity in the
meeting, you know what you can "play" to bring more balance to the discussion. (We'll go into detail about how to do this in Part III: Skills.)

Smart Choices or Defensive Reactions?

The multifaceted awareness I've described in the last three chapters is an invaluable asset. With it, you're far more focused, disciplined, and balanced, so that even when everyone else is thrashing about dysfunctionally on the dance floor of a meeting, you are up on the balcony, making more deliberate choices about how to contribute. This is a hallmark trait of social intelligence; this is the ability, as the psychologist Edward Thorndike put it, "to act wisely in human relations."[5] Without this ability, your beam of attention will bounce around like a small child on a candy binge.

> *Failure to focus inward leaves you rudderless, a failure*
> *to focus on others renders you clueless, and a failure*
> *to focus outward may leave you blindsided.*
> —DANIEL GOLEMAN

The problem is that the fiery, emotional part of your brain and the cool, rational part of your brain often conflict. And without the ability to see, label, and brake, your good intentions will be routinely hijacked by your defensive reactions. Unable to consistently align your actions with your intentions, at best, you'll act like a well-intentioned but bumbling fool. At worst, you'll come across as incompetent—a passive bystander, a backseat driver, an inert critic, an impotent whiner—droning on and on about the pitfalls of the status quo while never daring to do something about it. Or, perhaps worse still, you'll come across as an aggressive, egocentric, my-way-or-the-highway asshole[6] bent on getting your way at the expense of a good decision.

Strengthening your awareness is the first step to solving this problem. By building your awareness you'll be *less reactive* and manipulatable. When triggered, you'll respond in a smart and reflective way rather than a dumb, defensive one. You'll be less likely to react this way: "Paul's a jerk. It's impossible to do good work when he's in the room," and more likely to react this way: "Wow, what is it about Paul's behavior that triggered me so intensely?"

But here's the conundrum: It's extremely important to be able to do all this under pressure, but it's also far harder to do under pressure. So, to build this ability, you're going to need practice. The good news is that practice is the subject of the next chapter.

AWARENESS PRACTICES

Building Your Ability to Focus on Purpose

*Attention works much like a muscle—use it poorly
and it can wither; work it well and it grows.*

—DANIEL GOLEMAN

Just like a muscle, your ability to control your beam of awareness can be strengthened with a specific kind of training. These exercises—strength-training workouts for your mind—are called *mindfulness awareness practices (MAPs).* Given the importance of disciplined awareness for building your ability to stay in the sweet spot, I'll repeat the advice provided in *Conversational Capacity*: If you don't have a MAP, start one; and if you do have one, ramp it up.

Meditation, the most common form of practice, is widely misunderstood. It's best to think of the word *meditation* as you do the word *exercise,* as a broad term that encompasses a wide range of activities. Most exercises involve focusing your attention on a particular object, activity, or thought in order to strengthen your ability to control your monkey mind. The goal is to develop the ability to watch your mind at work so it's easier to catch your reactions and *choose* how to respond.

*Training your mind to be in the present moment is
the #1 key to making healthier choices.*

—SUSAN ALBERS

The mindful awareness that the practice of meditation strengthens enables you to monitor your emotional and cognitive reactions under pressure. It's a way to train your mind to stay at the bottom rung of the Ladder of Inference, noticing *when* and *how* your mind is trying to go *up* the rungs. The more disciplined your awareness, the more you're able to make conscious choices about how to make sense of the world around you. This gives you greater mental flexibility and more behavioral options because you're not just blindly accepting the view of "reality"—and the emotional reactions that go with it—that your brain tries to hand you.

Single-Point Attention Practice

Single-point attention practice is perhaps the most common and straightforward MAP. In this exercise, you center your focus on an object—your breath, a point on the wall, or the buzz of a fan—and when your mind inevitably wanders (because that's what minds do), you calmly recognize the drift and return to your point of focus. With regular practice, you become more and more capable of "watching" or "monitoring" your mind in action, which increases your ability to remain focused on the activity of your choosing. The main exercise is *catching* your mind when it wanders and then *bringing it back* to focus.

Do the Dishes

I prefer active meditation. A conversation or meeting is a busy, chaotic thing. So, if all my meditative practice is in a quiet room, I find it doesn't transfer as well to a louder, busier, context.

If your goal is to *be* more mindful in louder and busier places, then *practice* being mindful in louder and busier places. This means that even mundane activities—cooking a meal, doing the dishes, mowing the lawn, walking the dog, or taking out the trash—provide superb opportunities for strengthening your focus. The practice is similar to single-point attention practice. When you're doing the dishes, for example, stay focused on the act of doing the dishes. Then, when you notice your monkey mind taking over, merely notice it, label what's happening ("There goes my monkey mind again.") and refocus on the experience of doing the dishes.

Mindful meditation has been discovered to foster the ability
to inhibit those very quick emotional impulses.
—DANIEL GOLEMAN

Take Breathing Breaks

Take regular two-minute breaks to focus on your breathing. Breathe in and breathe out slowly and pay attention to the flow of the air. When your focus drifts, notice it and refocus on your breath. Do this several times a day.

"There are two reasons why taking just one mindful breath is so effective at calming the body and the mind," says Chade-Meng Tan, the chairman of the Search Inside Yourself Leadership Institute. "The physiological reason is that breaths taken mindfully tend to be slow and deep, which stimulates the vagus nerve, activating the parasympathetic nervous system. It lowers stress, reduces heart rate and blood pressure, and calms you down," he says. "The psychological reason is that when you put your attention intensely on the breath, you are fully in the present for the duration of the breath. To feel regretful, you need to be in the past; to worry, you need to be in the future. Hence, when you are fully in the present, you are temporarily free from regret and worry. That's like releasing a heavy burden for the duration of one breath, allowing the body and mind a precious opportunity for rest and recovery."

He continues with this observation:

The ability to calm the body and mind on demand has profound implications for leadership. Imagine that you're responding to a severe crisis with your peers and everybody but you is frazzled because you alone can calm down and think clearly. The ability to think calmly under fire is a hallmark of great leadership. The training and deployment of this skill involves paying attention, on purpose, in the present moment, non-judgmentally. The more you bring this quality of attention to your breath, the more you strengthen the parts of your brain involved with attention and executive control, principally the prefrontal cortex.[1]

Mindful Listening

Just as I can run mindlessly on a trail and not remember long sections of my route, I can also "listen" mindlessly to a person (I use quotation marks here because is it really listening if it's not mindful?) and not remember vast sections of the conversation.

> *Communicating is more than just expressing yourself*
> *clearly; it's about listening clearly—paying attention and*
> *blocking out all the mental clutter and distractions.*
> —ERIC J. HALL

This is all too common. Consider this excerpt from a *Wall Street Journal* article on the lack of listening in the workplace:

> Even before the age of digital distractions, people could remember only about 10% of what was said in a face-to-face conversation after a brief distraction, according to a 1987 study that remains a key gauge of conversational recall. Researchers believe listening skills have since fallen amid more multitasking and interruptions. Most people can think more than twice as fast as the average person talks, allowing the mind to wander.[2]

Listening mindfully, therefore, presents a useful way to practice controlling your beam of attention. You do this by placing your focus fully on someone as they talk with you, zeroing in on both what they're saying and how they're saying it. This is one of the most useful practices because the opportunities are endless. Meeting at work? Dinner with colleagues? Home with the family? On a plane with a single-serving friend? Negotiating with a client? All present opportunities for practice.

Mindful listening gets you out of your own experience and into the experience of others. It cultivates empathy, opens you up to more learning, and forces you to kick your ego to the curb and to be open to the other person or persons with whom you're talking.

As you listen, don't just focus on the intellectual content of the conversation, but to their words, their facial expressions, their tone of voice, and their sentiments: Are they excited? Nervous? Scared? Worried? Sad? Overjoyed? Melancholy? Intimidated? Angry?

But it doesn't just have to be people. You can practice mindful listening as you listen to music, the sounds of a city street, of rain hitting the roof of the house, the birds chirping outside your window, or to the sound of the wind blowing through the leaves of a tree. The key is to really listen, to keep your mind focused on the sound, and to let other thoughts go as they try and intrude on your focus.

Learn to Notice Your Beam

Today I pulled up to a red light in my Jeep. After a few seconds I realized I wasn't paying any attention to the intersection, the cars next to me, or anything at all in the world around me because my mind had drifted to thoughts about a meeting that I was facilitating the next day. Physically I was sitting at the intersection, waiting for the light to turn green. Mentally, however, I was someplace else. I took control of my beam of focus by consciously asking myself: "Where is my beam right now?"

Another way to build your mindful awareness, therefore, is to cultivate the habit of noticing *where* your beam is focused. It's surprising, a little disturbing even, when you first realize just how often you're not even conscious when your focus starts to drift. The question, *"Where is my beam right now?"* is a useful way to build the habit of paying attention to how you're paying attention, so ask it throughout day.

Here are two ways to strengthen this ability:

1. Once an hour take one minute and deliberately move your beam to one *external* object for 30 seconds, and to one *internal* object for 30 seconds.

2. Every so often throughout the day—perhaps even setting an alarm as a reminder—stop and ask yourself the question: *"Where is my beam right now?"*

Notice New Things

Mindfulness is "the simple process of noticing new things," according to Ellen Langer, the renowned mindfulness expert at Harvard.[3] To increase your mindful awareness, therefore, she suggests starting each day with the goal of noticing five new things—about yourself, your trip to work, your workplace, an issue, or a friend or colleague—anything at all. In this simple exercise, you're establishing the habit of looking for objects or events in your day that usually go unnoticed or unappreciated.

Get Outside

Get outside and into nature. Why does this matter? Getting outside, it turns out, is good for your brain. Consider the research of Gregory Bratman and his colleagues at Stanford University. They found that "volunteers who walked briefly through a lush, green portion of the Stanford campus were more attentive and happier afterward than volunteers who strolled for the same amount of time near heavy traffic."[4] Compared to strolling on a city street, walking in a natural environment does a better job of decreasing anxiety, worry, and other negative emotions, and increasing both a positive mental state and working memory.[5]

Marc Berman, a professor of psychology at the University of Chicago, discovered a similar benefit. "Berman conducted a study in which he sent volunteers on a fifty-minute walk through either an arboretum or city streets, then gave his subjects a cognitive assessment. Those who had taken the nature walk performed about twenty percent better than their counterparts on tests of memory and attention."[6]

Yoga

Start yoga and use it to deliberately hone your ability to remain focused and present in the moment. Done properly, yoga is a fantastic vehicle for expanding your awareness. Rather than describe this myself, I'll share a bit from Nora Isaacs and her article, "Bring More Mindfulness onto the Mat."[7] Notice the similarity between her description of mindful yoga and my take on mindful trail running:

> You're standing in Virabhadrasana I (Warrior I Pose). You actively reach through your back foot and allow your tailbone to descend away from your lower back as your arms reach up toward the ceiling. As you hold the pose you start to notice your front thigh burning, your shoulders holding tension, and your breath becoming labored. Still holding. Soon you get agitated and start to anticipate the joy you'll feel when the pose is over. Your breath becomes shallow while you await the teacher's instruction to come out of the pose. But she doesn't say anything. You label her a sadist. Still holding. You decide that you are never coming back to yoga. As your thigh starts to shake, you mentally check out. Frustrated, you drop your arms and look around the room.
>
> Now imagine this: You're standing in Virabhadrasana I, noticing the same sensations, having the same thoughts and feelings—anger, boredom, impatience, tension. But instead of reacting, you simply

observe your thoughts. You remember that this pose, like everything else in life, will eventually end. You remind yourself not to get caught up in your own story line. And, in the midst of feeling irritated while your thighs burn, you appreciate the sweetness of the moment. You may even feel a wash of gratitude that you have the time and privilege to do a hatha yoga practice. Then you bring your awareness back to your breath and witness the ongoing sensations and thoughts until the teacher guides you out of the pose.

You've just experienced the benefits of mindfulness—of bringing your awareness into the present moment, of noticing and accepting what is happening right now without judgment or reaction. And, no doubt, it feels a lot better than the first scenario (which you might recognize as something you've also experienced).

It doesn't have to be yoga. You can also do tai chi, qigong, or other mindfulness-based activities to strengthen this ability.

Take Care of Yourself

A tired brain is an undisciplined brain. Few things let your monkey mind out of its cage more quickly than being worn out. Feeling exhausted decreases your ability to concentrate your beam in a mindful way, hampering your ability to manage your emotions. So, a big part of learning to focus your beam is to take care of yourself. Get plenty of sleep, eat well, and exercise. Take care of your brain—and the body that houses it—if you want it to perform at its peak.

Unfocus, Focus. Unfocus, Focus

Your beam of focus, like a muscle, can get overused, strained, and weakened by overuse, so don't over focus. Let your brain wander. "The problem is that excessive focus exhausts the focus circuits in your brain. It can drain your energy and make you lose self-control," says Srini Pillay, an expert on mental focus. Research shows that ". . . both focus and unfocus are vital. The brain operates optimally when it toggles between focus and unfocus, allowing you to develop resilience, enhance creativity, and make better decisions too."[8]

Keep It Up

Ongoing practice is key. As with acquiring any discipline, you'll get out of it what you put into it. But it'll pay off rapidly. Research shows that even a little practice—done regularly—makes a big difference.

Building Your Personal Awareness

You're learning to control your beam of focus. Great. Now it's time to turn that beam inward. Here are a few ways you can strengthen your ability to recognize when you're at risk of losing balance, or, if you've left it, to catch it and quickly recover.

> *Self-awareness isn't a one-and-done exercise. It's a*
> *continual process of looking inward, questioning, and*
> *discovering the things that have been there all along.*
> **—TASHA EURICH**

Keep a Trigger Journal

Keeping a simple trigger journal is one of the most powerful ways to build your ability to recognize when you're at risk of leaving the sweet spot, or, once you've left it, catching it early. What is a *trigger journal*? It's an ongoing record of issues and situations that throw you off balance. When I lose discipline and allow my *min* or *"win"* tendencies to hijack my good intentions, for instance, I reflect on the experience by asking these questions and jotting down the answers in my trigger journal:

- *What was the trigger?*

- *What was my reaction? How did I let it affect my behavior?*

- *The next time I notice this trigger, what is a more balanced and effective way I might choose to respond?*

The primary goal of trigger journaling is not to identify your every trigger (I'm not even sure that's possible). The goal is to get in *the habit of noticing when* you're triggered.

Here's an example: I was recently getting off a plane after a long week of travel. It was 11:30 at night, and I'd been in New York all week, so I was exhausted. As I was pulling my bag out of the overhead bin to exit the plane, a man behind shoved past me, almost knocking me back in my seat. I immediately felt a flash of anger and outrage. But then a funny thing happened. I thought to myself, "Hey, I'm being triggered here. I gotta remember to write this one down." My trigger journaling practice helped me *catch*, *name*, and *tame* the reaction quickly, and this gave me the option to choose how to respond. (I still nailed the guy in the chest with my elbow, but it was a conscious choice, not an unconscious reaction—just kidding.) As I reflected back on that experience, I realized there were at least three triggers: I was *tired*; the actions of the other person seemed *disrespectful* (he shoved me aside); and the behavior seemed *unfair* (you're generally expected to get off a plane in order).

Reflect Back

Think about the times you've shut up when you should have spoken up or argued when you should have listened. What were the triggers? What were the earliest signs you were about to lose discipline and let your defensive tendencies put daylight between your behaviors and your intentions? Reflect on your past behavior by asking yourself these questions:

- *Under what circumstances do I let my tendency to minimize separate my intentions and my behavior?*

- *Under what circumstances do I let my tendency to "win" knock me off balance?*

- *How quickly can I catch myself when I leave the sweet spot?*

- *Do I catch myself before I lose balance or at the end of the meeting, or am I often driving home before I realize I was triggered?*

Focus on Feelings

Notice when you're triggered and reflect on the feelings associated with it. What were the physical and emotional precursors? How quickly did they escalate? The idea is to observe and flag those reactions so you can catch them earlier next time, and to dampen their effect on your behavior.

"Feelings arise within you—sadness, anxiety, annoyance, relief, joy— and you try to experience them from a different vantage point than is usual, neither clinging to the good feelings nor running away from the bad ones, but rather just experiencing them straightforwardly and observing them," writes Robert Wright in his book *Why Buddhism Is True*. "This altered perspective can be the beginning of a fundamental and enduring change in your relationship to your feelings; you can, if all goes well, cease to be their slave."[9]

As one executive told me, "I notice that when my need to '*win*' kicks into gear, I feel a tightening in my jaw muscles and a tense sensation in my chest. I now use these reactions as my 'early warning system.'" His awareness of how he's feeling in the moment gives him more control.

Check in with Yourself

Regularly focus your beam on your current emotional state: *"How do I feel right now?"* or *"What am I feeling and why am I feeling it?"* This helps you to *recognize* your emotions and to *label* them. Schedule this at a specific time—setting an alarm if necessary—to get in the habit of checking in on your internal state. "Every day at 15 minutes past the hour I'll do a quick internal check-in to see how I'm doing."

"Brake" a Habit

Research shows that exercising self-control of any kind builds your ability to exercise self-control in other areas and situations because you're using the same mental muscles. With this in mind I deliberately find activities that require *noticing, naming* and *taming, refocusing,* and *replacing.* They are not hard to find.

When I drive, for example, I tend to engage in ongoing commentary (some of it quite loud and colorful) about people doing stupid stuff on the road. Someone cuts me off on the freeway and off goes my mouth. Someone pulls out of a parking lot in front of me and off goes my mouth. Someone makes a sudden lane change without signaling and off goes my mouth.

But there's a downside to this. While this Tourette's-like behavior seems harmless to me, it drives my wife crazy. So as a loving, caring, considerate husband, obviously I've stopped doing it, right? Not exactly. I've discovered it's such a deeply ingrained behavior that it's a hard habit to "brake." So, in part to please her, I turned breaking this habit into a practice. When a reaction starts to flare up, I practice *seeing, labeling, braking, refocusing,* and *replacing.* When I want to mouth off and make rude comments about the driver who just cut me off, I try to maintain composure and laugh it off instead, or to make a sarcastic comment: "Thank you for cutting me off. Have a nice day." It's a hard habit to manage, but it's the difficulty that makes it such outstanding practice.

It's not just self-absorbed or irresponsible drivers. Our daily lives are filled with opportunities like this. The key is to see them and to use them:

- You prefer to kick back and read the news, but you *choose* to work on your proposal.

- You don't want to run on a cold morning—you'd rather stay in your warm bed—but you *choose* to lace up and hit the road.

- You want to make a vulgar hand gesture to the driver who just cut you off, but you *choose* to smile and wave instead.

- You want to order the biscuits and gravy for breakfast, but you *choose* to order the oatmeal.

- You want to tell your colleague his point of view is nonsense, but you *choose* to inquire into his perspective.

Assessments and Feedback

Review any personality or behavioral assessments you've taken for clues about your general predilections and habits. This can include 360-degree feedback, formal performance reviews, as well as personality or behavioral assessments like the Predictive Index® (PI) Behavioral Assessment, The Harrison Assessment®, the DISC® profile, the Birkman Method®, or the Hogan Assessment®. These assessments can provide powerful information about your tendencies and the situations in which they're triggered.

But don't just take the assessment at its word; use it as a starting point for conversations with your colleagues, employees, boss, family, and friends. Exploring where the people agree and disagree with the assessment is a powerful way to learn about yourself while also getting better at staying in the sweet spot.

Building Your Situational Awareness

Pay Attention to People, Patterns, and Purpose

Pay attention to the fit, or lack of it, between *patterns* of behavior and the *purpose* of the conversation or meeting. To do this, here are a few questions you can ask:

1. What are we trying to accomplish here? What is the problem we're trying to solve? What is the challenge we're up against, the decision we're trying to make, or the issue we're facing? What, in other words, is the *purpose* of this meeting or conversation?

2. Is the issue we're addressing *routine* (a clear problem with obvious solution) or is it more *adaptive* (a messy problem with no obvious or easy way to solve it)?

3. How do people seem to *feel* about the issue being discussed?

4. What *behaviors* are on display? How are people acting? Does the behavior of other people *support* what we're trying to do here, or does it work *against* it?

5. What about my *own behavior*? How well does it fit with our purpose?

6. If there's a *lack of fit*, what can I do to bridge it? Conversationally, what is being played and how can I play what's missing?

Score a Meeting

A simple way to improve our ability to focus on the patterns in a meeting is to *keep score*. You can do this by creating a simple template and then monitoring the conversation as it unfolds.

POSITION	THINKING	TESTING	INQUIRY
✓	✓		✓
✓	✓		
✓	✓		
✓			
✓			

When someone states a position, place a check mark in the "position" column. When someone explains their thinking, place a check mark in the "thinking" column. If they test it, place a check mark in the "testing" column." If there is an inquiry, place a check mark in the "inquiry" column.

After 10 or 15 minutes, when you have a clear view of the pattern of discourse, ask: *Does this pattern of conversation serve the purpose of the conversation?* If you're at a bar watching a game, then yes, this might be a perfect fit. But if your team is wrestling with a major decision, it's probably a lousy fit. And whenever there's a lack of fit, the question should always be: *What can I do to bridge the gap?*

Learn to Think Systemically

Systems thinking skills provide a particularly powerful way to build your situational awareness. As my colleague and close friend Chris Soderquist puts it, *systems thinking*—or what he refers to as *SysQ* (systemic intelligence)—helps you identify the "high leverage" places to intervene when you want to improve a process or relationship, or to address a problem. What is *high leverage*? It's the place you can intervene to make the biggest impact with the smallest investment and the lowest risk of unintended consequences. If that's not a great description of situational awareness, I don't know what is. Chris teaches people and teams how to use a variety of tools—ranging from *systems thinking questions, trend-over-time graphs, causal-loop maps, stock-and-flow diagrams,* and *dynamic simulation models*—to expand and improve how they're looking at a situation or issue. I'll talk about this again in Chapter 9, but if you'd like to learn more right away, you'll find a wealth of information about SysQ at findinghighleverage.com.

Readings

Whether it's single-point meditation practice, yoga, tai chi, running meditation, or some other activity, the goal is to find a mindful awareness practice (MAP) that works for you. I'd encourage you to talk with other people who practice in order to find out what they find most helpful. Here are a few books to consider:

- *10% Happier* by Dan Harris

- *Aware* by Daniel J. Siegel

- *Coming to Our Senses* by Jon Kabat-Zinn

- *FOCUS* by Daniel Goleman

- *Fully Present* by Susan L. Smalley and Diana Winston

- *Insight* by Tasha Eurich

- *Mindfulness for Beginners* by Jon Kabat-Zinn

- *Mindfulness in Plain English* by Bhante Henepola Gunaratana
- *Mindfulness* by Ellen Langer
- *Mindsight* by Daniel J. Siegel
- *Running with the Mind of Meditation* by Sakyong Mipham
- *Search Inside Yourself* by Chade-Meng Tan
- *Start Where You Are: A Guide to Compassionate Living* by Pema Chodron
- *The Art of Communicating* by Thich Nhat Hanh
- *The Art of Noticing* by Ellen Langer
- *The Mindful Brain* by Daniel J. Siegel
- *The Mind's Own Physician* by Jon Kabat-Zinn and Richard J. Davidson
- *The Places That Scare You* by Pema Chodron
- *Wherever You Go, There You Are* by Jon Kabat-Zinn
- *Why Buddhism Is True* by Robert Wright

If you want to wield more powerful influence and take more constructive action, mindful awareness—the ability to direct and concentrate your attention on the subject of your choosing—is a bedrock skill to cultivate. But building disciplined focus takes dedicated practice. It's akin to running. Just as completing a marathon requires a strong, disciplined body, high mindful awareness requires a strong, disciplined mind.

Want to Learn More?

For a regularly updated list of practices, readings, and other resources check out conversationalcapacity.com

PART

II

MINDSET

That's your responsibility as a person, as a human being—to constantly be updating your positions on as many things as possible. And if you don't contradict yourself on a regular basis, then you're not thinking.

—MALCOLM GLADWELL

THE CONVERSATIONAL CAPACITY MINDSET

Turning Your Mind into a Workshop

If you haven't changed your mind lately, how do you know it's working?
—ALICE DREGER

This is the most important section of the book. It outlines the essential disposition that determines whether you're flexible, open, and constructive in a challenging conversation, or rigid, defensive, and destructive. *Awareness* is vital, and the *skills* are important, but when it comes to working in the sweet spot under pressure, your *mindset* is pivotal.

What do I mean by mindset? Your *mindset* is the values, attitudes, and goals—conscious or unconscious—that inform your behavioral choices. A mindset is not what you *say* you value, or even what you *think* you value; it's what you *actually* value. It's what matters to you, the ideas and actions on which you place the most importance. If awareness is what you're *noticing* in a situation, and the skills are what you're *doing*, the mindset is who you're *being*. The conversational capacity mindset drives your behavioral choices and infuses your candid and curious behavior with authenticity. So, for our purposes in this section, *mindset* refers to *the values with which you approach a significant conversation*.

Given it's monumental importance, in this chapter I'll share with you the distinctive aspects of the *Conversational Capacity Mindset*. They are the values that inform how you respond to difficult circumstances and issues, and help you remain candid and curious and focused on learning, even when your *min* and *"win"* tendencies are doing their damnedest to knock you off balance.

The Basic Discipline: Refocusing

Awareness is essential to the basic discipline of conversational capacity. When you're being triggered, it enables you to *catch it, name it*, and *tame it*. But to remain candid and curious you must next *refocus* by setting your mental sights on a loftier set of goals. The mindset does just that. It provides something on which to fix your beam of attention so that even when your defensive inclinations are doing their best to knock you off-kilter you're still able to align your behavior with your intentions. Put differently, this mindset provides a conversational compass for staying on track in situations where it's easy to lose your bearings; it provides a navigational beacon that helps you stay true to your course even in the confusing fog of a high-pressure conversation.

At its core conversational capacity is a mindset in action.

Staying "Mindset Forward"

In a conversation about something important, rather than let your reactions be driven by arrogance, anger, fear, cowardice, resentment, vengeance—or any other self-centered motives—you rise above yourself and focus on *learning*. It is from this learning-focused mindset that your balanced behaviors flow. Your actions are guided by purpose rather than defensiveness because you're more interested in thinking clearly and being effective than in inflating your ego.

But this mindset presents a challenge. In my experience, and in teaching this discipline to thousands of other people, maintaining this mindset under pressure is extremely difficult. Why? In challenging circumstances your defensive reactions shove your mindset into the backseat and seize the wheel. To stay in the sweet spot, therefore, a huge challenge is to remain *mindset forward*.

Your Mental Workshop

To help you deal with this challenge, I'm going to share with you a way to keep learning in the driver's seat. When you're facing a tough problem, big decision, or important issue, rather than letting your mind be sidetracked by your defensive reactions, you should stay mindset forward by turning your mind into a *workshop*. Rather than treat your mind like a temple to sanctify or a fort to protect, treat it like a workshop to use.

Rather than treat your mind like a temple to sanctify or a fort to protect, treat it like a workshop to use.

I mean workshop in the traditional sense, as a place you actually *build* something. When you're facing a tough conversation or a challenging meeting, I suggest you mindfully step into your mental workshop and take the ideas, issues, decisions, problems, or challenges that you're facing and "work" them. To do this, you concentrate on two things: the *product* you're creating (the *what*) and the *process* by which you create it (the *how*).

Your Workshop Product

The *product* of your mental workshop is *more rigorous, intelligent decision-making.* You're working hard to create the clearest view of the situation, problem, or decision that you're facing because what's most important to you—what *drives* your behavior—is the desire to think more intelligently about the issues you are up against so that you and others make the *smartest choices and take the most effective action.* (And when you think about it, what else should it be? Mollycoddling your ego? Reinforcing your ideological framework? Feeling warm and fuzzy? Looking smart? Manipulating others to see things your way and to do what you want?)

This may seem obvious, but vigorous, clear-headed thinking doesn't happen automatically. The psychologist Cordelia Fine explains the basic problem:

A brain with a mind of its own belies our strong sense that the world is just as it seems to us, and our misguided belief that our vision of "out there" is sharp and true. In fact, it appears that our attitudes are the muddled outcome of many struggling factors, she says. Tussling against our desire to know the truth about the world are powerful drives to protect our self-esteem, sense of security, and pre-existing point of view. Set against our undeniably impressive powers of cognition are a multitude of irrationalities, biases, and quirks that surreptitiously undermine the accuracy of our beliefs.[1]

In her book, *Blind Spots*, Madeleine L. Van Hecke reinforces the precariousness of our perceptions:

. . . we all have blind spots, blind spots that are built into the ways that we naturally think, just as blind spots are part and parcel of a car's mirrors. Our mental blind spots can account for much of what people ordinarily label stupidity.

She then points out how these blind spots affect our everyday experience:

When we feel dim-witted, whatever it is that we should have known, or should have realized, or should have thought about, seems so obvious in retrospect. How could we have missed it? When others seem dense to us, whatever we grasp seems so clear that we cannot fathom how they could have missed it.[2]

Concerned about such cognitive distortions, you work hard to compensate for the inevitable biases, blind spots, and bullshit that so readily infect your perceptions. (Clearly recognizing that your mind twists reality in secretive and self-serving ways, by the way, is a great way to stay curious because you're always wondering: "What am I missing? How is my view off-kilter?") Vigorous, clear-headed thinking doesn't happen automatically. It takes hard work. You have to craft it.

Vigorous, clear-headed thinking doesn't happen automatically. It takes hard work. You have to craft it.

In short, when you're in your workshop, you're engaged in the process of *learning*. Rather than clinging to your current perspective like it's a sacred relic, treat it as a "work in process," something still in development. Passionately *refocused* on thinking sharp and acting smart, you're not protecting your point of view; instead you're sharpening it. Your picture of reality is just an instrument you use to make sense of the world. With this in mind, you're not just aware of your habitual *min-"win"* reactions, you're kicking them to the curb so that you can focus on getting smarter.

You're not naïve. You're not seeking a perfect view of "reality."* You're just doing your best to make the smartest choices possible, given constraints such as time and information. To paraphrase Nate Silver, you're trying to be more and more right and less and less wrong.[3] To do this, you're saying to yourself, in essence:

- *If working with others to make the smartest choice means I'll be less comfortable than I prefer to be, so be it. That's a price I'm willing to pay.*

- *If working with others to make the smartest choice means I'll be less certain than I prefer to feel, so be it. That's a price I'm willing to pay.*

Your Workshop Process

... it's not always the people who start out the smartest who end up the smartest."

—CAROL DWECK

What is the *process* you employ to produce this learning? There are four main activities:

1. Pooling perspectives

2. Leaning into difference

3. Integrating perspectives

4. Critical thinking

Pooling Perspectives

Given that your mental models of "reality" tend to be skewed, incomplete, and self-servingly biased in a disturbing number of ways, you work hard

---

* I use quotations marks around the word to honor this observation of the mythologist Joseph Campbell: "There is no way you can use the word 'reality' without quotation marks around it."

to improve them. But how do you catch an erroneous assumption? How do you better identify biases and blind spots? How do you know where you're missing information? How do you learn to spot the inevitable gaps in your maps?

One powerful way to detect and correct such mental flaws is to engage people who see the world through a different lens. An essential part of the process in your workshop, therefore, is the *pooling of perspectives to expand and improve your thinking.* You recognize that your view on any issue is limited and the best way to expand and improve it is to pull in perspectives that highlight or emphasize aspects of the issue you tend to overlook. You're seeking to view the issue through other lenses. (A decision might make perfect sense from a finance perspective, but it might look very different when you expand your view by looking at it through a legal lens.)

In his book, *The Opposable Mind*, Roger Martin explains the value of engaging people with dissimilar mental models: "There's much to be gained from the recognition that no model has a lock on reality, but that all models reflect reality from a particular angle," he says. "It becomes possible to assemble a fuller, though probably not complete, model of reality by incorporating a variety of other models."[4]

The raw materials in your mental process, you could say, are varied ways of thinking about an issue or a challenge. With this in mind, you mine the perspectives of others for insight and knowledge.

Leaning into Difference

In your mental workshop you're not just working to increase viewpoint diversity; you're doing it with a particular bias. To expand and improve your thinking, you're *leaning into difference.* By "leaning in" I mean you're not just tolerating difference, you're placing a premium on it. You're not just casually interested in different points of view; you're pursuing them because they turbocharge learning. You actively seek out and explore dissimilar ideas, interpretations, and information because they provide the greatest probability of sparking an insight. You know that the best way to guard against your confirmation bias, and to sharpen and strengthen your thinking, is to engage with people who see the world differently. They're more likely to spur those aha moments when a blind spot in your mental map of reality is unexpectedly illuminated. "Oh, I never thought of it that way before."

Strength lies in differences, not in similarities.
—STEPHEN COVEY

While pooling perspectives places an emphasis on *expanding* your thinking, leaning into difference places the emphasis on *improving* it. "Opposing models," says Roger Martin, "are the richest source of new insight into a problem. We learn nothing from someone who sees the problem exactly as we do."[5] You know that to overcome your confirmation bias you must question your kneejerk perceptions by actively seeking out contrasting points of view.

With this mindset, you're always looking for the cop to your architect.* If you have a human resources background, for example, you're wondering what the issue looks like from the perspective of the sales team, engineering, or production. If you're a conservative politician, you're wondering how the issue looks from a progressive point of view, or vice-versa. With a disciplined focus on producing insight, solid judgment, and wise choices, you're not doing all this in a quest for comfort confirmation or agreement. You're doing it to learn. If *pooling perspectives* leads to greater knowledge, *leaning into difference* is the path to greater.*wisdom*.

If pooling perspectives *leads to greater knowledge,*

leaning into difference *is the path to greater* wisdom.

Placing a premium on different points of view magnifies your ability to make informed choices because it facilitates more *double-loop learning*.† After all, the best way to understand and *see* your assumptions, beliefs, and filters is to contrast them with alternative ways of thinking and perceiving reality. It's like international travel. You experience your own culture more clearly after living in another culture because the contrast helps you *see* your own culture, something that used to be largely invisible, by pulling it into the light.

As I pointed out in my first book, Abraham Lincoln understood this. Facing an adaptive challenge of historic proportions—a civil war and the utter failure of the American experiment—he did something unusual. He pulled people into his cabinet with political agendas that clashed not only with his own views but with each other's. He didn't create this hornets' nest of conflicting perspectives because he yearned for comfortable cabinet meetings, nor did he do it because he wanted to get his way all the time. He

---

* If this analogy doesn't ring a bell, revisit Chapter 6 in *Conversational Capacity*.
† See Chapter 7 in *Conversational Capacity* to review the concept of double-loop learning.

did it because he knew a room full of contrasting points of view would help him make wiser, more informed decisions about the *adaptive realities* he was facing. The diversity of Lincoln's cabinet—and his ability to leverage it—helped him to see and think more clearly.

It's no different in your team, organization, or community. When you're up against big decisions, conflicts, changes, and challenges, the potential for profound learning isn't in the *sameness* around the table—it's in the *difference*. If you can orchestrate balanced dialogue that fosters open-minded exposure to the varied and conflicting perspectives, you gain a huge advantage that is unavailable to less capable people and teams. You gain the ability to think in a more expansive and integrative way about your most pressing problems. You have a greater field of vision and clearer set of choices in an adaptive situation because, as author Margaret Heffernan puts it, you have "thinking partners who aren't echo chambers."[6]

Pooling perspectives with a bias toward difference is important for two main reasons. It increases your capacity for *integrative thinking* and it reduces your risk of *intellectual inbreeding*.

Integrating Perspectives

So, you're in your workshop pooling perspectives and placing a strong emphasis on different points of view. Now what? Well, here's where it gets interesting. Rather than getting mired in a pool of conflicting assessments, you elevate the problem-solving process by rising above the conflict. You do this by treating contrasting viewpoints as a creative opportunity, not a frustrating conundrum. Instead of feeling trapped between one view or the other, or between one choice or the other, you leverage varying perspectives to create a more integrated, higher-order solution.

To do this you employ *integrative thinking*, the ability to combine varying and contrasting perspectives to craft a more sophisticated understanding of an issue. In his book on the subject, *The Opposable Mind*, Roger Martin says that people who can think this way have the "ability to face constructively the tension of opposing ideas and, instead of choosing one at the expense of the other, generate a creative resolution of the tension in the form of a new idea that contains elements of the opposing ideas but is superior to each."[7]

When faced with seemingly contradictory ways of making sense of something, conventional thinking tends to focus on this *or* that. Integrative thinking, by contrast, opens the door to fresh ideas and novel solutions by focusing on this *and* that.[8] "Integrative thinking shows us a way past the binary limits of either/or," says Martin. "It shows us that there's a way to integrate the advantages of one solution without canceling out the advantages of an alternative solution." Remembering the cop and the architect example, you know that leaning into conflicting "ladders" allows you to see and think more, and to find solutions that are invisible, or only partly visible, when viewed from just one perspective or another. You're able, as Martin puts it, "to produce a synthesis that is superior to either opposing idea."[9]

The problem faced by Steve and Phil provides a perfect example of what this looks like in action. At first, each party framed the other as the source of the trouble. "Phil needs to dial it down," thought the team. "The team needs to toughen up," thought Phil. But to solve the problem *both* the team and Phil had to make adjustments. The eventual solution was an elevated hybrid of these conflicting mental models. It *integrated* both ways of making sense of the problem into a more elegant and effective way forward.

This integrative approach transforms how you react to people with different perspectives and information because your bias for learning leads you to see the different perspectives and information as opportunities to expand and elevate your own thinking, not as petty nuisances to avoid or attack. Rather than cave in or argue when someone shares a contrasting point of view, you get curious: "What can this person's perspective teach me about how I'm looking at this issue?"

Viewing alternative perspectives as something to leverage for learning moves a conversation to a higher plane. It shifts the exchange from "Your view versus my view," to "You and I with our differing views versus the problem we're facing." It transforms people whose ideas conflict with your own from asses to assets. (I stress this point in my work with state legislators around the United States by asking them to reframe how they react to people with different political views—as valuable partners, rather than obstacles—in making more intelligent policy decisions.)

Viewing alternative perspectives as something to leverage

for learning moves a conversation to a higher plane.

INTELLECTUAL INBREEDING

It's important to recognize that whenever you're up against a tough problem or an important decision you always face a monumental choice between strong and smart thinking, or weak and sloppy thinking; between moving forward with an intelligent choice, or fumbling around with a dumb one. It's hard to overemphasize how pivotal this is. If you surround yourself with people who see things the way you do, or only listen to people with similar views, you trap yourself in an ego-enhancing echo chamber. You remain an ignorant slave to your insular thinking and the confirmation bias that gives it safe haven.

To avoid this trap, enlarge and enrich your worldview by valuing learning over ego-enhancement. You should do this because you're keenly aware that failing to consider other perspectives puts you at serious risk of a noxious malady: *intellectual inbreeding*. Reducing the number of new perspectives coming in from outside sources has the same impact as reducing the number of new genes coming into a population; pretty soon your view of the world is as messed up as the banjo-playing kid on the porch in the film *Deliverance*.

Think about it. If you're convinced that your narrow view of "reality" *is* reality, you're doomed to suffer from ridiculous and unnecessary levels of self-inflicted stupidity. Few things are as off-putting as arrogant, closed-minded people who are so shut off to learning that they're impervious to the views of others. They go through life catering to their *confirmation bias,* a sad and depressing tactic that puts them increasingly out of touch with the world around them because they routinely sacrifice learning on the altar of ignorance.* I'm sure you've worked with people like this.

> *Progress is impossible without change, and those who*
> *cannot change their minds cannot change anything.*
> —GEORGE BERNARD SHAW

Few things are more refreshing and engaging, on the other hand, than open-minded people who are interested in new ideas and eager to improve how they see the world around them. But being open like this takes discipline. Leaning into difference to expand and improve your thinking will inevitably put you up against your *min-"win"* tendencies. It inevitably leads to being wrong, uncomfortable, or both. So, this mindset confronts you with pivotal choices: *Do I want to avoid emotional discomfort or do I want to get smarter? Do I want to "feel right" and get my way or do I want to become more informed?*

---

* To be clear, the idea isn't that these people are inherently unintelligent—they might be capable of brilliance—it's that they're using weak, sloppy, insular thinking. The point is that there is a fundamental difference between these two kinds of thinking, and if your goal is to make smart choices you first need to adopt a smart approach.

Critical Thinking

When you're in your workshop your mind is open to fresh ideas and perspectives. You're not just sitting around passively willing to accept a new view if it happens to knock on the door and present itself; you're actively seeking them out, eagerly pursuing more expansive and effective ways of making sense of the world around you. But an open mind is not a gullible mind. With this mindset, you're intelligently open-minded, not uncritically open-minded.[10] For a perspective to influence your view it must pass muster.

What determines what you let in and what you don't? *Evidence*. Smart thinking is evidence-based thinking.

> *When you are studying any matter, ask yourself only what are the facts and what is the truth that the facts bear out. Never let yourself be diverted either by what you wish to believe, or by what you think would have beneficent social effects if it were believed. But look only, and solely, at what are the facts.*
> —BERTRAND RUSSELL

So, with this mindset you're not just carelessly, casually, or lazily open-minded. You're *critically* open-minded. You're constantly vetting ideas and evaluating input.

Critical thinking, a form of intellectual self-discipline, helps you identify where your biases, ego-needs, and blind spots distort how you're making sense of an issue or a situation. In your workshop—focused on learning, getting smarter, and making better decisions—you're striving to get outside your own head so you can look at the world in a clearer fashion. You're evaluating and critiquing your mental models in order to sharpen and refine them.

You pay a steep price when this ability is weak. In an academic research article with an interesting subject and an unorthodox title: "On the Reception and Detection of Pseudo-Profound Bullshit," several researchers describe the problem with having an open mind unencumbered by critical thinking: "Our results suggest that this tendency—which resembles a general gullibility factor—is a component of pseudo-profound bullshit receptivity."[11]

> The authors also draw an interesting distinction between types of open-mindedness ... reflexive or uncritical open-mindedness, in which a person is accepting of information but doesn't pause to evaluate inherent conflicts or other features, and reflective or active open-mindedness, in which a person seeks information for the purpose of critical thinking.[12]

What? You mean that an open mind without a critical filter will soon overflow with flawed, weak, claptrap thinking? What a surprise. The good news is that you can avoid this fate by adopting a more active and reflective approach in which you're curious and open-minded but you also sport a fully functional "Baloney Detection Kit," the set of critical thinking tools championed by Carl Sagan. (I'll bet that's not what he originally wanted to call it!) Focused on thinking more clearly, you're actively weighing what you hear, sorting what's useful from what's not, what's accurate from what isn't, what's nonsense from what's really going on. You're as unwilling to *accept* an idea simply because it conflicts with your own perspective as you're willing to accept one simply because it reinforces it.

> *You're as unwilling to* accept *an idea simply because it conflicts with your own perspective as you're willing to accept one simply because it reinforces it.*

A great example of someone applying critical open-mindedness to a serious problem is American physicist Richard Feynman and the role he played in the investigation of the Space Shuttle *Challenger* disaster. In a public meeting, members of the Rogers Commission, the body appointed to investigate the disaster and its causes, were talking with people from Morton-Thiokol and NASA about the events the evening before the launch of *Challenger*. In that conversation, Morton-Thiokol managers asserted that the opinions of the seal experts about whether or not to launch were evenly divided. The decision was, the way they were framing it, a coin toss.

But while other members of the commission were ready to uncritically accept the managers' assertions, Feynman was not. Here's his account of the incident:

> It struck me that the Thiokol managers were waffling. But I only knew how to ask simpleminded questions. So I said, "Could you tell me, sirs, the names of your four best seals experts, in order of ability?"
>
> "Roger Boisjoly and Arnie Thompson are one and two. Then there's Jack Kapp and, uh . . . Jerry Burns."
>
> I turned to Mr. Boisjoly, who was right there, at the meeting. "Mr. Boisjoly, were you in agreement that it was okay to fly?"
>
> He says, "No, I was not."

I ask Mr. Thompson, who was also there.

"No, I was not."[13]

When asked about the views of the other two experts, who were not in the room, it turns out one was unsure about whether or not to launch and the other was probably a yes. "So," Feynman said to the Morton-Thiokol managers, "of the four, we have one 'don't know,' one 'very likely yes,' and the two who were mentioned right away as being the *best* seal experts, *both said no*. So this 'evenly split' stuff was a lot of crap. The guys who knew the most about the seals—what were *they* saying?" Under more curious but critical investigation it was clear the decision to launch was not a coin toss.

By-Products

When you're working in your mental workshop you're not just producing smart choices and effective action. The process also generates precious by-products: *commitment,* c*onfidence,* and *trust.*

Commitment

Making informed and *effective* choices is your North Star. A choice, however, is unlikely to be effective if people don't buy into it. With low internal commitment you may get compliance (if you're lucky), but you're unlikely to get people's A-game. And why bother putting a lot of work into making a smart decision if no one will raise a finger to put it into action?

> *If you don't like your job, you don't go on strike. You just go in every day and do it really half-assed—that's the American way.*
> —**HOMER SIMPSON**

The good news is that an invaluable by-product of the workshop process is *internal commitment,* or buy-in, to the choices that do get made, which greatly increases the likelihood they'll be implemented effectively. When people feel committed to a decision, they're more likely to roll up their sleeves to help with implementation and far less likely to open a bag of Corn Nuts.*

Research shows that people feel more commitment to a decision if it meets two standards:

---

* Don't remember this reference? See pages 68–71 in *Conversational Capacity.*

1. **Respect for the process.** "Studies show that people are willing to accept an unfavorable outcome if they believe the decision-making process was sound," writes HBR.com's Amy Gallo. "This is often called 'procedural fairness.' You might say to your employees, for example: *'Here's the process that was followed, the people we spoke with, and where things came out.'* "[14] It's not about agreement, in other words, as much as it is about a process that is clear, fair, and rigorous. People need to see that the decision was meritocratic rather than self-serving or politically convenient.

2. **Involvement in the process.** People want to feel their thinking has been taken into account. People feel more ownership for a choice if they feel they've had some say in the matter, that they've been listened to, and that their point of view is playing a useful role.

When people respect the process by which a decision is reached, and when they feel part of that process, they tend to have more buy-in and less resentment. They're more likely to give the decision a thumbs-up than a middle finger.

Confidence

Another important by-product is greater *confidence* in your decisions and choices. This confidence flows from two things:

1. Because the issue has been considered so rigorously, you have more confidence in the *quality* of the choice. As one manager told me: "I find that as my conversational capacity goes up, I'm way more confident in my decisions because I know I'm using the best thinking around the table to make them."

2. Because the higher internal commitment increases the likelihood people will bring their best efforts to the implementation, you have greater confidence it will be *implemented* effectively.

Trust

Your conversations are more purpose-driven than ego-driven, more focused on working with others to learn than on being right or comfortable, so your conversations cultivate more trust and respect. When you're able to align your behavior with your intentions and act in a way that is candid yet curious, courageous yet humble, you're viewed as more trustworthy and authentic. Such congruence and balance are impossible, however, if you lack the ability to recognize when your *min* and *"win"* tendencies threaten to separate your actions from your objectives. It is in this way that trust and conversational capacity are inextricably linked.

To Sum Up

The product of your mental workshop is *clear thinking*, and the process is *learning*. When you're up against a tense situation or tough problem, rather than treat your mind like a temple to sanctify or a fort to protect, roll up your sleeves and treat it like a workshop to use. Recognizing you're either dedicated to informed choice or willful ignorance, muster the discipline to focus on learning and start working on the issue.

As you do this, your conversations will be less egotistical and more purposeful; less about looking good, feeling right, or avoiding emotional discomfort and more about making meaningful progress and constructive change. This learning-focused mindset will infuse your use of the candor and curiosity skills with authenticity. (I'd rather talk with someone who has this mindset in place but is a little rusty with the skills than someone who is using the skills but doesn't really mean it.)

> *Your job as a leader is to be right at the end of the meeting,*
> *not at the beginning of the meeting.*
> —DAVID M. COTE

Remember when you're in your workshop, you're not trying to create agreement but learning. You're working hard to help whoever is making a decision to make the smartest decision possible. With this in mind, you refuse to accept the worldview that your mind hands you by constantly seeking to expand and improve it. In pursuit of insight, knowledge, and wisdom you're always asking several important questions:

- *What is the problem we're trying to solve?*

- *What do I think we should do to address it? Why do I think this? And what am I seeing that others are missing?*

- *What do others think about the problem and how to address it? What are they seeing that I'm missing?*

- *What are we all missing? Do we have a collective blind spot?*

By asking questions like these, you acknowledge the choice between intelligence and ignorance, and choose to start the process of learning. And whether it's to yourself or out loud to others, by saying "OK, let's take this issue into the workshop" is a simple way to do just that.

EXPANDING THE SWEET SPOT

Eight More Balanced "Character-istics"

To change old values ... work at developing new values.
—DOUGLAS LaBIER

The "sweet spot" in a conversation is where candor and courage are balanced with curiosity and humility. It's in this sweet spot where the best conversations occur, especially when you're toiling in difficult circumstances, grappling with challenging issues, or working across tricky boundaries.

Candor ➡ ● ⬅ Curiosity

Courage ➡ ● ⬅ Humility

When you're in the sweet spot, you're direct and clear about your own views, but you're also keen to explore new ideas and divergent perspectives. But as Steve demonstrated, being honest and direct doesn't just require candor; it can also take tremendous courage. If you're to raise tough issues, speak hard truths, and confront brutal facts, you must marshal the gumption to speak up, even when your ideas are unpopular, inconvenient, or controversial.

But because few things provoke defensiveness and hinder learning more effectively than arrogance, when you're in the sweet spot you're also intellectually humble. You make yourself vulnerable by testing your own perspectives and working hard to explore those of others. You're *more interested in making a difference than in making an impression.* (And when you think about it, the best way to make an impression *is* by making a difference.) Your curiosity and humility, in other words, prevent you from coming across as just a candidly courageous asshole.[1]

The Sweet Spot Expanded

As I reflect on the people who've built their conversational capacity and used it to inspire constructive change, I realize that there's more to it than just candor and courage balanced with curiosity and humility. There's a larger suite of counterbalanced traits by which they strive to operate. Because these traits are all aspects of character, a better way to describe them is "*character*-istics." In this chapter, I'll share them with four main goals in mind:

1. To provide an expanded suite of counterbalancing characteristics you can cultivate to build your conversational capacity.

2. To create a deeper appreciation for why leadership is so hard and yet so precious.

3. To reinforce the idea that in order to build healthier, more effective organizations, we need to become healthier, more effective people.

4. To expand your notions about the personal work you must do if you're to be effective in your leadership quest.

What are these additional attributes? Here is a list:

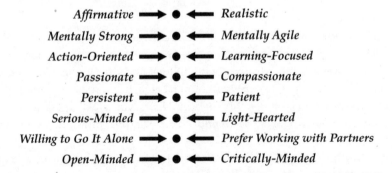

Affirmative ➡ ● ⬅ *Realistic*

Mentally Strong ➡ ● ⬅ *Mentally Agile*

Action-Oriented ➡ ● ⬅ *Learning-Focused*

Passionate ➡ ● ⬅ *Compassionate*

Persistent ➡ ● ⬅ *Patient*

Serious-Minded ➡ ● ⬅ *Light-Hearted*

Willing to Go It Alone ➡ ● ⬅ *Prefer Working with Partners*

Open-Minded ➡ ● ⬅ *Critically-Minded*

Let's explore each pair of characteristics and the essential role they play when you're trying to inspire and orchestrate meaningful change.

Affirmative → ← Realistic

As I've helped people from all over the world build their capacity to work in the sweet spot as they engage the important issues they're facing, the more I appreciate one characteristic that rides high above all others. None of the other aspects of mindset matter if it's missing. What is this pivotal piece of mental software, you ask? It's an *affirmative bias:* a willingness to focus on what *can* be done, as opposed to what can't be done; to see the opportunities in a challenging situation, not just the limitations; and to adopt an optimistic approach to a messy predicament, rather than a pessimistic one.

An affirmative bias is not just shallow positive thinking. It's more than just faking a smile while discounting or denying the ugly aspects of the situation. With an affirmative bias your eyes are wide open. You're keenly aware of the unwelcome nature of the predicament you're facing, yet you're confident in your ability to do something constructive about it. Even with a no-nonsense view of the hard realities you're up against, you still adopt a mindset that says: "It's possible I can do something productive here." You're passionate. You're affirmative. You're ready to take action. "Let's roll up our sleeves and work hard to improve this screwed-up situation," you say to yourself and to others, "and while we're at it, let's *learn* something along the way." You're adopting an attitude that says "yes" to the mess.[2]

> *Optimistic people play a disproportionate role in shaping our lives. Their decisions make a difference; they are inventors, entrepreneurs, political and military leaders—not average people. They got to where they are by seeking challenges and taking risks.*
> —DANIEL KAHNEMAN

This dual focus is akin to a concept—"the Stockdale Paradox"—that Jim Collins made popular in his bestselling book *Good to Great*. This paradox is named after Vice Admiral James Stockdale, a former prisoner of war, who described the paradoxical mindset needed to sustain yourself through intense difficulty: "Retain faith that you will prevail in the end, regardless of the difficulties," he says. "And at the same time confront the most brutal facts of your current reality." This dual focus is key. Collins then asked

Stockdale about the kind of people who didn't survive. "Oh, that's easy," he said. "The optimists."

> Oh, they were the ones who said, "We're going to be out by Christmas." And Christmas would come, and Christmas would go. Then they'd say, "We're going to be out by Easter." And Easter would come, and Easter would go. And then Thanksgiving, and then it would be Christmas again. And they died of a broken heart.

> This is a very important lesson. You must never confuse faith that you will prevail in the end—which you can never afford to lose—with the discipline to confront the most brutal facts of your current reality, whatever they might be.[3]

There are two reasons this aspect of the mindset is so essential: First, it determines your focus. It sets the filter by which you make sense of the world around you. With an Eeyore mindset, you focus on what's impossible, on all the reasons things will fail. Your mind scans a situation looking for excuses, and they're always easy to find. As Richard Bach put it, "argue for your limitations and sure enough, they're yours."[4]

But with an affirmative bias, you intentionally dial into what's possible. You hold the view that something useful can be done and that you can make a difference. Your mind scans the situations looking for opportunity. This is a radical and transformative filter by which to operate in life.

> *Just because you're naked*
> *doesn't mean you're sexy,*
> *Just because you're cynical*
> *doesn't mean you're cool.*
> **—TOM ROBBINS**

There is a second reason that an affirmative bias is such a powerful aspect of the mindset: without it, you fail before you start, or worse still, you fail because you never start. "You don't always win when you try," says Alex Lifeson, "but you always fail when you don't."[5] The awareness and skills don't matter if you're convinced the situation is hopeless.

> *What's needed is an affirmative belief that a solution exists and that something positive will emerge. In fact this is a skill of the imagination . . .*
> **—FRANK BARRETT**

Steve personifies this balanced approach. He didn't look at his circumstances and think, "This is a real mess, and someone should speak up. But I'm just the new guy here. There's not much I can do." He thought instead, "This is a real mess. But just because I'm the new guy doesn't mean I can't make a difference. But I'm not stupid. I know it won't be easy." Even more impressive, Steve maintained his affirmative stance while confronted with pessimistic points of view. Assuming it would go poorly, his fellow team members not only avoided the conversation themselves, they pressed Steve to do the same. One even referred to Steve's intention as "career suicide."

You don't always win when you try, but you always fail when you don't.
—ALEX LIFESON

While there's no way Steve would have raised the issue with Phil without the belief that he could help solve the problem, Steve wasn't blindly optimistic either. He recognized the risks and prepared for them. This is an important point: *Without an* affirmative bias *Steve wouldn't incur the risk of speaking to Phil; but without a* realistic view *of the situation he wouldn't put as much effort into preparing for it.* By holding a belief that the problem was solvable, while simultaneously accepting all the hard facts, Steve exemplifies the affirmative bias in action.

In order to carry a positive action we must develop here a positive vision.
—DALAI LAMA

Mentally Tough → ← Mentally Agile

Another indispensable characteristic is *mental toughness*. The word "fortitude" is close to this aspect of the mindset, but it's not a perfect fit. The requisite mental stance is one of grit, determination, resilience, gumption, or a tenacious stick-with-it-ness.

Mental toughness is important in three ways:

- First, it gives you the strength to deal with the inevitable stresses, tensions, confusion, and frustrations of exercising leadership.

- Second, it gives you the strength to keep your mind centered on *purpose* and not let fear, ego, or discouragement knock you off balance. It takes mental strength to control your thoughts, direct your beam of attention, regulate your emotional reactions, and keep your behavior and your intentions aligned, regardless of circumstances. This is the key to living intentionally. Without mental toughness, your behavior is undisciplined and reactive. You're doomed to living a life that is little more than one knee-jerk reaction to one circumstance after another. When you're mentally weak you're highly triggerable.

- Third, it is the key to more robust thinking. As tempting as it may be, you have the strength to avoid simple, easy assumptions about a situation. You're not weak-minded. Your thinking is more rigorous and disciplined. Your baloney detection kit is in full use.

> *Strong minds suffer without complaining; weak*
> *minds complain without suffering.*
> **—LETTIE COWMAN**

In Japanese there is a word, *ganbaru*, that conveys this mentally tough stance. Loosely translated, it means "to stick with something difficult until it's complete." The common phrase *ganbatte kudasai* is often translated into English as "please hang in there." But it actually has a far deeper and more intense meaning: "Be tenacious, stick with it even under intense doubt or pressure, don't cave in—you can do it. I believe in you because I know you've got more strength than you think!"

Other languages share similar notions. *Sisu*, for example, is a Finnish concept that captures the essence of this mindset extremely well. Emilia Lahti, a native of Finland and a leading expert on the topic, explains it this way:

> The small Nordic country of Finland has a cultural construct known as "sisu," used to describe the enigmatic power that enables individuals to push through unbearable hardships. The term dates back hundreds of years and is a central part of Finnish collective discourse. Sisu is fortitude, perseverance and indomitable determination in the face of extreme adversity. . . . Sisu provides the final empowering push, when we would otherwise hesitate to act.[6]

To balance your mental toughness, you also need *mental agility*—the ability to adopt a jazz-like approach to novel situations, and to learn and adapt to unfamiliar circumstances with cognitive dexterity. "What we need to add to our list of . . . skills," says my friend and colleague Frank

Barrett, author of *Yes to the Mess*, "is improvisation—the art of adjusting, flexibly adapting, learning through trial-and-error initiatives, inventing ad hoc responses, and discovering as you go."[7]

The ability to adjust your mental models to new information, ideas, or evidence gives you a far greater capacity for adaptive learning, enabling you to respond to unfamiliar circumstances and tough new realities in a flexible rather than rigid way. Intellectually nimble, you're able to shape your thinking to fit the problem rather than frame the problem to fit your thinking. You're curious, leaning into difference, and less attached to being right because you know you are smarter when you are open to other points of view and dumber when you're trapped in your own.

You're able to shape your thinking to fit the problem

rather than frame the problem to fit your thinking.

As Steve worked with Phil to address the challenge in their team, he knew it would be difficult and he prepared accordingly. He was courageous in giving it a go, humble in how he prepared, strong in his determination to make a difference, yet flexible and learning-focused in how he handled it.

Passionate → ← Compassionate

Driven by a deep sense of purpose and driving passion to spark constructive progress, you throw yourself into the work of creating a stronger team, organization, or community. You have a wholehearted ambition to make a difference.

Passion is one great force that unleashes creativity, because if you're passionate about something, then you're more willing to take risks.
—YO-YO MA

But while passionate about inspiring change, your strong conviction is tempered with empathy and a genuine concern for others. You're aware that change is hard, and that others may feel threatened, insecure, or afraid of the changes you're advocating. You realize that even constructive adjustments to the status quo are hard for some people. So, your passionate enthusiasm and hard-nosed dedication to the cause is balanced with empathy, understanding, concern, and warmth.

I find that compassion is closely associated with personal awareness and humility. The more aware I become about my own weaknesses, emotional reactions, and cognitive errors, for example, the more compassion I have for others. I'm less judgmental when I see others behaving poorly because I'm all too aware of how often I behave poorly.

Serious-Minded → ← *Light-Hearted*

You don't just rush into important situations with your thought process half-cocked, making decisions in a casual, half-assed manner. You respond in a rigorous, serious-minded way. You're disciplined, deliberate, and careful as you strive to make useful sense of the predicament you're facing and how to address it.

But at the same time, you remain lighthearted and humorous. You focus on the funny moments, not just the frustrating ones. "There's a humorous side to every situation," said George Carlin. "The challenge is to find it." With this in mind you pay attention to the ironies and absurdities in a situation, not just the irritations and dysfunctions.

Most important, you're not afraid to laugh at yourself or at the predicament you're in. This is a vital balance to strike when you're doing adaptive work. Humor lowers defensiveness, and when directed at yourself humor is a powerful guard against arrogance, self-deception, and narcissism. Able to hold both attitudes in your mind at once, you simultaneously recognize the gravity of an issue and still laugh at how you and others are responding to it. This balance fosters an atmosphere that lowers defensiveness and increases learning—and, in an adaptive context, learning is the key to progress.

> *As you proceed through life, following your own path, birds will shit on you. Don't bother to brush it off. Getting a comedic view of your situation gives you spiritual distance. Having a sense of humor saves you.*
> —JOSEPH CAMPBELL

It's for this reason, I've found, that people and groups with high conversational capacity tend to laugh more. Less ego-driven, uptight, and self-protective, and more purpose-driven, vulnerable, and self-possessed, they're able to remain light-hearted and learning-focused even when things go sideways. This means their conversations and meetings are not just more effective—they're often more fun.

Persistence → ← Patience

With unflappable focus and realistic expectations you're raising issues no one else will raise and working hard to resolve those issues productively. Like a hiker ascending a steep mountain pass, you continue pushing forward, one step at a time, even in the face of resistance or setback. You're persistent and tenacious even as you pursue change.

> *Persistence is probably the single most common quality of high achievers. They simply refuse to give up. The longer you hang in there, the greater the chance that something will happen in your favor. No matter how hard it seems, the longer you persist the more likely your success.*
> —JACK CANFIELD

But at the same time, you're bright enough to know that making constructive change is more like a long trail run than a short walk to the mailbox, so you're patient. You pace yourself. You don't expect instant change. You're willing to take two steps forward and one step back because you know that if you're smart, persistent, and patient, progress is not only possible, it's probable.

Action-Oriented → ← Learning-Focused

Motivated to make a productive difference, you operate by a core set of ideas:

- A problem won't get solved unless you *solve* it.

- An opportunity isn't an opportunity until you *take* it.

- An obstacle isn't an obstacle once you *overcome* it.

With these ideas in mind, you don't just sit back and observe, analyze, research, and plan, and then once you've got things all figured out, finally jump in and take action. You've got *an action mindset*. You want to make change and you're active in pursuing it. You're engaging problems, confronting nonsense, raising issues, asking tough questions, and suggesting improvements.

But you're not just jumping in on blind impulse. You're acting intelligently. You know that the best way to learn about a situation is to try and change it. Put differently, you're holding your theory of change—your idea for *what* needs to happen and *why*—like a hypothesis that you test and revise as you go along. "I took some action," you say to yourself. "What did I learn about the problem? What new information did I gain? What differing mental models of the situation did I encounter? What insights did I spark, and how might these fresh insights make my next action more focused and effective?"

Acknowledging all this, you adopt a curious, "learn as you go" attitude. Viewing action as an essential part of the learning process, you use your interventions to pry open the doors of discovery. As Frank Barrett, an expert on jazz sensibilities and leadership effectiveness, puts it, much like a jazz musician, you're *performing* and *experimenting* at the same time.[8] This approach prevents you from getting stuck in analysis paralysis—endlessly holding off action until you have a clear way forward—but it also keeps you from being rigidly attached to your initial perspective and plan.

To some people, the idea that learning and action are so closely related seems contradictory. To their way of thinking, you're supposed to formulate a strategy and then execute it. You *plan* and then you *do*. But while this might work for simple problems, in an adaptive context—where there is no obvious solution and learning is the key progress—they're actually two sides of the same coin. Learning with no action and you're an armchair academic. Action with no learning and you're a crash-test dummy.

Learning with no action and you're an armchair academic.

Action with no learning and you're a crash-test dummy.

Steve's approach to working with Phil illustrates this duality. He didn't wait until he understood the problem completely before talking with Phil. He recognized that the only way he could figure out the problem was *by* talking with Phil. The information he gained from his conversation inspired entirely new ways of framing the problem, and, as a result, a more integrated way of addressing it.

Willing to Go It Alone → ← Prefer Working with Partners

You're prepared to take action alone if necessary. You're neither waiting for permission, nor for someone to back you up before you act. You're willing to perform solo. But at the same time, you have a strong preference for partners—people with similar convictions and concerns who might work with you to address the issues at hand. You realize that leadership is rarely a solo act. It tends to come from a team.*

And not just any partner will do. You specifically seek out people who share a common purpose, but also expand your horizons; people who will give you sharp feedback and provide strong support. Dean Williams explains this in his book *Leadership for a Fractured World*:

> You need people around you who can help expand your boundaries rather than reinforce your boundaries. You need people to partner with you in the creative exploration of ideas and strategy—people that push you, challenge you, and help you grow multidimensionally as a change agent and as a human being. If you are going to provide leadership . . . you personally must value the power of interdependence in the form of partners and collaborators in increasing your leadership capacity.[9]

In addition to expanding your boundaries, Williams shares another key attribute of the cohorts you're pursuing:

> In seeking partners, look for people who bring a unity of purpose and complimentarity—that is, they share the greater mission or higher purpose you are championing. Although their styles and perspectives might be different, people with a shared purpose can play off one another to produce something that is distinctive.

Partnering with such people is like playing jazz. As Frank Barrett puts it, "Jazz involves jamming with people who don't see things exactly the same way."[10]

So, while you're willing to fly solo, you're seeking partners who share your sense of purpose, expand your thinking, complement your style and skills, and provide support. That's a tall order.

---

* See "Real Leadership Rarely Comes from Just One Person," on pages 193–195 of *Conversational Capacity*.

There is still another important variable. They need to be *stalwart*: "Creative work is messy work, so you need a collaborator who has a stomach for it and who is not going to flee when the going gets tough or when you are feeling raw and vulnerable," says Williams. "It can be painful at times as you must explore numerous pathways to discover what works, even if that entails going down paths that may turn out to be dead ends. A good partner understands that this is a critical feature of the creative process, and, therefore brings patience and persistence to the relationship. They support you in your leadership journey."[11]

Again, Frank Barrett reinforces this idea:

> Jazz players don't innovate by isolating or breaking off from others. They don't wait for inspiration. They don't think of themselves as creating something out of nothing. They innovate by being tightly coupled to a diverse group of specialists, noticing the potential in people, ideas, and utterances. In a sense they are engaged in constructive [dialogue].[12]

Open-Minded → ← Critically-Minded

This characteristic takes you right back to your mental workshop, so there's no need to spend much time on it here. Suffice it to say that you're pooling perspectives and leaning into difference to expand and improve your thinking, but at the same time you're vetting and evaluating the information you're taking in. You're open and inquisitive, but your B.S. detector is on high power.

The Ball Is in Your Court

In this chapter, I've dramatically expanded what it means to work in the sweet spot by sharing a suite of characteristics that will help you exercise more effective leadership, do more engaging work, and foster more useful change. The ball is now in your court. Given the kind of leadership you want to exercise and the issues you want to address, what characteristics do you need to cultivate?

Given the kind of leadership you want to exercise

and the issues you want to address, what

characteristics do you need to cultivate?

It's not a casual choice. Building this mindset—this deliberate way of thinking, of seeing, of being—is not easy. There is no magic pill. There is no optical device you can surgically implant that allows you to see the world in a different way. If you want to adopt this mindset and strengthen it, you'll need to do the work. What is that work, you ask? That is the focus of Chapter 9 in which you'll learn how to cultivate this mindset and put it into action.

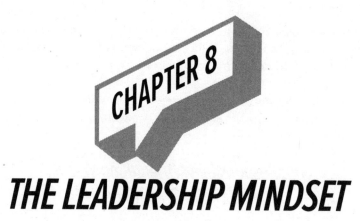

THE LEADERSHIP MINDSET

Taking Responsibility and Being Constructive

> *. . . the productive person animates that which he touches.*
> *He gives soul to that which surrounds him.*
> **—ERICH FROMM**

In this chapter, we'll explore *the leadership mindset,* an indispensable mental stance for anyone yearning to wield more constructive influence. But before we do, it's important to remember a key point I made in the Introduction: Real leadership isn't about stepping in and taking charge, armed with all the right answers. And it isn't about your position, expertise, or authority. *Real leadership comes from the kind of work you're doing.* Leadership is about helping people and groups solve tough problems by spurring integrative learning. When you take responsibility for inspiring and effecting adaptive change, no matter your station, you're exercising leadership.

If your goal is to do this, you need to deliberately adopt and strengthen a *leadership mindset* that stems from two dispositions: the *responsibility orientation* and the *constructive orientation.* These orientations differ from the counterbalancing characteristics of the sweet spot. Rather than being mutually balanced, they are two sets of opposing traits. Each one sits on one end of a continuum with a *contrasting* orientation at the other end.

To adopt this leadership mindset you'll need to cultivate both a strong sense of *responsibility* and a *constructive* stance. So, let's take a closer look at both sets of opposing characteristics: first the *responsibility* versus the *victim* orientation, and then the even more vital distinction between the *constructive* and the *destruction* orientation.

Victim Orientation ◄──────► Responsibility Orientation

Destructive Orientation ◄──────► Constructive Orientation

The Responsibility Orientation Versus the Victim Orientation

The Responsibility Orientation

A person with a *responsibility orientation* has what psychologists refer to as an *internal locus of control*. They see themselves as intentional agents in their own lives and as active shapers of circumstance. They take responsibility for their decisions because they see their choices as a way to influence and change the situations that they're in. "A person with an internal locus of control," says Brian Tracy, "feels that he or she is in charge and is making the decisions that determine the direction of his or her life."[1] So if they get a bad performance review, for example, they immediately begin reflecting on what *they* may have done to score so poorly, and then try to figure out steps *they* can take to get a better review next time. They see themselves, not their context, in control of their fate.

Responsibly-oriented individuals tend toward the *growth mindset* outlined by Carol Dweck. "Individuals who believe their talents can be developed (through hard work, good strategies, and input from others) have a growth mindset. They tend to achieve more than those with a more fixed mindset (those who believe their talents are innate gifts)."[2]

ROBERT SMALLS

To illustrate the *responsibility orientation* let me share the extraordinary and inspiring story of Robert Smalls, an underappreciated American hero. He was a man who took impressive action in a system devised to prevent it. Smalls, you see, was a slave in the American South during the Civil War. Legally, he was the *property* of his master. This is a difficult fact to grasp, much less to overemphasize. It wasn't just that Smalls lacked freedom; in this society, he wasn't even considered a full human being. "Slaves had no constitutional rights; they could not testify in court against a white person; they could not leave the plantation without permission. Slaves often found themselves rented out, used as prizes in lotteries, or as wagers in card games and horse races."[3]

It's hard to imagine a situation that could make it more difficult to adopt a responsibility orientation. The horrific, cold-blooded system of slavery was *designed* to victimize people—to emotionally and mentally break them so that they would not, or could *not*, take responsibility for their plight.

But, despite his circumstances, Smalls responded to his predicament with remarkable boldness. Late one night, after a year of careful planning, he stole the ship on which he'd been working, the *Planter*, a cotton transport ship that the Confederacy had seized and converted into a gunboat. He then snuck aboard his wife and 16 other slaves before donning the captain's hat and bluffing his way through multiple Confederate checkpoints, including the heavily armed Fort Sumter, by using the appropriate coded signals he'd memorized.

But escaping the Confederacy was only the first challenge. The situation grew even riskier when he cleared Confederate waters and approached the powerful Union navy blockading Charleston harbor. This was the most perilous part of the escape because he risked being attacked. A Union ship was just about to fire on the approaching Confederate gunboat, in fact, when at the last minute a Union sailor cried out: "I see something that looks like a white flag."[4]

Smalls surrendered to the Union, declaring to the officer in charge, "Good morning, sir! I've brought you some of the old United States guns, sir!" With this courageous act he secured freedom for himself, his wife, and his fellow passengers. Although he was a 23-year-old slave, Smalls's actions were called "one of the boldest and most daring things of the war."

But he didn't stop there. After escaping from slavery, he maintained his passionate *responsibility orientation* and kept up the fight, first by helping persuade Abraham Lincoln to admit African-Americans into the military to fight against the South, and, after the Civil War ended, by getting elected to the South Carolina State Legislature and then to the U.S. House of Representatives.[5]

Robert Smalls is an awe-inspiring example of the *responsibility orientation* in action. "Although born a slave," he later said, "I always felt that I was a man and ought to be free, and I would be free or die."[6]

This remarkable story reinforces several concepts from the last chapter. For example, Smalls's life is a great example of *patience* and *persistence*. He planned the escape for a year. He had both a *realistic view* of his predicament and an *affirmative bias*. His story is also an obvious example of *courage* and *conviction*. Smalls would have been executed if he'd been caught, and he had to clear no less than four Confederate checkpoints to get out of the harbor. (Imagine how he must have felt at every one of those encounters, with the lives of his fellow passengers, including his wife, hanging in the balance.) Then, even after escaping the Confederates, there was still a good chance he'd be attacked by the Union navy before he had the chance to surrender.

What's so remarkable about this story is that Smalls accomplished this astounding feat in a system that was *designed* to victimize. But even though the risks were high, Smalls found a unique opportunity and took advantage of it. By escaping the Confederacy, working to convince President Lincoln to allow African-Americans to fight for the Union army, and then by getting elected to public office (in the same state in which he'd originally been a slave), Robert Smalls chose to stand up, speak out, and make a difference for himself, for his family, for his friends, and for his country.

I find this story both inspiring and humbling. *Inspiring* in that it sets a high standard for the difference a single person can make, even when conditions conspire against them. *Humbling* because when I'm in a tough situation, and taking less responsibility than I should for my plight, reflecting on the life of Robert Smalls helps me frame my predicament in a more modest way.

RESPONSIBLE SELF-TALK

One of the clearest signals that you've got this mindset is your *self-talk*. In a tough situation, responsible self-talk sounds like this:

- *The status quo won't do.*

- *I can do something constructive here.*

- *What can I do to make this messy situation a little better?*

- *It may not be in my job description, but it's the right thing to do.*

- *I'm willing to take an intelligent risk.*

- *If I'm to be effective I need to take responsibility for my tendencies and behave in a more deliberate and disciplined way.*

- *I am responsible for my behavior and my effectiveness. I'm not dependent on other people or on circumstances to do my best work and put forward my best efforts.*

It's not always easy to tell where you should take more, rather than less, responsibility for a challenge, problem, or opportunity. M. Scott Peck put it this way:

... the problem of distinguishing what we are and what we are not responsible for in this life is one of the greatest problems of human existence. It is never completely solved; for the entirety of our lives we must continually assess and reassess where our responsibilities lie in the ever-changing course of events.[7]

But with a *responsibility orientation*, your bias is toward taking more responsibility rather than taking less responsibility. You focus on what you *can* do rather than on what you *can't*. This is the key. There is no way to exercise leadership without taking responsibility.

There is no way to exercise leadership

without taking responsibility.

The Victim Orientation

Contrast the *responsibility orientation* with a characteristic sitting at the other end of the spectrum, the *victim orientation*. People with this frame of mind have an *external* locus of control. They see themselves as passive pawns in the process, as victims of circumstance. And because they take little responsibility for their decisions, they have an *irresponsibility orientation*. Their choices, as they see them, are dictated to them by their situation.

"The person with an external locus of control," explains Brian Tracy, "feels that others are in charge, and that he or she is controlled by external factors and influences about which he can do very little. They feel that their boss, their bills, their childhood experiences, or their current marriage or relationship controls their life." Rendered rudderless by their lack of responsibility, they allow events to determine their choices and the direction of their lives. When they get a bad performance review, for example, they immediately begin blaming other people and circumstances for their low scores because they see external factors, not their own choices, as responsible for their plight.

Undisciplined and reactive, people with a *victim mindset* are fragile and triggerable. This creates a vicious cycle. Their self-image as a victim is magnified by their inability to manage their emotional tendencies and the counterproductive reactions they unleash. Then, when their behavior and intentions part ways, they accept no responsibility for their own lack of discipline, and instead blame other people and circumstances for their own incompetence. In this way, at its worst, the *victim orientation* spawns a downward spiral. With each passing day, these people feel less as active agents of change and more as passive victims of circumstance. Given all this, the victim *syndrome* is a more apt description.

VICTIM SELF-TALK

Again, a strong clue that you're re trapped in this sewer of a mindset can be found in your *self-talk*:

- *It's not my fault.*

- *It's not my job.*

- *There's nothing I can do about this predicament.*

- *This is someone else's problem.*

- *It's not my fault my behavior was so reactive; other people provoked me.*

- *This is above my pay grade.*

- *I'm not taking this dumb risk. Let some other idiot do it.*

- *If other people behaved differently, and if circumstances were improved, I could be so much more effective.*

The *leadership mindset* is so important to your ability to take action, wield influence, and make a difference because it profoundly affects the degree to which you take responsibility for two things:

1. It determines whether you'll engage the status quo or accept it. Taking action and trying to promote constructive change is an act of responsibility.

2. It also determines whether you'll take charge of *your own behavior* in tough conversations, and whether you'll put in the work required to gear up for them. Without a *responsibility mindset*, Steve wouldn't have put so much careful preparation into managing his own reactions in the conversation with Phil. He probably wouldn't have raised his concerns at all. Similarly, with a *leadership mindset* you don't just recognize your triggers; you own them. And in doing so you take responsibility for your effectiveness by doing the hard work of preparing for important encounters. This stands in stark contrast to people with a *victim orientation,* who blame other people and imperfect circumstances for their own inaction and incompetence.

The Constructive Orientation Versus the Destructive Orientation

The second and more significant distinction is the contrast between the *constructive* and the *destructive* orientations.

The Constructive Orientation

People with a *constructive orientation* strive to build things up rather than tear them down. Even in the midst of setbacks, they remain realistically optimistic and focus on what *can* be done rather than what *can't* be done. With this characteristic, which Erich Fromm described as "biophilic"[8] (loves life), a person is always trying to make things healthier, smarter, and more effective. With a constructive orientation, you're not just trying to make things different; you're trying to make things better.

> With a constructive orientation, you're not just trying to
>
> make things different; you're trying to make things better.

Concerned about the people around them, constructive people celebrate when others excel or succeed, and offer support when others fall down or fail. They focus on the strengths and good intentions of others rather than their weaknesses and imperfections. They're loving rather than hating, encouraging rather than discouraging, kind rather than mean, and positive rather than negative.

It's in the nature of these people to nurture—themselves, others, their teams, organizations, communities, and the environment—so they're driven to create, to build, and to improve. Looking for ways to make positive change, they view problems as opportunities for learning and progress. Focused on promoting constructive progress rather than on inflating their own ego, they have a mutually beneficial relationship with their organization or community. People with a *constructive* mindset are always trying to make the world around them more vibrant and healthy. That said, when you have a *constructive mindset*, you're not a naïve, holier-than-thou Dudley-Do-Right. You have a pragmatic, clear-headed view of the mess you're in, the challenges you face, and your personal limitations. The difference is in your choices. You choose to play a constructive role and prompt significant change. You embody the realistic yet affirmative mindset we explored in the last chapter. Even when things are really screwed up and people around you are shutting down, giving up, or going negative, you direct your energies toward *progress, growth*, and *learning*.

Here again Steve provides a great example. He took responsibility to inspire constructive progress, but not to look good or to stroke his ego. He did it out of a genuine desire to make Phil, the team, and the organization more effective. And that's not the only example in that situation. Two of Steve's colleagues partnered with him to help him prepare. Despite disagreeing with his decision to address the issue, they supported Steve by helping him create a conversational game plan for the encounter. They even called him at home the night before to provide encouragement and support.

CONSTRUCTIVE SELF-TALK

A constructive orientation is also reflected in your *self-talk*:

- *What can I do to make this situation better?*
- *What is the most useful thing to do here?*
- *What can I do to make this conversation smarter and more effective?*
- *What responses will promote progress rather than hinder it?*
- *How can I support other people who are trying to do something productive?*
- *What behavior will foster more learning and less defensiveness?*

The Destructive Orientation

People with a *destructive orientation* delight in tearing things down rather than building things up. When faced with problems or setbacks, they focus on what *can't* be done rather than what *can*. Obsessively selfish and caustic, they refuse to lift a finger to make things better, and they're often looking for opportunities to make things worse.

Destructive people are annoyed when others succeed or excel, and they are pleased when others fall down or fail. They focus on the imperfections of others and prey on their vulnerabilities. They feel they can only win if others are losing. (Consider the CEO who walked around his office taking swings with a baseball bat, musing out loud about which of his people might get fired next, and who declared, "It's not just enough to fly in first class; I have to know my friends are flying in coach."[9]) They're contemptuous rather than compassionate, discouraging rather than encouraging, cynical rather than confident, callous rather than kind, and negative rather than positive. They have more apathy or animosity than commitment or concern.

Focused on inflating their ego rather than on promoting progress or providing help, their relationship with their team, organization, or community is parasitic. Interested only in what's in it for them, they suck the blood out of the host for their own self-centered ambitions and needs. They see relationships as transactional and opportunistic, and plagued by a zero-sum attitude, they use them to further their own selfish needs with little regard for shared goals or the well-being of other people. When a problem crops up, destructive people respond in unhelpful ways. Rather than work to address the issue, they let it fester or, worse, they inflame it. They often seek opportunities to make mischief or cause trouble, and then they use those problems for their own advantage. People with a destructive orientation make the world around them a darker, lesser place.*

People with a destructive orientation make the world around them a darker, lesser place.

To *experience* what it's like to be in the presence of someone with a malignant mindset like this, watch the 1999 film *The Green Mile* and pay attention to the character Percy, the malevolent, dark-souled prison guard, played by the actor Doug Hutchison. (As you watch the film, contrast Percy's orientation with the more constructive mindset demonstrated by the character Paul, played by Tom Hanks. Pay close attention to how differently Percy and Paul respond to the same people and events.) For a literary example, consider Shakespeare's character Iago in *Othello*, widely regarded as one of the most nefarious and destructive characters in literature.[†]

---

* For a more rigorous perspective on the destructive orientation, explore the research on what psychologists refer to as the "dark triad" of personality: narcissism, Machiavellianism, and psychopathy.

† *Schindler's List* provides another cinematic experience. Compare the actions of Oskar Schindler (Liam Neeson) with the actions of Amon Goeth (Ralph Fiennes).

DESTRUCTIVE SELF-TALK

You know you're on the destructive side of the scale when your self-talk sounds like this:

- *What's in this for me?*
- *This is not my fault.*
- *Who can I blame for this?*
- *I can't be bothered. Let some other chump deal with this problem.*
- *How can I turn this mess to my advantage?*
- *What can I do to cause some trouble?*
- *Who is out to get me?*
- *Things are "FUBAR" and someone needs to pay for it.*
- *Why is everyone out to get me?*

Where Are You on This Continuum?

The Malignant Mindset		The Leadership Mindset
Victim Orientation	⟷	*Responsibility Orientation*
Destructive Orientation	⟷	*Constructive Orientation*

All your choices and actions—about what to eat, with whom to associate, what to read, whether or not to exercise, whether or not to bring up an issue or suggest a solution, what ideas will occupy your mind—fall somewhere on the continuum between *constructive* and *destructive*. It's the patterns that count. A constructive decision every so often probably won't do you much good. And a destructive reaction every once in a while might not do much harm. As with diet or exercise, it's the trend *over time* that matters. If your goal is to take action, wield influence, and make a difference, you must consciously adopt a responsibly *constructive orientation*, and then align your behavior with that worldview.

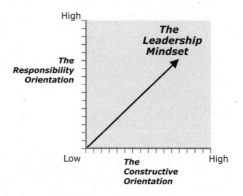

What are the dominant patterns in your life choices? Are they mostly responsible and constructive with the occasional slip into victim and destructive? Or are they the opposite? Perhaps you're somewhere in the middle, bouncing back and forth, depending on the day? These are important questions to consider, for the choices you make lead to the character you cultivate:

> An old Cherokee is teaching his grandson about life. "A fight is going on inside me," he said to the boy. "It is a terrible fight and it is between two wolves. One is evil—he is anger, envy, sorrow, regret, greed, arrogance, self-pity, guilt, resentment, inferiority, lies, false pride, superiority, and ego." He continued, "The other is good—he is joy, peace, love, hope, serenity, humility, kindness, benevolence, empathy, generosity, truth, compassion, and faith. The same fight is going on inside you—and inside every other person, too."
>
> The grandson thought about it for a minute and then asked his grandfather, "Which wolf will win?"
>
> The old Cherokee simply replied, "*The one you feed.*"[10]

I encourage you to get far more intentional about the characteristics you feed day-to-day. Get engaged and strive to make a meaningful difference in the world.

My primary goal with this book, after all, is to provoke you to spark *adaptive learning* around issues that really matter, all while building your *conversational capacity* and cultivating your better angels. That's right. I'm saying that if you're willing to put in the effort, you can do meaningful work, inspire productive change, and become a more grounded, balanced, and fulfilled person in the process. That's not a bad deal.

STRATEGIES FOR EMBRACING AND STRENGTHENING YOUR MINDSET

Building Your Ability to Place Learning Over Ego

$$\frac{Learning}{Ego}$$

As I said earlier, awareness and skills are important, but what really separates a person who can stay in the sweet spot from a person who can't is how they're thinking. At its core, conversational capacity is a mindset in action.

In this part of the book you learned how to use your mind like a workshop in which sharper thinking and smarter choices are the product. When you're in your mental workshop your behavior isn't driven by fear, anger, resentment, vengeance, or a desire to be comfortable or liked; it's driven by a desire for learning. The big challenge, therefore, is cultivating your ability to stay *mindset forward* even in circumstances that conspire against it.

Cultivating this mindset is the hardest work you'll do as you acquire this discipline. It's also the most important. Your mindset affects your tactics, tone of voice, body language, and facial expressions. And unless your mindset has shifted, what difference does high awareness make? Sure, the skills or balancing candor and curiosity are practical, but unless your mindset is different, why bother using them?

So, the question becomes this: How do you build your *conversational capacity* mindset? The answer to the question is the same as the answer to: "How do you become a runner?" You don't read yourself into being a runner; you lace up and run yourself into being a runner. In a similar way, to build your conversational capacity you don't read yourself into this mindset; you think and act yourself into it. In this chapter, I'll provide ways to strengthen your mindset and keep it in your behavioral driver's seat under pressure.

> *It infuriates me to be wrong when I know I'm right.*
> —MOLIÈRE

Keep an "Indianapolis Journal"

A few years ago, I flew to Indianapolis to deliver a keynote address at a conference. I landed at the airport, hopped in my rental car, and prepared to drive to my hotel. I'd traveled to Indianapolis a couple of times in the recent past, so I remembered how to get to the location. If you'd been with me and asked: "Craig, do you need directions?" I'd have confidently declared: "No thanks. I've been here before. I know where I'm going. It's an easy drive." Had you persisted I might have even gotten snarky. "Look, I travel for a living. I'm good at this. Thanks for your concern, but I'll say it again: I know where I'm going. I don't need directions." I was that *certain* my mental map was correct. Then, armed with this supreme confidence, I zipped out of the airport and promptly got lost.

I later realized *why* I got lost. It turns out that the hotel in my head, the one I thought I was driving to, is in *Wichita*. That's right. I had my cities confused. So, I was driving to an illusion—the hotel in my head does not *exist* in Indianapolis—yet I was absolutely certain that I *knew* where I was going. I was totally convinced I was right, but I was absolutely wrong. That's funny. (It's funny now, anyway. It wasn't funny while it was happening.)

> *There is no way you can use the word "reality"*
> *without quotation marks around it.*
> —JOSEPH CAMPBELL

My Indianapolis experience was a powerful learning moment that continues to influence how I hold my views of "reality." A central idea in my work, after all, is that you can dramatically improve your conversational capacity by learning to hold your perceptions of "reality" like hypotheses rather than truths. But this is easier said than done. Your brain doesn't present to you with a view of "reality" that seems hypothetical. Like a friend all too eager to please you, it often hands you a flawed interpretation of an issue or situation, saying, in essence: "Trust me. This is how things really are." No wonder the psychologist Cordelia Fine says you should "never trust your brain."[1]

I now routinely ask myself a simple question: "Am I having another 'Indianapolis moment' here?" That's a powerful question and I suggest you start using it too. These cognitive disconnects are sacred learning moments if you're open to them. Better still, keep an "Indianapolis Journal" and document your own Indianapolis moments, and those of friends, or even examples you see in the news, on film, or in literature. This simple practice reinforces bedrock aspects of the mindset: curiosity; humility; holding your views of reality as formulations rather than facts; thinking critically; and mental agility— thereby increasing the likelihood you'll pool perspectives, lean into difference, think more critically, and test your views.

As Kathryn Schulz points out: "Most of us don't have a mental category called 'Mistakes I Have Made.' "[2] An Indianapolis Journal is a way to remedy that. You're creating, very deliberately, a "Mistakes I Have Made" file. You're not just noticing when you're wrong—or when you've been wrong— you're writing it down. You're leaning into your wrongness!

When you get into the habit of recognizing your Indianapolis moments, you'll quickly realize that when it comes to acting on faulty maps of "reality," you and I are not alone. You'll regularly see and hear examples in the stories of friends, colleagues, family, and even in the news. Pilots of a Delta Air Lines flight, for example, mistakenly landed their Airbus A320, with 130 passengers on board, at Ellsworth Air Force Base in South Dakota when they thought they were landing at their real destination, the airport in Rapid City, seven miles away. Oops.

I keep my Indianapolis Journal on my desktop right below my "Trigger Journal," and I make new entries several times a week. Sometimes I record my own errors; sometimes I record the stories of others. (This is made easier because in my workshops I often conduct an activity to see who can come up with the funniest Indianapolis story, which gives me access to a wide range of examples. If you'd like to share a story, please send it my way.)

Your mindset matters. It affects everything—from the business and investment decisions you make, to the way you raise your children, to your stress levels and overall well-being.

—PETER DIAMANDIS

Ask Three Big Questions

There are three simple, but powerful, questions that help you build the mindset and keep it in the driver's seat of your behavior. A number of people I've coached found that simply keeping these three questions in front of them during a meeting helps them stay grounded and learning-focused under pressure. (One executive even emailed me to say: "These questions work so well in helping me control my *"win"* tendency I thought about getting them tattooed on the back of my hand!") Teams also report that reviewing these three questions before a meeting, or even writing them on the board, has a positive impact on team behavior. What are the questions?

1. *What am I seeing that others are missing? (Do they have a blind spot? I need to speak up because others may have blind spots that my perspective could illuminate.)*

2. *What are others seeing that I'm missing? (Do I have a blind spot?)*

3. *What are we all missing? (Do we have a collective blind spot?)*

Increase Your SysQ

Boosting your ability to think systemically is another high-leverage activity that enhances multiple aspects of your workshop mindset, from pooling and integrating perspectives, to critical thinking and making smart decisions. It also boosts your situational awareness, an important skill we explored in the last section.

A person with *high systemic intelligence*—or what my close friend and colleague Chris Soderquist refers to as *SysQ*—is better at recognizing long-term trends, seeing how issues play out across organizational or community boundaries, framing problems in a more actionable way, and finding the most high-leverage places to take action. Here are specific ways that cultivating your systemic intelligence reinforces aspects of the conversational capacity mindset:

- *Pooling and Integrating perspectives.* Boosting your systemic intelligence increases your ability to *pool perspectives* in a way that helps you pinpoint high-leverage solutions that aren't immediately visible or obvious—the essence of *integrative thinking.*

- *Critical thinking.* Building your SysQ also improves your *situational awareness* and your *critical thinking* by helping you identify causal relationships, weigh variables in a more useful way, catch and adjust your assumptions (and those of others), and learn where you need more information if you're to make the best decision. It allows you to make more useful sense of a situation you're facing so you can zero in on interventions that will have the greatest impact with the fewest unintended consequences.

A suite of powerful tools is available to help you increase your SysQ (and that of your team or organization), ranging from basic systems thinking questions and behavior-over-time graphs, to causal loop maps and stock-and-flow diagrams. If you'd like to learn more, Chris Soderquist—who I refer to as the "Carl Sagan of systems thinking"—has a great website with a host of tools and information at findinghighleverage.com.

Employ Integrative Thinking

When you're in your mental workshop, the operative question isn't: "What should we *do* to solve this problem?" The question is: "What should we *think* to solve this problem?"[3] The best way to answer this question is to mine divergent viewpoints for insight and then integrate the best of each perspective to engineer a superior solution. You can do that by following these steps:

1. Explore the varying notions about how to address this issue. Delve into difference; seek out alternative views; lean into contrarian perspectives.

2. What is *useful* about each view? What isn't?

3. What assumptions constrain how you and others are making sense of the problem? About yourselves? About your organization? About your market or community? About your customers or clients or the people you're trying to serve?

4. To enhance your decision-making, adopt a different kind of thinking: Rising above "this-*or*-that thinking," indulge in "this-*and*-that thinking." Treat the choices you're facing as building blocks for creating a more elegant, higher-order solution. To do this, ask questions such as these: *As we look at each list, how can we integrate the ideas so that we achieve what we like and jettison what we don't? How can we find a better path forward than the limited options we're currently facing?*

5. Then make short presentations and discuss what you're learning. What new opportunities or ideas emerged? Repeat the process if need be.

To learn more about integrative thinking, I'd suggest two books:

- *Creating Great Choices: A Leader's Guide to Integrative Thinking* by Jennifer Riel and Roger Martin

- *The Opposable Mind: Winning Through Integrative Thinking* by Roger Martin[4]

Cultivate an Anti-Confirmation Bias

Left to its own devices, your mind naturally seeks out confirming ideas and information. It likes to think in a rut. But you can force it out of its comfort zone and dramatically increase your mental agility by exploring opposing ideas. To do this, establish the habit of delving into ideas, research, perspectives, and information that *contrast* with your current take on things. Lean into difference. Talk to people with whom you disagree. You're not doing this to agree with every perspective you explore; you're doing it to learn.

Madeleine Van Hecke makes a compelling case for doing this:

> Becoming more aware of our blind spots, as individuals, and as groups—organizations, businesses, ethnic and religious communities, political parties, states, and nations—deepens our understanding of the issues we grapple with and often points to the way toward their resolution. The most direct path to discovering our blind spots is to intentionally bring perspectives other than our own to the table. This means that we absolutely need other people, people who are unlike ourselves, to help us see what we cannot see on our own . . . From this perspective other people and their differing viewpoints—however blind they may be in some ways—truly have something priceless to offer. From this point of view, our own perspective—however blind it may be in some ways—always has something to contribute as well.[5]

Mental agility is closely related to curiosity, so a simple practice is to entertain the opposite assumption. If you *love* a decision, for example, get curious about how people who *hate* it are looking at the issue. Do they have different evidence? How are they interpreting the situation differently? What concerns them most?

Make sure your worst enemy doesn't live between your own two ears.
—**LAIRD HAMILTON**

Learning to do this well helps you learn to hold your views more carefully. When it comes to the value of holding your perspectives as hypotheses, Dean Williams frames it as well as anyone:

> . . . one must hold onto one's doubts. Excessive certainty about the rightness or righteousness of one's cause, as with a crusader, might diminish one's curiosity, questioning, open-mindedness, and experimentation. Without curiosity, questioning, open-mindedness, and experimentation, real solutions to complex problems will be elusive.[6]

Skepticism toward your own way of looking at the problem or challenge is not only healthy, it's rational. As human beings, our finite cognitive capacity guarantees that no one person enjoys a complete view or perspective about any issue or problem. The more complex the issue, the less your view will accurately represent it. In the process, you'll build patience, stamina, and the discipline to hold steady even when listening to a belligerent blowhole who is advocating a repugnant idea.

Treating Listening as a Discipline

Learning to listen with intense focus is another high-leverage practice. Listening well requires mental strength, mindful awareness, curiosity, and even humility. It's also the gateway to learning. It does no good, after all, to test your views, or to inquire into the views of others, if you don't listen to the responses you get.

But when people say they're listening, they're often doing little more than waiting for their turn to talk, formulating their response, or thinking about something else entirely. "Did I turn off the lights before I left the house this morning?"

Here are four simple ways to use listening as a practice:

1. **Practice mindful listening.** Be in the present. Focus your beam of attention on other people—on both what they're saying and how they're saying it.

2. **Practice engaged listening.** Pay careful attention to the people you're listening to while resisting the temptation to guess what they're trying to say or to make rash judgments. Actively seek to understand their view and the underlying logic that informs it.

3. **Listen for something new.** Turn a conversation into an Easter-egg hunt for learning. Listen intently for fresh insight or information. It may be something about the issue you've not considered, or perhaps something about the people with whom you're talking.

4. **Listen for contrast.** Listen to people who see things in a different way, not necessarily to find common ground—although it's a big bonus if you can—but in order to understand and to learn. Holding steady while listening to people, even when they're spouting a repugnant view that curdles your milk, quickly strengthens your muscles in multiple areas: mindful awareness, mental strength, curiosity, patience, and persistence.

Build Your Overall Discipline

Cultivated discipline lasts longer than fickle motivation.
—**JOCKO WILLINK**

Tim Ferris, in an article about Jocko Willink, a former Navy SEAL, explains why building your discipline is so important:

Having spent 20 years in the U.S. Navy—with time spent commanding Task Unit Bruiser at SEAL Team 3—Willink intimidates not only with his extensive military career, but also physically. He is the recipient of the black belt in Brazilian jiu-jitsu and has been known to tap out 20 Navy SEALs per workout. On top of all that, Willink is also a business founder and bestselling author of the book *Discipline Equals Freedom: Field Manual.*

No doubt, with all of this expertise in business, sport, and combat, it would be natural to assume that Willink must be incredibly motivated, right? Actually, he would beg to differ, as he says, "Don't count on motivation; count on discipline."

"The more you practice," he says, "the better you get, the more freedom you have to create." Discipline in any area of your life will increase your skills, productivity, and, he reveals, will "set you free."

Don't feel like exercising? Don't feel like starting that business proposal? Trust an expert U.S. Navy SEAL and remember that your lack of motivation truly does not matter. "You do it anyways," Willink says. "You grit down."[7]

So rather than depend on fickle motivation, grit down and increase your discipline. "I believe that self-control is our greatest human strength, and the easiest thing that we can improve upon," says Nathan DeWall, a professor of psychology at the University of Kentucky, who went from obesity to running 100-mile foot races by building his discipline.[8]

Build Your Mental Toughness

Mental and physical agility run on the same track.
—JOHN J. RATEY AND RICHARD MANNING

While you are building *your discipline*, go the extra mile and build *your mental toughness*, too. Here's the difference. You're building discipline when you accomplish your daily goal of running 10 miles. You're taking it a step further—and building your mental toughness—when you choose to do it during the coldest, wettest, most miserable part of the day. You build mental toughness by *accomplishing your goal in a way that lets your body know your mind is in charge.* Cold showers are proven to be good for you, but they're a miserable experience, so from time to time turn off the hot water and force yourself to tolerate the frigid spray. It's healthy, and it provides yet another way to show your body that your mind is in the driver's seat.

When I trail run I have a rule: I always run uphill. I can walk downhill if I need to, but if I'm heading up a long hill and I need to stop, I start to walk back down the hill. Once I've caught my breath, I turn around and continue running up the trail. This is a painful practice, but it helps me push my performance to higher levels (I don't waste any time catching my breath because I know I'll have to run back up the distance I just walked down) and it builds mental toughness.

Cultivate an Affirmative Bias

"Our brain evolved to scan for problems and it is skilled at finding problems when it looks," says Loretta Breuning, author of *The Science of Positivity*. "Negativity will engulf you unless you build yourself a positivity circuit. To guard against or combat a negative bias, spend one minute looking for positives, three times a day for forty-five days. This trains your brain to look for positives the way it is already trained to look for negatives."[9]

If you're in a position of authority, cultivating an affirmative bias is particularly important because you have the attention of the people below you in the hierarchy and they take cues from how you're framing an issue or situation. Pay attention to what you're doing with that attention. What signals are you sending to your team? What can you do to cultivate a more affirmative orientation in your organization? What questions can you ask? How well are you at maintaining the balance between keeping a clear-headed, evidence-based, no-nonsense look at current reality *and* an affirmative bias for how to move forward?

Sometimes you won't recognize that you've been sucked into the morass of negative assumptions until you're too far gone. To pull yourself out of that dark place, challenge your negative assessments in a rigorous way by asking yourself double-loop questions:

- *If my negative assumptions have no more validity than my affirmative assumptions (they're all just untested hypotheses at this point), then which assumptions are the most useful? Which assumptions make me less a passive victim and more an active agent? Which assumptions are more likely to spark the most learning and progress?*

- *What examples can I think of in which someone facing similar circumstances (or even more difficult ones) was still able to do something productive?*

- *Where in the universe does it say, beyond the shadow of a doubt, that the situation I'm facing is hopeless?[10]*

- *What opportunities vanish if I cling to this negative assessment? And if I adopted an affirmative mindset, what new possibilities might open up?*

- *What messages am I sending to my team, and are those messages helping them deal with the challenges we're facing, or getting in the way?*

Sharpen Your Baloney Detection Kit (BDK)

Familiarize yourself with Carl Sagan's Baloney Detection Kit (BDK). I'm not going to describe it here, but you can find descriptions online or read about it in his brilliant book, *The Demon-Haunted World: Science as a Candle in the Dark.*

Ask Questions That Challenge Your Worldview

- *Why do I think what I think?*

- *How might others be making sense of the issue differently?*

- *How might my previous experience, or the lack thereof, be influencing my interpretation of this situation?*

Refocusing

Once you've seen, labeled, and braked, refocus on what really matters:

- *I can feel my need to be right urging me to argue my point. But the goal here is to make the smartest decision we can, so let me see if there are contrarian points of view and explore what others are seeing that I am not.*

- *Uh-oh. There's my* minimizing tendency *telling me to play it safe and avoid this issue. But if we're to make progress it needs to be addressed. So, let me put my view on the table and check it with the team.*

Focus on the Good

Get in the habit of directing your beam of attention on the positive aspects of your surroundings. As you walk along a street, instead of focusing on the trash on the sidewalk, watch the birds on a bench. Rather than focus on the traffic in front of you, notice the trees above you. As Mr. Rogers's mother suggested, when things are going horribly wrong, rather than focus on the people causing the trouble, focus on the people stepping in to help.[11]

Change Your Self-Talk

Practice what psychologists refer to as "cognitive reappraisal":

- Instead of thinking, *This situation is hopeless and it's not my job to fix it,* deliberately shift to, *Yes, the situation is a mess, but if we work together and work smart we can do something about it.*

- Instead of thinking, *I can't make a difference here, so why waste time trying?,* think instead, *I can make a constructive difference here, or at least learn something by giving it a try.*

- Shift your thoughts from, *Clearly I'm the only person who cares around here; everyone else is just a self-protecting bureaucrat,* to *People may see things differently, and they may be frustrated, but they probably want things to improve as much as I do.*

Another simple way to change your self-talk is to ask yourself more affirmative, responsible, and constructive questions:

- *What can I do to make a constructive difference in this messy situation?*

- *We should never waste a crisis, so how can I use what is happening to spark some learning and progress?*

- *People seemed to be focused on the downside to this decision, but I wonder if there's an upside?*

- *Everyone is focusing on what's wrong with this situation, but what are the opportunities it presents us? How might we take advantage of those opportunities?*

- *We've got two strong, opposing views here. I wonder how we might combine them to generate an even smarter response to the situation we're facing?*

- *With whom might I partner to help shift the focus of the team, organization, or community on this issue?*

> *The state of your life is nothing more than a reflection of the state of your mind.*
> —**WAYNE DYER**

Celebrate Mistakes

Celebrate slipups for the learning they provide. Embracing your frailties and blunders breeds learning, compassion, and humility. Frank Barrett explains it this way:

> ... errors violate expectations. Essentially, they disrupt routines and unthinking behavior. They wake us up and demand we pay attention to something that previously was in the background. We are forced for the moment to look again, to become curious, to ask about our own approach, clearly showing how mistakes are a powerful tool for growth and learning. We have to disengage ourselves from patterns and pay attention in new ways. An error can energize us to investigate strange outcomes and can lead to discovery. When we make a mistake, it's not possible to comfortably live inside our assumptions and comfortable beliefs. We're forced to confront our biases; we have to explore alternatives.[12]

Here are questions you can use to learn to do a better job of this:

- *What was the cause of my mistake? What led me to be so ineffective?*

- *Did other people see me make the mistake? How do I think they judged me?*

- *Have I seen other people make a similar mistake? How did I judge them?*

- *What can I learn from all this?*

- *What can I do to ensure that the next time I'm in a similar situation I respond in a more constructive way?*

- *Do I need to strengthen some aspect of my awareness? My mindset? My skills? Some combination of them all?*

Goof Off

"The time you enjoy wasting," said Bertrand Russell, "is not wasted time." It's easy to overdo it when you get excited about a goal. One way to build this mindset is to occasionally get your mind off building it. Take time to relax and goof off.

Emma Seppalla, author of *The Happiness Track: How to Apply the Science of Happiness to Accelerate Your Success*, points out the dangers of overdoing it. "Although overwork can appear to be the most productive route, it actually fails us in two major ways that are critical to our success: creativity and problem-solving skills, on the one hand, and social connections, on the other." And these skills, she points out, are essential to taking our work or product to the next level. Emma goes on to make this point:

> Here's how overworking fails our problem-solving skills and creativity: research by former Harvard psychology professor Dan Wegner suggests that too much concentration on set goals can lead to the exact opposite of the desired goal. He coined the term *ironic processes* to describe the failure of positive mental processes when performed under conditions of stress. For instance, the more you obsess about having to hit a perfect golf tee shot, the more likely you are to choke; or the more you try to maintain a strict diet, the more likely you are to eventually binge.[13]

So, if you're working hard to build your conversational capacity, make sure you enjoy periodic timeouts and just take it easy.

Look for the Humor

Look for the humor in a situation, especially when it's about you. It's a great way to increase your humility, and research shows it can increase your persistence. Looking for what's funny—and relishing it—is not wasting time; it's an investment in your ability to stick with a challenging task.[14]

Rethink Risk

Assess the risk of the situation in a different way. Sure, there are hazards associated with speaking up and making a difference, but rather than just focusing on the dangers—something we're naturally prone to do—deliberately focus on the opportunities as well. Instead of emphasizing what might happen if you speak up, for example, consider what might happen if you don't speak up. Yes, speaking up can be a risk, but what's the risk of remaining silent?

Study People Who've Done It

Put things into context by studying people who have overcome bigger obstacles than you're facing; people like Malala Yousafzai, Temple Grandin, Abraham Lincoln, Mahatma Gandhi, Martin Luther King, Jr., Lech Walesa, and even Steve. If they were able to make a difference in their situations, why can't you?

Cultivate a Constructive Orientation

Consider this big question: *What are the patterns of choice in your life?* Are they mostly constructive, with the occasional slip into destructive? Or the opposite? What is the trend over time? This is an important question to consider, for the choices you make lead to the character you cultivate, and the character you cultivate influences the choices you subsequently make. We're all somewhere on this continuum. The goal is to be more conscious about where you are and to deliberately choose activities that push you toward *The Leadership Mindset*. Be more focused and deliberate about the wolf you feed.

Questions to Continually Ask

Here are questions to continually ask:

- *Are there more useful ways to frame this issue?*

- *What are my blind spots in this situation?*

- *What biases are distorting my perceptions?*

- *How might I be seeing things that others are missing?*

- *How can I frame the changes I'd like to see so that people respond more positively to the idea?*

- *How can I help others get their ideas into the conversation?*

- *What perspectives are we all missing, and how can we find them?*

- *Are we avoiding issues that need to be addressed?*

- *If things were to change for the better, where would be the most high-leverage place to begin that work?*

- *What can I do to improve the status quo?*
- *How can I play what's missing to bring more balance to this meeting or conversation?*

Watch Films

Watch dramas and documentaries that demonstrate people making progress on tough issues against tough odds. Here's a short list to get you started:

- *A Beautiful Mind*
- *Dead Poet's Society*
- *Gandhi*
- *Rabbit Proof Fence*
- *Sophie Scholl*
- *Temple Grandin*
- *The King's Speech*
- *To Kill a Mockingbird*
- *Twelve Angry Men*

What would you add to the list?

Suggested Readings

Here is a list of readings to help you strengthen particular aspects of the *conversational capacity* mindset:

- "Level 5 Leadership" by Jim Collins (HBR article)
- *13 Things Mentally Strong People Don't Do* by Amy Morin
- *A Mind of Its Own* by Cordelia Fine
- *Being Wrong* by Kathryn Schulz
- *Dare to Lead* by Brené Brown
- *Emotional Agility* by Susan David

- *Grit* by Angela Duckworth
- *Leadership for a Fractured World* by Dean Williams
- *Leadership Without Easy Answers* by Ron Heifetz
- *Making Great Choices* by Jennifer Riel and Roger Martin
- *Mindset* by Carol Dweck
- *Mistakes Were Made (but Not by Me)* by Carol Tavris and Elliot Aronson
- *On Being Certain* by Robert Burton
- *On Bullshit* by Harry G. Frankfurt
- *On Thinking* by Edward DeBono
- *Real Leadership* by Dean Williams
- *Team of Rivals* by Doris Kearns Goodwin
- *The Abilene Paradox* by Jerry Harvey
- *The Demon-Haunted World* by Carl Sagan
- *The Heart of Man* by Erich Fromm
- *The Lost Art of Listening* by Michael P. Nichols
- *The Opposable Mind* by Roger Martin
- *The Person and the Situation* by Lee Ross and Richard Nesbett
- *The Power of Vulnerability* by Brené Brown
- *The Science of Positivity* by Loretta Graziano Breuning
- *What Do You Care What Other People Think?* by Richard Feynman
- *Willpower* by Roy Baumeister and John Tierney
- *Yes to the Mess* by Frank J. Barrett

Want to Learn More?

For a regularly updated list of practices, readings, and other resources, visit conversationalcapacity.com

PART III

SKILLS

Knowledge is of no value unless you put it into practice.
—**ANTON CHEKHOV**

CANDOR SKILL #1

Stating Your Position

> *Language is the magnificent faculty that we use to*
> *get thoughts from one head to another . . .*
> — **STEVEN PINKER**

Without specific skills for putting the ideas into action, the mindset we explored in the last section is little more than a bumper sticker. It is the focus on skills—specific behaviors you can learn, practice, and adopt— that separates this work from most of the other training and development advice on the market today. Think about it. Most of the guidance on interpersonal effectiveness, team building, or leadership development focuses on improving your *intentions:*

- *You should always communicate in a way that builds trust.*

- *To have a good meeting, always leave your emotions at the door.*

- *To be a good manager, you should be an active listener.*

- *Always create outcomes where everybody wins.*

- *Never make assumptions.*

- *Always separate the person from the problem.*

- *Be open to new ideas and perspectives.*

- *To increase your stature and influence, always speak authentically.*

These books, trainers, and "thought leaders" tell you what you should be doing but fail to provide the underlying skills to *do* what they're counseling you to do. Instruction like this ignores two problems.

The first problem is that they fail to show people *how to implement the advice*—the actual *behaviors* needed to employ it. This problem is similar to someone asking a friend, "How do you play the piano?" and having the friend respond: "It's not that hard. You just sit on the bench, place your hands on the keyboard, and use your fingers to hit the appropriate notes." Sadly, a lot of the advice about communication falls into this trap. But teaching communication skills by just *telling* people how they should communicate is like teaching people to play tennis by just *telling* them how they should hit the ball.

The second problem is something I highlighted with the subtitle of Chapter 2 of *Conversational Capacity:* "Why Good Intentions Are Never Enough." Even if the advice you're giving is sound, if you're not also showing people the internal barriers that make implementing the advice difficult, you're still not being helpful. If I told you to balance candor and curiosity under pressure, for example, and also shared the *skills* for doing it, I'd still be providing inadequate counsel if I didn't help you recognize the powerful tendencies that make implementing that advice so challenging: the primal fight-flight reactions that often hijack your good intentions.

Only advice that hits all fronts—*awareness, mindset,* and *skills*—can be translated into effective action. Anyone advocating ideas about how to improve your effectiveness but failing to address these three factors is providing feeble counsel. They're suggesting you adopt better intentions while providing little in the way of actionable skills for acting on those intentions when it counts. They're selling what Chris Argyris refers to as "good advice that isn't useful."[1]

Only advice that hits all fronts—awareness, mindset,

and skills—*can be translated into effective action.*

The Four Foundational Skills

With all that in mind, now that we've explored *awareness* in Part I, and *mindset* in Part II, let's turn our attention to the *skills*. Navigating a tough conversation without keen awareness and a guiding mindset, after all, is like trying to find an unfamiliar destination using a GPS unit without a satellite connection. You're soon lost. But even a satellite connection isn't enough if you lack a steering wheel—a way to take your directions and put them into action. Without awareness you can't *see*. Without a mindset you can't *navigate*. Without skills you can't *steer*.

Fortunately, just as there are basic skills in any sport (for example, throwing, hitting, running, and catching in baseball), there are also basic skills you can master for balancing candor and curiosity:

1. **Candor**

   a. **Stating a clear, succinct position** *that shows others where you currently stand on an issue.*

   b. **Explaining the thinking** *behind your point of view in an accessible way to show others how you arrived at your position. (The first candor skill tells people where you stand on an issue; the second candor skill shows them how you got there.)*

2. **Curiosity**

   a. **Testing** *your perspective to discover ways to improve it.*

   b. **Inquiring** *into the views of others in the pursuit of learning.*

It is the adept use of these four skills, backed by disciplined awareness and a mind set on learning, that helps you remain constructive, balanced, and learning-focused under pressure. The goal of this section is to help you do just that. In this chapter and the next I'll help you strengthen your facility with the *candor* skills. Then, in the two chapters that follow, I'll show you how to build your competence with the *curiosity* skills.

Without awareness you can't see. *Without a mindset*

you can't navigate. *Without skills you can't* steer.

The Basic Discipline

The skilled use of these four behaviors helps you align your actions with your mindset. This is the next step in "The Basic Discipline" of conversational capacity I've been sharing with you all along. In a conversation, you're first *catching, naming,* and *taming* your emotional reactions. You then *refocus* on learning and head to your workshop. The next step is to *replace* your habitual reactions with the appropriate skills for remaining balanced. If your need to *minimize* is being triggered, for example, the candor skills will help you maintain equilibrium. If your need to *"win"* is threatening to knock you out of the sweet spot, the curiosity skills are the ticket.

The Candor Skills

A writer uses words, sentences, and paragraphs to get *thoughts* out of her head and into the minds of her readers. A composer uses notes to get *music* out of his head and into the minds of his performers and the ears of his listeners. An engineer creates a schematic to get a *design* out of her head and into the minds of other people. In the same way, when you converse you're using language to get an *idea* out of your head and into the heads of others.

To do this well, you need to be as clear and accurate as possible. The adept use of two candor skills serves this very purpose: *stating your position* and then *explaining the thinking* behind it. There are multiple reasons to hone your ability to use these skills well:

- *They are the antidote for the formidable minimizing tendency.* When you're being triggered to acquiesce or shut down, the deft use of the candor skills helps you stay in the sweet spot.

- *They enable you to test your thinking to expand and improve it.* There is no way to do this if you can't get your ideas out of your head and into the heads of others in a lucid way.

- *They give you more power in a conversation by increasing the degree of influence of you and your view.* Dacher Keltner, author of *The Power Paradox*, defines *power* as "your capacity to make a difference in the world by influencing the states of other people."[2] Again, your ideas are unlikely to have much influence if you can't express them in a clear and potent manner.

- *They help you convey your ideas in a way that makes them harder to misunderstand.* Karl Popper once said: "It is impossible to speak in such a way that you cannot be misunderstood." He's probably right, but that doesn't mean you can't communicate in a way that limits the chances it'll happen.

- *You'll inspire more learning in others.* By sharing how you're seeing things you can help other people see things *they* might be missing, to entertain perspectives they may not have considered, to help them sharpen their own thinking, and to perceive ideas in a more useful way. When you don't speak candidly you deprive others of aha moments.

- *It'll make you a sharper thinker.* This more rigorously responsible approach to being candid will also make you smarter in two ways: by forcing you to be more conscious about *what* you think and *why* you think it; and as I pointed out above, putting forward your view in this rigorous and responsible way helps you to test and improve it.

Candor Skill #1: Stating Your Position

A well-crafted position distills your main point—your thought, concern, suggestion, or feeling—to its essence. It provides a synopsis of your idea or view. This is important. You're working to expand and improve your thinking, after all, and it's hard to do this well if you're not stating a clear point of view in the first place. By summarizing your central idea in no more than one or two sentences you provide the base for a more grounded, less ambiguous conversation. It's the first step in thinking smarter—and helping others to do the same.

I'm often asked why I call it a "position." The reason is simple. Because it's a clear description of where you *currently stand* on an issue. "I think we should hold off on another acquisition for at least six more months," for example, is a direct statement of your position on the subject. But a clear position need not be such a strong, fixed opinion. Consider these three statements that would clearly inform others where you stand on the matter at hand:

- *I think there are two ways we can solve this problem and I'm not sure which is best.*

- *This decision really scares me.*

- *I'm confused.*

Topic Sentences

Stating your position in a conversation serves a similar purpose as a good topic sentence in effective writing:

- "Topic sentences reveal the main point of a paragraph."[3]

- "It introduces the main idea of the paragraph."[4]

- "A topic sentence (also known as a *focus sentence*) encapsulates . . . an entire paragraph."[5]

- "A topic sentence . . . tells the reader what the paragraph is going to be about. All other sentences in the paragraph should support that idea."[6]

- ". . . a topic sentence makes a claim of some sort . . ."[7]

- ". . . the topic sentence must be the unifying force in the paragraph."[8]

- ". . . acts as a signpost for the argument of the paper as a whole . . ."[9]

An effective *position statement* reveals your central point; it serves as a signpost to the perspective you're putting forward. Crafted effectively, it signals to the listener the general hypothesis you're about to explain and test.

The Price of Doing It Poorly

When you fail to state your position you risk the following consequences:

- *You'll have less influence.* Without a clear position, your ideas will get less traction. I've never ever heard anyone say to a colleague: "Your advice didn't really catch my attention until you stated it in a weak and ambiguous way. But once you obfuscated the idea, I immediately saw the value of your suggestion." There's little value in thinking through an issue and generating a good idea if you can't communicate it effectively.

- *You'll be misunderstood.* A weak or fuzzy position promotes confusion: "Sure, I like that idea, and that's probably the way to go, but I'm wondering if we might also consider doing something a little less bold, you know, a little less, in your face? I mean, I'm probably off-base here, right? So, we should probably just do what you're suggesting. Sorry." It's hard to tell where this person stands on the issue. It seems like they have a concern, but what is it? Is it a big concern, or a minor one? Given what they're saying and how they're saying it there is no way to know.

- *You'll make a poor impression.* Put forward a waffling, rambling, or fuzzy point of view and you risk appearing uninformed, confused, or wishy-washy. Worse, you might come across as duplicitous, disingenuous, or passive-aggressive.

The Four Characteristics of a Good Position Statement

Given its importance, let's explore how to do it well in more detail. An effective *position statement* exhibits four traits: it is *clear*; it is *concise*; it is *compelling*; and it includes *no unnecessary harshness*.

IT IS CLEAR

If your goal is to help others understand your point of view, you need to explain it intelligibly. To do this, you should avoid trying to sound sophisticated or smart, or to impress people with your grandiloquent, Brobdingnagian vocabulary. Use simple, direct language. Nothing signals intelligence better than the ability to present an idea in an accessible way.

In his brilliant book, *On Writing Well*, William Zinsser makes this point about writing that also holds true for speaking: "Managers at every level are prisoners of the notion that a simple style reflects a simple mind. Actually a simple style is the result of hard work and hard thinking; a muddled style reflects a muddled thinker or a person too arrogant, or too dumb, or too lazy to organize his thoughts." Zinsser goes on: "How can the rest of us achieve such enviable freedom from clutter? The answer is to clear our heads of clutter. Clear thinking becomes clear writing [and speaking]; one can't exist without the other."[10]

The key point is this: Your position should signal to people where you stand on an issue in plain, crisp language. In 1942, for example, out of a concern about nighttime air raids, the U.S. government issued this memo about blackouts:

> Such preparations shall be made as will completely obscure all Federal buildings and non-Federal buildings occupied by the Federal government during an air raid for any period of time from visibility by reason of internal or external illumination.

A masterful communicator, President Franklin Roosevelt stripped the point down to its essence by using more down-to-earth language. "Tell them," he said, "that in buildings where they have to keep the work going to put something across the windows."[11]

IT IS CONCISE

"Concision," says Thomas Kane, "is brevity relative to purpose."[12] Avoid muddling your point with a lot of unnecessary words or ideas. Do like President Franklin Roosevelt and distill your perspective down to its essence. In *Elements of Style*, William Strunk and E.B. White share advice that holds true for this verbal skill just as it does for writing: "Vigorous writing is concise. A sentence should contain no unnecessary words, a paragraph no unnecessary sentences, for the same reason that a drawing should have no unnecessary lines and a machine no unnecessary parts."[13]

Concision and clarity often go hand in hand. For example, look again at the way President Franklin Roosevelt's clarified the main point of the memo. It's not only easier to understand, it's half as long:

- "Such preparations shall be made as will completely obscure all Federal buildings and non-Federal buildings occupied by the Federal government during an air raid for any period of time from visibility by reason of internal or external illumination." [38 words]

- "Tell them that in buildings where they have to keep the work going to put something across the windows." [19 words]

The basic rule is this: Keep it tight. "The notion that this acquisition is beneficial to the short- and long-term performance of our organization is fallacious and ill-advised" is less efficient and effective than simply saying: "This acquisition is a bad idea."

IT IS COMPELLING

An effective position is also *compelling*. It communicates why others should care, and why they should pay attention to what follows. Here's an example: A few years ago, I wrote a letter to the executive in charge of customer service for a national furniture company after an exasperating experience at a local store. I could have started by saying, "I'm unhappy about the customer service at your store in Palmdale." That's not a bad position. It meets the first two criteria. It's clear. It's concise. But it's not very compelling. I imagined the executive reading this lackluster position and thinking, "Yawn. Another generic complaint," before responding in an equally humdrum way.

I wanted to get his attention, to express my frustration, and explain why it should matter to him and to his business. So, this is how I started off: "Unless frustrating and losing customers is a key part of your business strategy, you've got a major problem in your Palmdale store." It worked. Not only did the executive respond with active interest, exploring my experience in detail and suggesting how he would remedy the problem, shortly thereafter I received a call from the CEO.

One way to make your position compelling is to make it *specific*. Again, Strunk and White provide advice about good writing that applies equally well to crafting an effective position: "The surest way to arouse and hold the reader's attention is by being specific, definite, and concrete."[14]

When Steve prepared for his talk with Phil, he and his colleagues worked to make sure his position was clear, concise, and compelling—that it showed Phil why he should care in specific, concrete ways. Steve's first attempt in their preparatory role-playing was: "Phil, people are afraid to talk to you." But as they practiced, he found that framing his position this way prompted Phil (or the person pretending to be Phil in the role-play) to misinterpret the message and respond with something like, "OK. I get that. I'm not the easiest guy to work for. Give me the names of the people who are struggling and we'll get them some help. Perhaps some assertiveness training will do the trick."

But with additional thought and practice—which came about as he and his colleagues experimented in some rough-and-tumble role-play—he crafted a position that was more clear, concise, and compelling: "Phil, I've never worked for someone who's more open about his need for timely and accurate information as you, and I applaud that. But despite your good intentions, I think you act in ways that make it really hard for people to do what you're asking." This position, stated in two sentences, is more specific, and, as a result, more compelling.

IT CONTAINS NO UNNECESSARY HARSHNESS

Here's another important rule for crafting an effective position: It should contain *no unnecessary harshness*. Notice I did not say "no harshness." That cannot always be avoided. Sometimes the information you need to convey is going to be tough for others to hear. Your goal is to make your point clearly, concisely, and compellingly, and to do it in the least abrasive way possible. You are trying to spark learning, not dampen it.

This can be difficult to pull off. Your *minimizing* tendency often tempts you to mince words or water down your point, while your *"win"* tendency often tempts you to be overly aggressive, sarcastic, condescending, or dismissive. There is a sweet spot between those two points that can be hard to find, especially in a tough conversation.

Steve's conversation provides yet another good example: "Phil, it seems a few people are just a little nervous about talking with you because, well, you can be—and this is not a fault—really passionate sometimes." This watered-down position doesn't serve Steve's goal of helping Phil identify a potential gap between what he wants (people telling it to him like it is) and what is happening (people *not* telling it to him like it is).

But Steve could have undermined the purpose of the conversation if he had erred in the other direction and expressed an *unnecessarily* harsh position: "Phil, you act like a Philistine by verbally abusing people in nearly biblical ways and yet expect them to 'tell it to you like it is.' I can only think of three reasons you'd do that—ignorance, insincerity, or foolishness. Which is it?"

By inviting both misunderstanding and defensiveness, both approaches subvert the purpose of the feedback: to make things better. Steve finally settled on a more balanced approach that was direct and no-nonsense, but without any unnecessary harshness: "Phil, I've never worked for someone who's more open about his need for timely and accurate information as you, and I applaud that. But despite your good intentions I think you act in ways that make it really difficult for people to do what you're asking."

Clarifying Points

It Can Be a Feeling

Stating how you're feeling is often a great way to frame your point. A clear position can declare confusion, uncertainty, or ambivalence:

- *This decision makes me very nervous.*
- *I feel conflicted about the best way to go on this change process.*
- *The thought of making this change scares me.*
- *I love this idea for two big reasons.*
- *I feel torn between these two options.*

It Can Be Tentative

You can lower defensiveness by letting people know you're not wedded to your current position and that you're holding it hypothetically just by the way you put it forward:

- *Here's my "going in position" on the issue . . .*

- *Right now, I'm looking at the situation like this . . .*
- *My current take on this problem is . . .*

It's More Authentic

Speaking in such crisp, no-nonsense terms is more authentic, which generates more trust and respect.

It's Easier in Some Circumstances, Harder in Others

This skill is harder for some people than it is for others. It is also harder in some circumstances than it is in others. The Flamethrower, for example, was a natural with this skill.* When his internal reaction to a colleague's suggestion was, "That won't work," he'd simply say, "That won't work." That's 10 out of 10 on the position clarity scale.

But if you're like me and struggle with a strong tendency to *minimize*, this skill takes more practice to master. I tend to sacrifice a clear position to avoid being confrontational, rocking the boat, looking like a nonteam player, hurting feelings, or making myself look foolish. So, putting forward an effective position is an unnatural act, and I've worked hard to strengthen my ability to do it well. I realized that if I didn't learn to state my views directly, I risk the three problems I mentioned earlier: I'm more likely to be misunderstood; to have less influence; and to appear ill-informed, weak-minded, or two-faced.

In situations where your need to *minimize* is being triggered, a well-crafted position is often the first casualty. But it's exactly what's necessary if you're to stay in the sweet spot.

---

* Don't remember the Flamethrower? Revisit pages 46–47 and 104–105 in *Conversational Capacity.*

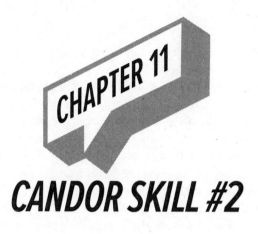

CANDOR SKILL #2

Helping Others See Your Thinking

Simple can be harder than complex: You have to work hard to get your thinking clean to make it simple. But it's worth it in the end because once you get there, you can move mountains.
—**STEVE JOBS**

To get a thought out of your head and into the heads of others, putting forward your position is a start, but if your goal is to pool perspectives in the pursuit of learning, this skill, by itself, is inadequate. Like an elementary school child doing long division homework, you need to show your work. You must explain how you arrived at your position. You need to share your *thinking*.

A useful analogy is mapmaking. When you're helping other people see your point of view, you're doing your best to present the mental map—the cognitive cartography—you used to arrive at your position. Your position tells others *where* you stand on an issue. Your thinking shows *how* you got there.

Your Thinking Has Two Facets

To describe your mental map in an accessible way you do your best to share the *evidence* you're using and how you're *interpreting* that evidence. Your view on any issue is always a mix of these two components, and if you're going to lay your thinking on the table so others can examine it, you need to share both.

When Steve chose to raise his concern with Phil, for instance, he prepared for his conversation by exploring important questions with his colleagues: *What is leading us to our concerns? What are we seeing or hearing?* The answers to these questions allowed Steve to share specific, concrete examples of what he was seeing and hearing in the workplace: the hallway conversations, examples of Phil's reactions in meetings, the coaching he provided to the shell-shocked project manager, as well as the new nickname people had for their interactions with Phil—"The Gestapo Interrogation." He went on to add another compelling piece of evidence: "It's so bad that I was actively counseled by a lot of my colleagues not to even come in here and bring this up with you. One even suggested it would be 'career suicide.'"

But Steve also prepared for his conversation by thinking through his *interpretation* of this evidence, and how he and others were making sense of it. "I'm concerned that if this continues people will be increasingly afraid to bring up important information and the impact on the business will be dire." This is not evidence—it's how Steve is *making sense* of the evidence—but it's a pivotal part of his thinking.

Explaining Your "Ladder"

For another example, reflect back to the story of "the cop and the architect" in Chapter 6 of *Conversational Capacity*. As the cop and the architect walked around the city of Chicago together, they each ascended the Ladder of Inference in very different ways. When asked to describe the city one stated, "It's a dump," while the other declared, "It's beautiful!" They each experienced the city differently because they each focused on different aspects of the environment, which led them to *interpret* the city in contrasting ways. As I wrote in *Conversational Capacity*:

> Whenever we talk with other human beings, to one degree or another, we're just like the cop and the architect. We all filter the world around us in distinct, biased, and incomplete ways. If our conversational capacity is high, we know that we each have a unique take on "reality," and we want to get our "ladder" into the conversation as clearly and candidly as possible.[1]

The process for doing this is fairly simple. Put out a clear position, and then explain the thinking behind it. By explaining your thinking to others, you're describing how you've gone up your ladder.

Evidence

When it comes to your cognitive cartography, not all mental maps are created equal. There are two basic paths to a point of view:[2]

1. Biased, myopic, *opinion-based* thinking.

2. Rigorous, expansive, *evidence-based* thinking.

If your goal is to double down on ignorance, cling to your current perspective, and make half-baked choices, the first kind of thinking is optimal. If, on the other hand, your goal is to learn, to create more accurate mental maps, and make more intelligent choices, the second kind of thinking is the only way to go. It's that simple. Dull thinking or sharp thinking. Those are your options.

Some people prefer the first kind of thinking. You probably know a person who wields fervent opinions unencumbered by evidence. They accept ideas or views with little data, especially if those views support their current thinking. Such people live in what one engineering team I worked with referred to as the DFZ, "the data-free zone." Research shows such people are more inclined to believe in conspiracy theories and pseudo-profound bullshit. At it's most softheaded extreme, these sloppy "thinkers" are prone to conspiracy theories and spend a lot of money on stuff sold on late-night TV via infomercials. They tend to believe everything they read on the Internet. "Dude, I just joined the Flat Earth Society!" or, "Did you hear that NASA found life on Uranus but they're covering it up? No. Seriously. My friend saw the photos online."

Most of us fall somewhere in the middle, neither perfectly rational and evidence-based thinkers, nor mouth-breathing morons plagued by an allergic reaction to facts. When your aim is rigorous thinking and smart choices, however, you focus your beam of attention on *evidence*. This imposes a degree of discipline on how you look at the world by forcing you to ask important questions:

- *Why do I think what I think?*

- *How valid is my perspective?*

- *Do other people see it differently? If so, what evidence do they have? How might they be interpreting the evidence in ways I'm not?*

Questions like these encourage you to hold your views like hypotheses to be tested rather than truths to be sold. It is this dedicated focus on evidence-based thinking that separates smart, discerning, rational people from dense, bias-driven dullards.

I'm coming on strong here, but it's hard to overemphasize the point. With high conversational capacity, you're not engaged in the childish sport of "Whose opinion is the sexiest?" or "What's the most convenient way to think about this issue?" and you're not playing the kiss-ass game of "Let me find out what the boss or the group thinks so I can espouse an agreeable opinion." No. Dedicated to learning and aware of your cognitive limitations, you ground your thinking on evidence rather than convenience, comfort, authority, bias, eloquence, flashy presentation, or social standing.

Basic Kinds of Evidence

There are different kinds of evidence you can provide to help people see how you've reasoned to your position:

- *Directly observable (sensorial) evidence.* As you walk up a city street, for example, you might *see* people sipping coffee at a sidewalk cafe, *smell* the tacos being sold by a food truck, *feel* the warmth of the sun on your face, and *hear* the siren of a passing ambulance. In a meeting, you might focus your attention on the words on the agenda, the comments of your manager, the body language of your colleagues, the sound of the gardener's leaf blower outside, or the smell of coffee brewing in the break room.

- *Validated evidence.* This is evidence backed up by scientific methods. For example, to support your view, you might provide a research paper from a peer-reviewed journal.

- *Statistically or mathematically measurable evidence.* To help others see how you arrived at your view, you might share a financial spreadsheet, a profit-and-loss statement, or an engineering schematic.

- *Analogic information.* You might compare similar things: "This isn't that different from our acquisition in 2008 . . ." or "Here are examples of two other companies, similar to ours, that have tried to make this same change and failed."

- *Systemic analysis.* By providing an organizing framework for evidence, systems thinking tools—such as behavior-over-time graphs, causal-loop maps, or stock-and-flow diagrams—help you describe the underlying structure of an issue or problem (what systems thinking expert Chris Soderquist calls the "physics of a system") in a rigorous, evidence-based way.

- *Anecdotal evidence.* Less rigorous and more prone to error, anecdotal evidence might include your previous experience with a comparable decision, or conversations you had with someone who had a similar experience.

Why Your Thinking Matters

Rigorous, evidence-based reasoning is pivotal to informed decision-making. It's the only way to prevent sexy bad ideas from trumping boring good ones. Remember, your goal is not to bounce your opinions back and forth in a game of poppycock Ping-Pong. It's to pool, evaluate, and improve the thinking being used to make sense of an issue, to solve a problem, or to make a decision.

Rigorous, evidence-based reasoning is pivotal to informed decision-making. It's the only way to prevent sexy bad ideas from trumping boring good ones.

Interpretation

Imagine an engineering team has developed a new idea for their product that they believe will provide a major boost to the business. Excited about their work, they pitch it to the management team. After explaining their idea in technical detail to the team they switch off the presentation and say, "So what do you think?"

The sales director jumps in immediately: "This is fantastic! We'll make a fortune! We're obviously going to do this. How soon can we start?"

The corporate attorney, having heard the same presentation, responds to the sales director with a simple question: "Do you like prison food?"

These contrasting reactions aren't due to evidence—the sales director and the corporate attorney each witnessed the same presentation. Their contrasting reactions are due to their *interpretations* of the evidence. They're using different intellectual filters to process the information, and this leads them to divergent conclusions. When interpreted through the sales lens, the evidence presented by the engineers leads to a strong position: "This idea is *fantastic*." But when interpreted through a legal lens, the same evidence leads to a conflicting position: "This idea is a *felony*." Their differing areas of expertise lead them to screen and weigh the evidence in very different ways.

The main point is this: Very often it's not the evidence you're paying attention to that makes your perspective unique; it's how you're making sense of it. So, when you're in your mental workshop laboring to produce smart choices, you need to consider both the evidence *and* how you're filtering it. Both are essential if you're to get your entire Ladder of Inference into the open so others can respond to it. To do this you're asking yourself important questions:

- *How have I gone up the ladder on this issue?*
- *What is the evidence I'm focusing on?*
- *What are my gut reactions to it?*
- *Where are these reactions coming from?*
- *What are the logical assumptions I'm making?*
- *What do I think the evidence is telling us?*

Ladder of Inference

The version of the Ladder of Inference I shared in my first book, *Conversational Capacity,* provides a useful way to think about how the *evidence* you pay attention to and how you then *interpret* that evidence leads to your *position* on an issue.

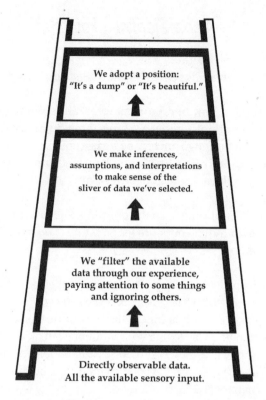

We adopt a position: "It's a dump" or "It's beautiful."

We make inferences, assumptions, and interpretations to make sense of the sliver of data we've selected.

We "filter" the available data through our experience, paying attention to some things and ignoring others.

Directly observable data. All the available sensory input.

Here again, Steve provides a good example. After sharing with Phil what he was *seeing* and *hearing* around the company (*evidence*), he explained to Phil how he was making sense of it all, and what concerned him about the evidence he was sharing (*interpretation*): "My biggest concern is that if this continues you'll get less and less information about what's really going on in the business and the consequences could be severe." By providing both the evidence and how he's making sense of it, Steve shared how he was "going up the ladder" with Phil.

Again, illustrating your thinking by clearly describing both your evidence and how you're e interpreting it fosters more learning on two fronts:

1. **It makes you smarter by helping you improve your thinking.** There is no way to effectively *test* your view if you don't put it forward clearly. You're candid, in other words, *because* you're curious.

2. **It makes other people smarter.** You're making sense of an issue in a unique way and your views can help other people detect and correct blind spots, biases, and errors in how *they're* making sense of the situation.

A Few Clarifying Points

Don't Overdo It

Francis Flaherty shares this gem in his book, *Elements of Story*:

> Don't ask Barbara how her morning went. She's the type who will give you a *full* accounting—everything about breakfast (bran muffin, orange-peach-mango juice, used up last coffee filter), everything about the trip to work (left 10 minutes late, made up the time on the Taconic State Parkway), and about everything else.
>
> Barbara is not wandering from the question. She just thinks that her listener has a boundless appetite for facts and a Texas-size capacity to absorb them.

Flaherty then provides sharp advice that applies equally well to how you put forward your thinking: *"Don't be like Barbara."*[3]

It's better to explain your ladder in bite-sized chunks than to share too much information and risk losing your audience because they can't keep up with your train of reasoning. You don't want people to check out or cut you off by saying, in essence: "I'm sorry to interrupt, but does your train of thought have a caboose?"

Over-explaining is often a sign you're trying to sell your view rather than describe it. It can also come across as haughty and condescending, as if you're underestimating the intelligence of your audience. So don't overload your listeners. The additional gem of information you think you're providing may instead be the straw that breaks the camel's back.

> *[Thinking] improves in direct ratio to the number of things*
> *we can keep out of it that shouldn't be there.*
> **—WILLIAM ZINSSER**

Instead of sharing all you know, lay out just enough to illustrate your key point so you can test it. If your colleagues want to know more about your perspective, they can always ask for more information. (In fact, you'll be *testing* your view shortly, which provides that very opportunity.) Remember, the conversation serves a purpose—improving your mental maps of reality so you can make better choices. So share only enough information to serve this purpose and no more. This can be accomplished verbally, with reports, or with visuals such as systems-thinking tools like causal-loop maps trend-over-time graphs, or stock-and-flow diagrams. Whenever you're trying to share your view with others, the important question to ask yourself is: "What's the most efficient way to clearly share my thinking about this issue?"

What About Gut Feelings, Hunches, or Intuition?

People often say: "You should keep your emotions out of the conversation," or, "Before the meeting begins, remember to leave your emotions at the door." This is bad advice for two reasons:

- First, it's impossible to do; you can't just turn your emotions on and off at will.

- Second, it's counterproductive. Research shows that emotions are essential when it comes to making decisions. Without them you have no preferences.[4]

Research also suggests that you should particularly pay attention to your gut feelings when you have a lot of experience with the subject matter. They're often the product of tacit knowledge.[5]

So here is more practical advice: Rather than attempt to keep your emotions out of a conversation, work instead to prevent your emotions from running away with the conversation. Don't negate your feelings; treat them responsibly. How do you do this? Rather than suppress your feelings, intuitions, or hunches, treat them, instead, like hypotheses by explaining and testing them:

- *My gut is telling me this is a really bad decision, but I can't quite find an explanation for why I feel this way. Is anyone else feeling the same way, and, if so, are you any closer to the underlying reasons than I am?*

- *I really love this idea, but I'm not sure if that's because it fits with what I've done before or if it's genuinely the best way to go. Where are others on this decision, and what are your thoughts? I'd be particularly interested in hearing from someone who has reservations about it.*

- *This decision scares me. Is anyone else feeling this way, or am I just overreacting?*

Often others will see this as an opportunity to bring up their own concerns or fears. If no else is feeling the same way, back off and see if the feeling goes away, or investigate further to see if you can discover some of its underlying causes.

It'll Make You Smarter

This practice will force you to get more rigorous about how you perceive "reality" and how you explain your perceptions to others. Knowing you're going to show people your road map forces you to be more disciplined about how you share your ideas. You're less likely to make a flippant comment, toss a half-baked idea on the table, or showboat your opinions, after all, when you know you'll need to disclose the thinking behind them.

Knowing you must back up a claim by explaining your thinking also imposes a degree of discipline on how you formulate your views. It forces you to evaluate your mental model, to more curiously think it through, and to ask yourself these critical questions:

- *Why do I think what I think?*

- *How valid is my perspective? On what is it based?*

- *Are there gaps or blind spots in my way of looking at the situation?*

- *Where am I wrong about this?*

- *Do other people see it differently, and, if so, how have they gone up the ladder?*

This self-reflection encourages you to hold your views like hypotheses rather than truths, a bedrock trait of someone with high conversational capacity. Full of healthy doubt and skepticism, you're more curious than dogmatic, more inquisitive than rigid, and more open-minded than opinionated. You're better equipped to marshal your intelligence in the service of your goals, and to detect and correct errors and gaps in your thinking, which makes you, quite simply, *smarter.*

> *Many highly intelligent people are poor thinkers. Many*
> *people of average intelligence are skilled thinkers. The power*
> *of a car is separate from the way the car is driven.*
> —EDWARD DE BONO

You'll Have More Influence

Evidence-based thinking is more *influential.* If the architect, for example, just said, "It's beautiful," without explaining *why* in a rigorous way, it's unlikely he'd affect the police officer's point of view. But if he claimed it was beautiful, and then *explained* what he witnessed and how that led him to his position, he'd be far more likely to influence the cop's perception of the city. In a similar way, if Steve failed to explain the underlying thinking that informed his position, Phil would have been far less likely to give any credence to Steve's concerns.

You'll Be Less Manipulatable

Learning to craft and explain your own thinking in a more rigorous way also makes you less prone to the manipulative nonsense of others. You aren't swayed by a claim just because of the person's authority, good looks, charm, or wit. When someone makes a claim, you paraphrase the classic line of Cuba Gooding Jr.'s character in *Jerry Maguire*: "Show me the *evidence*." This thorough thinking, described best, perhaps, in Carl Sagan's "baloney detection kit,"[6] means you are far less likely to blindly accept the views of others precisely because you are being so disciplined about managing your own.

A Parting Note on the Candor Skills

If you're wondering why I'm pounding this issue of rigorous, evidence-based thinking so hard, consider this observation by Carl Sagan:

> In hunter-gatherer, pre-agricultural times, the human life expectancy was about 20 to 30 years. That's also what it was in Western Europe in Late Roman and in Medieval times. It didn't rise to 40 years until around the year 1870. It reached 50 in 1915, 60 in 1930, 70 in 1955, and is today approaching 80.[7]

What do we have to thank for these impressive gains? It isn't opinion-based decision-making, and it isn't a greater use of Ouija boards, Magic 8 Balls, or the Psychic Friends Network. No, it's the greater use of more rigorous, evidence-based reasoning in the fields of public health and medicine. We're making more effective decisions about how to improve our health and extend our lives because our approach to the challenge is now largely grounded in an evidence-based pursuit of informed treatment.

So let me wrap up by reemphasizing a point I made at the beginning of this chapter: There's a spectrum of quality when it comes to thinking. At one end you have weak, opinion-based reasoning; at the other end, you have more robust evidence-based reasoning. The more you're focused on working with others to make the most informed and effective decisions possible, the further you should move to the right.

Opinion-Based Reasoning ◄────────► *Evidence-Based Reasoning*

From here on out, I expect you to pay attention to how candid you're being in the moment. Do you have ideas or concerns that you're not putting forward? How might you get your thoughts out of your head, through your mouth, and into the conversation in a productive, learning-oriented way? How clearly are you stating your position? How effectively are you articulating your thinking? Reflect on meetings. Use drive time, for instance, to consider questions such as these:

- *How candid was I in the meeting today?*
- *Were there things I should have said but held back? Why?*
- *What triggered me to withhold my view?*
- *How can I become more aware of this next time it happens? What was I feeling?*
- *What were the signs I was minimizing?*
- *What is a more productive way to handle it the next time I notice this happening?*
- *How could I have said what I needed to say in a constructive, learning-focused manner?*

Your thinking is a tool you use to make sense and to make choices. So treat it—and share it—with discipline and respect.

CURIOSITY SKILL #1

Testing Your Hypothesis

> *People who claim to be absolutely convinced that their stand
> is the only right one are dangerous. Such conviction is the
> essence not only of dogmatism, but of its more destructive
> cousin, fanaticism. It blocks off the user from learning new
> truth, and it is a dead giveaway of unconscious doubt.*
>
> **—ROLLO MAY**

You're learning how to be candid in a more rigorous and responsible way. That's important. But stop there and you'll end up, as the Flamethrower put it, "All push. No pull."* The key to staying in the sweet spot is to now employ your curiosity.

Curiosity, remember, is an indispensable part of the "production" process in your mental workshop. It's the reflection of a mindset that places learning over ego and the bettering of your mental models over being comfortable or feeling right. It's what distinguishes open-minded people who manage their worldview from closed-minded people who are trapped in it. When properly focused, curiosity leads to sharper thinking and smarter choices because it helps you catch and correct the inevitable disconnects between the mental maps you're using to make sense of a situation or issue

---

* If the story of the Human Flamethrower doesn't ring a bell, revisit pages 46–48 and 104–105 in *Conversational Capacity*.

and the actual events on the ground. By the time you finish this chapter and the next, you'll better understand the importance of cultivating your curiosity, and more important, the skills you need to strengthen to put that curiosity into action.

But curious about what? To answer that, I invite you to revisit three questions I first shared in Chapter 9:

1. *What am I seeing that others are missing?*

2. *What are others seeing that I'm missing?*

3. *What are we all missing?*

With these questions in mind, the next step is to seek answers. As you'll no doubt recall, there are two skills that help you counter your rigorous "push" with some genuine "pull":

- *Testing* your own hypotheses.

- *Inquiring* into the hypotheses of others.

Testing

Between 560 and 547 BCE, Croesus ruled as the king of Lydia, a country in what today is Turkey. Concerned about the growing power of the Persians, he thought it best to attack them before they grew any stronger. Before making his decision, however, he consulted the oracle at Delphi, who told him, "If Croesus goes to war, he will destroy a great empire."

Emboldened by the oracle's response, Croesus made the necessary preparations and attacked the Persians. The Persians quickly overpowered the Lydians, captured their city, put Croesus in chains, and ordered him to be burned alive.

The oracle had spoken correctly: Croesus had destroyed a great empire—*his own.* By failing to consider other, less favorable interpretations of the oracle's portent, he based a major decision on his flawed, self-serving interpretation. By construing what he was hearing to fit his expectations, Croesus suffered a major disconnect between the mental map he was using to make the decision to go to war and actual events on the ground. Croesus experienced, you could say, a disastrous "Indianapolis moment."*

---

* For a review of "Indianapolis moments" and "Indianapolis journaling," revisit the concept in Chapter 10.

Holding Your Perspectives with a Bias for Learning

You've shared your view and explained it clearly. That's a good start. The goal now isn't to sell it, convince others you're right, or cajole them into seeing things your way—*it's to learn*. This is where a curious mind is invaluable. With a mind focused on learning, you're now asking yourself these important questions:

- *What are others seeing that I'm missing?*

- *Do I have a blind spot?*

- *Am I misinterpreting the oracle?*

How do you discover, for example, where your thinking is off-kilter? How do you know where your mental model needs some work? How do you detect and correct any mental errors in your analysis? How do you recognize where your perceptions of "reality" are being distorted by a cognitive bias? How do you know if you're missing some evidence, or making—like Croesus—erroneous assumptions? How do you know if *you're* having an "Indianapolis moment"?

It's simple. You *test* your thinking.

> *Our decisions, opinions, perception, and memory can all*
> *be set adrift by our emotional undercurrents, often without*
> *our even noticing that our anchor has slipped.*
> —CORDELIA FINE

With an effective test, you're treating your view like a *hypothesis* rather than like a *truth*; a *premise* rather than a *fact*; a *provisional point of view* rather than a *rock-solid veracity*. How do you do this in a conversation? Like a scientist publishing his or her research in a peer-reviewed journal, you subject your point of view to scrutiny.

This is common practice in a range of disciplines. For example, a doctor rarely looks at a patient and immediately begins treatment. She first works to properly diagnose the patient's condition. She may have an idea about what's ailing her patient, but she tests her assumptions to ensure she's looking at the problem correctly. Only then does she take action. She approaches the problem-solving process in this manner because her goal is to make the most informed and effective choices about how to treat her patient.

In your mental workshop, you're doing the same thing. Your goal is to expand and improve your thinking by subjecting it to scrutiny. You do this by showing people that you're holding your view like a hypothesis you want to evaluate rather than a truth you're trying to protect or to sell. This is unlikely to make you feel comfortable or "right," but if you want to sharpen your thinking, it's the only way to go.

The point of testing your hypothesis is to proactively detect and correct errors in how you're making sense of things. You're trying to spark double-loop aha moments *before* you make important choices. You don't want to wait until you're lost and confused before you realize that the view of reality you're using to reach your destination is flawed.

Is It Really That Necessary?

"Testing sounds like a royal pain in the ass," you might be thinking. "Is it really that important?" It is. *Test*, originally a word from Latin describing a small container used to evaluate gold and other precious metals, had by the Late Middle Ages developed the meaning familiar to us today: a "trial or examination to determine the correctness of something."[1] As I'm describing it here, *testing* is straightforward in concept: You're conducting a trial or examination to determine the correctness of your thinking.

It may be simple in concept, but it's challenging in practice. The difficulty stems from how your mind works. Despite being riddled with errors, distortions, and blind spots, your brain hands you a view of "reality" that seems rock solid (which explains why "Indianapolis moments" are so commonplace). The problem, therefore, is that your brain is so adept at tricking you in this way—making you feel you can trust it—testing your view doesn't *feel* necessary. Learning to do it wholeheartedly, therefore, is no easy task.

But while difficult, it's vital to your goal of thinking clearly and making smart choices. A disturbing number of *cognitive biases* distort how the human mind makes sense of the world, from *the hindsight bias* and *the bandwagon effect*, to *the Dunning–Kruger effect* and *the fundamental attribution error*. The most pernicious of them all, the grand distorter, is *the confirmation bias*—the tendency in which once you've adopted a view your brain seeks information that supports that view and in turn misses or dismisses information that contradicts that view. Thanks to your confirmation bias, you have a penchant for getting stuck in your narrow way of seeing things.

Part of the problem is that cognitive errors are seen as bad; they're viewed as a sign that you're not as smart as you should be. Ironically, that's the *wrong* way to frame the issue. "Of all the things we are wrong about, this idea of error might well top the list," says Kathryn Schulz, author of

Being Wrong. "It is our meta-mistake: we are wrong about what it means to be wrong. Far from being a moral flaw, it is inextricable from some of our most humane and honorable qualities: empathy, optimism, imagination, conviction, and courage. And far from being a mark of indifference and intolerance, wrongness is a vital part of how we learn and change. Thanks to error, we can revise our understanding of ourselves and amend our ideas of the world."[2]

> *Do not feel absolutely certain of anything.*
> —BERTRAND RUSSELL

With that in mind, you adopt an *anti-confirmation bias* and test the views your brain hands you. You treat with great suspicion the view of "reality" your mind is serving up because you're more interested in making informed and effective choices than in protecting a flawed viewpoint. This opens the path to smarter thinking because you're actively struggling against your self-serving brain by leaning into difference, seeking contrarian perspectives, and asking people to challenge how you're currently making sense of things. And if additional evidence or more cogent reasoning can improve your mental map, you change it. (Remember, with your new mindset, getting smarter takes priority over stroking your ego. If you're *not* going to test your views, stop wasting other people's time and talk to yourself in a mirror instead.) The basic idea is that when you're focused on clearer, cleaner, more rigorous thinking, you're working extremely hard not to buy into your brain's own bullshit.[3]

You're Candid Because You're Curious

This is a big point. Remember, one reason you're being so rigorously forthright with the candor skills is so you can *test* your view of reality. And there is no way to test your view if it's not clearly explained and open to scrutiny. In this way, candor and curiosity are intimately related. Focus on pooling perspectives to expand and improve your thinking in pursuit of making the smartest choices possible. When you do so you're not *just* candid and curious, you're candid *because* you're curious.

> You're not just candid and curious,
> you're candid because you're curious.

What the Skill Is

Trying to improve your thinking by thinking about your thinking can trap you in a cognitive cul-de-sac, so to be a more flexible and adaptive thinker, you need to contrast your thinking with outside perspectives. Testing, therefore, is a form of mental discipline by which you refuse to blindly accept the view of reality presented to you by your brain. Because you're holding your view like an educated guesstimate rather than an absolute certainty, you're less attached to your take on things and more open to alternative views. Testing is the triumph of learning and humility over ignorance and arrogance.

> *Testing is the triumph of learning and humility*
>
> *over ignorance and arrogance.*

With an effective test you're not just sitting back passively hoping other people will provide a contrasting perspective; you're *inviting* and *encouraging* them to do so. You do this by showing people you're holding your position and the thinking that informs it hypothetically. Rather than holding your view close to your chest like a poker player with a good hand or holding it over your head like a Kendo stick with which to whack opposing perspectives, you hold it up like a notional view of "reality" so others can see it and provide feedback. "Here is how I've made sense of this situation," you're saying, "and I'd like you to help me improve it. What am I missing? What have I got wrong? What are you seeing that I'm not?"

Why does this help? It is far easier for people who see things differently to engage with you when other people see you're holding your views skeptically, as something you're trying to vet and improve rather than something you're trying to sell or defend. A good test, therefore, encourages people to climb over their *minimizing* hurdle and into the conversation with you. Better still, when done well, it dramatically lowers or even removes the hurdle. In this way, by testing your own views and pulling more ideas and information into the conversation, you can increase the intelligence of the entire conversation or meeting, even when others in the conversation are unfamiliar with the skills.

What the Skill Is Not

Let me also emphasize what the skill is not. It's not a *gimmick*—a superficial invitation to push back the unsupported by genuine curiosity. It's also not a *trick* designed to lure people into the open so you can take a cleaner shot. And it's not based in weakness and insecurity; it's grounded in strength and confidence. It's not that you're unsure of yourself or afraid to formulate a thought; it's that you're conscious of your mind's limitations and you're acting accordingly. Few things signal strength and confidence more than being in command of your behavior and using that discipline in the pursuit of rigorous thinking and smart choices.

Sample Tests

I shared a range of tests in my first book *Conversational Capacity*. Here are a few more to add to your repertoire. (Many of these came from clients or from participants in my workshops):

- *I have strong feelings about this issue, so I really need to hear from people who see it differently. I don't want my preconceived notions to get in the way of making the best decision.*

- *What might be two or three unintended consequences of this decision?*

- *My thinking has betrayed me so many times in the past. Does anyone see how it might be trying to fool me again this time?*

- *Help me find the flaws in how I'm looking at this situation.*

- *This is an important decision and I want to explore it from all angles. So, I'm not ending this meeting until we've heard at least three concerns about what I just proposed.*

- *I want to make sure my idea holds water. So, let's try and shoot a few holes in it.*

- *I've been here for twenty years and I have strong opinions about how things are supposed to look and run around here. So, I'd like to hear from some of the newer people on the team. You're no doubt looking at this decision with fresher eyes than I am.*

- *To help me think through this decision in a careful way, let's identify all the reasons we shouldn't do it.*

- *I don't want my presence to get in the way of your ability to tell me what I need to hear. So, I'm going to leave the room for thirty minutes. When I come back in half an hour, I'd like to see at least three concerns about what I'm suggesting up on a flip chart and we'll work through them together.*

- *I'm the finance person, so I tend to see everything through a finance lens. I'd like to hear from someone with a different functional perspective.*

- *I know I've got a strong "win" tendency and I've never made it easy for you to challenge me publicly before, but this is way too important and I need your input. So, let's do this: Break into pairs for fifteen minutes and come up with two things you like about what I'm suggesting, and then, more important, two things you don't. Then we'll go around and hear what each pair comes up with.*

Here's a particularly strong one: Executives at a major international bank see *conversational capacity* as a key part of their "risk management culture." As one executive put it: "If we don't have people willing to raise their hands when we're about to make a really stupid decision, we're going to make a lot of really stupid decisions." Taking a cue from Edward De Bono's *Six Thinking Hats*, we developed a pair of powerful tests they employ with big decisions:[4]

- **Test 1.** The "Black Hat" test:

  - *Let's take thirty minutes to find everything wrong with this decision. What are the risks? Why shouldn't we do this? Why would our competitors laugh in our faces if we made this choice?*

- **Test 2.** The "Yellow Hat" test:

  - *Now that we've kicked the daylight out of the idea, let's look at it again through a different lens: What do we like about the decision? What are the risks of not doing it? Why would our competitors laugh in our faces if they saw us letting this opportunity slip by?*

"If we don't have people willing to raise their hands

when we're about to make a really stupid decision,

we're going to make a lot of really stupid decisions."

We've found that even the biggest minimizer in the room has little problem raising a concern or a criticism during the first test, because that's the objective. This flips the minimizer's dilemma on its head: he's now uncomfortable *not* raising a concern because he's supposed to be raising concerns.

The Stronger, the Better

Here's a basic rule for testing: the stronger, the better. Nick Hornby nails this point in his hilarious book *A Long Way Down*. After a life-shattering series of bad decisions that wrecked his marriage, ruined his career, and trashed his sense of self-worth, the main character, Martin Sharp, reflects on the limitations of his own thinking: "If thinking inside the box were an Olympic sport, I would have won more gold medals than Carl Lewis," he says. He then continues with the following reflection:

> Here's the thing: The cause of my problems is located in my head, if my head is where my personality is located. . . . I had been given many opportunities in life, and I had thrown each of them away, one by one, through a series of catastrophically bad decisions, each one of which seemed like a good idea to me—to me and my head—at the time. And yet the only tool I had at my disposal to correct the disastrous course my life seemed to be taking was the very same head that had caused me to fuck up in the first place. What chance did I have?[5]

Recognizing that more than awareness is needed, Martin then contemplates what he needs if he is to improve his thinking. His initial insight is about *awareness*:

> Quite clearly I needed two heads, two heads being better than one and all that. One would have to be the old one, just because the old one knows people's names and phone numbers, and which breakfast cereal I prefer, and so on; the second one would be able to observe and interpret the behavior of the first, in the manner of a television wildlife expert.

I love the idea of having two minds: one making sense out of things and making choices about how to deal with it, and the other observing the first at work, like a "wildlife expert." (He's talking about cultivating his personal awareness by learning to direct his beam of attention internally.) Martin goes on to explain why this is important: "Asking the head I have now to explain its own thinking is as pointless as dialing your own telephone number on your own telephone: Either way, you get an engaged signal. Or your own answer message . . ."

Martin then wakes up to the idea that people who will *challenge* his thinking are the key to improving it: "It took me an embarrassing amount of time to realize that other people have heads," he muses, before admitting that their heads do a far better job of detecting and correcting errors in his own views of reality.

But Martin doesn't stop there. Going deeper, he recognizes not all feedback is created equal. When you're looking for a catalyst for profound learning, some sources are more powerful than others: "Friends and lovers might try to throw a kindly light on the episode, but because I had only ex-friends and ex-lovers, I was ideally placed. I only really knew people who would give it to me with both barrels." He follows with this thought:

> I knew where to start, too. Indeed, so successful was my first phone call that I didn't really need to speak to anyone else. My ex-wife was perfect—direct, articulate, and clear-sighted—and I actually ended up feeling sorry for people with someone who loved them, when not living with someone who loathed you was so obviously the way to go. When you have a Cindy in your life, there aren't any pleasantries to wade through: There are only unpleasantries, and unpleasantries are an essential part of the learning process.

Martin wraps up with the wry observation: "Ex-wives: Really, everybody should have at least one."

Emphasize the Test

To prepare for his conversation with Phil, Steve and his learning partners spent a lot of time on exploring how to employ this skill. At first Steve was experimenting with the fairly "casual tests" I provide in my workshop handouts (a list very similar to the one in *Conversational Capacity* on pages 88–89), such as "What is your reaction to what I just said?" But in their role-playing it became obvious such casual tests were far too weak. Steve was hitting Phil with a very strong position, and a laid-back test didn't provide sufficient balance. The *position* put forward by Steve is hard on Phil, after all, so the test should be just as hard, or harder, on Steve. After some trial-and-error practice, Steve and his colleagues came up with this much brawnier test: "This is really hard to come in here and say, and I'm sure it's hard to hear. Push back on my point of view if you think I'm being unfair."

This illustrates a good rule of thumb: At the very least, seek relative parity in the intensity of your position and the strength of your test. Even better, place an even stronger emphasis on the test.

Coda

Testing your view is a pivotal skill for three reasons:

- First, it's rare. You aren't taught to test your thinking this way in a conversation. (In school, for example, you're rewarded for having the *right* answer, not for discovering you're sporting a *wrong* one.)

- Second, it helps you counter your brain's automatic and self-serving preference for information that supports your current position.

- Third, an effective test can prevent your candor from pushing people away from the table when your goal is to pull them toward it.

It's not easy work, explains Cordelia Fine:

> While the veil our brain stealthily drapes over reality can never be whipped away entirely, there are other reasons for us not to be completely disheartened. We can be encouraged by the fact that determined efforts on our part to see the world accurately can help counteract distortion. If precision is important enough to us, we are capable of greater conscientiousness in gathering and considering our evidence.[6]

Testing your perspective by subjecting it to public scrutiny is the strongest signal that you're in your workshop focused on thinking clearly. It is so important, in fact, that your conversational capacity can be measured by your ability to hold your views hypothetically under pressure.

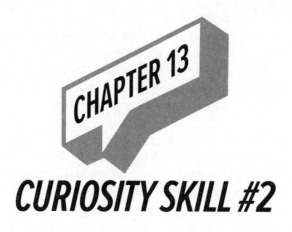

CURIOSITY SKILL #2

Inquiring into the Hypotheses of Others

*There is no such thing as a weird human being. It's just that
some people require more understanding than others.*

—TOM ROBBINS

With the first three skills, you're putting *your* view into the conversation
and testing it. But the beauty of this discipline is that there's an additional
tool in your mental workshop that helps you expand and improve your
thinking by leveraging how other people are making sense of things: genuine *inquiry* into their views.

It's one thing to test a view you're holding, but *inquiry*—a word that
stems from the old Latin *inquīrere* meaning "to seek to learn" or "to look
into"[1]—helps you identify gaps in your thinking for which you didn't even
know to test. Inquiry in a tough conversation is like a flashlight in a dark
cave—an essential tool that illuminates ideas and information that might
not otherwise see any light.

Other people have views—all of them different from yours in either
large or small ways—and in the spirit of learning, you're working just as
hard to *pull* them into the conversation as you're at putting yours forward.
With this skill, in other words, you're *inviting* the perspectives of others into
a conversation.

To inquire means to search and discover. Inquiry is the act of exploration, a questioning with an agenda to see new possibilities. [Inquiry] always begins with a question—an honest desire to learn about something—as its premise.[2]
—FRANK BARRETT AND RONALD FRY

What, for instance, can the way in which others are making sense of this issue teach you about a decision you're facing? There is no way to know unless you encourage them to speak up, clearly and candidly. How do they view the world differently? Get curious and inquire. Do they have information you don't have access to? Are they interpreting the information in a different and perhaps more useful way? Again, it's simple: Ask and find out.

I stated in the Introduction that a key goal of this book is for you to be able to make every conversation or meeting smarter because you're in the room. Genuine *inquiry* is a powerful yet underestimated way to achieve that goal. It provides another tool for turning the thinking of others into a profound source of learning. Here are a few key points about this deceptively complex skill.

Inquiry Is Different from Testing

Both *testing* and *inquiry* are curiosity skills, yes, but they each play a distinct role in a conversation: You *test your* hypotheses. You *inquire* into the hypotheses of *others*. Recognizing that no one has a perfect handle on the truth, you're holding your views *provisionally*, but you're also treating the views of others *conditionally* as well. You're treating everyone's perspective *hypothetically*, as another important but imperfect lens through which to look at an issue.

It's a Process

It's not as simple as just asking a simple question. You may need to ask a few questions to fully understand how someone else is making sense of an issue. As Edgar Schein says: "Humble Inquiry is the fine art of drawing someone out, of asking questions to which you do not already know the answer, of building a relationship based on curiosity and interest in the other person."[3] Inquiry, that is to say, is the *process* of asking as many questions as necessary to explore and understand another's position.

"Humble Inquiry is the fine art of drawing someone out, of asking questions to which you do not already know the answer, of building a relationship based on curiosity and interest in the other person."

You're Not Seeking Agreement

Here's another important distinction: You're not inquiring into the views of others in the pursuit of agreement; you're doing it in *the pursuit of learning.* After a conversation that never leaves the sweet spot you may still disagree with the person with whom you're talking, but you've both probably learned something about the issue you're exploring. You're inquiring into the perspectives of others with the goal of getting smarter, not reaching consensus.

It Can Be Used in Multiple Ways

There are a range of ways that genuine inquiry can be employed to bring more depth and balance to a conversation:

When Someone Reacts to Your Point of View

You're in a meeting, and you've put forward a suggestion, explained it, and tested it. Suddenly one of your colleagues blurts out: "There's no way that'll work." At this point you have three basic options:

1. *Minimize* and shut down.

2. Kick into *"win"* mode and argue.

3. *Inquire* into their reaction to find out where it's coming from.

If you're in your mental workshop and learning is your primary goal, option three is the obvious choice: "I appreciate your candid reaction. Tell me more. What specifically about my idea doesn't work for you?" You don't have to agree with their reaction, but you certainly want to *understand* it.

When Someone Reacts to Another Person's Point of View

When someone reacts to a colleague's comment in a conversation or meeting, you can help keep the conversation in the sweet spot with *an inquiry*. For example, "Take a minute and tell us more, Rupert. What leads you to think Kim's idea is so risky?"

When Someone Is Not Participating in a Conversation

When colleagues have shared neither their view nor their thinking you can *invite* them to share their perspectives. If you're in a meeting where a discussion about an important decision is taking place and you notice that Maria and Trey haven't shared their observations, you can bring more balance to the conversation, and perhaps spark some useful insight, by asking them to *share their points of view*: "Maria, we've been bouncing this topic around for a while now. I'd love to get your take on the decision. What do you think about the issue?" or, "Trey, we've not heard from you yet. As you've listened to the conversation unfold, what are you thinking? I'd love to get your thoughts and reactions."

When Someone Isn't Being Clear

When people aren't being clear, you can ask them questions to clarify their position. For example: "Bethany, maybe I'm a little slow, but I didn't grasp your basic point, and I want to make sure I understand how you're thinking about this. Do you like the idea or do you not?"

When Someone Is Being Verbally Aggressive

It may seem counterintuitive, but inquiry is a powerful way to deal with verbal hostility. Picture, for example, someone blurting out in a meeting: "You're an idiot if you really think that's a good idea!" This could easily send you flying out of the sweet spot. But if you're on your conversational game, you might respond in a more curious, humble, and learning-focused manner: "Well, it certainly wouldn't be the first time I've been an idiot. You seem to be seeing this very differently than I do, so help me out. What am I missing? What are you seeing that I'm not?"

This is a powerful way to respond. You're not only more likely to gain additional information; you're also holding your colleague responsible for explaining their view. In a meeting with people using these skills, therefore, it's harder for anyone to get away with a flippant, gruff, or sarcastic comment because someone will inquire and ask them to explain, but in a curious rather than a castigatory way. In this way, the skilled use of inquiry into an aggressive comment tends to de-escalate the encounter. People being aggressive are pushing their view, and when you respond by pulling more of their thinking into the conversation, it reduces their need to push so hard. "Look, I'm sorry I called you an idiot. That was terrible thing to say. But I still don't like your idea."

"No problem," you might then respond. "What specifically about my suggestion doesn't work for you?"

Steve demonstrated the power of doing this well. When Phil blurted out, "I think you're making a mountain out of a molehill," Steve's inquiry into that strong position helped him understand and evaluate it, but it also held Phil accountable for explaining it: "I don't think I'm making a mountain out of a molehill, but maybe I'm missing something. What makes you say that? What are you seeing that I'm not?"

When Someone Presents a View, But Fails to Explain It

If a teammate puts forward a position but doesn't show you how she got there, you can *invite* her thinking into the conversation. If you're in a meeting and a colleague says, "I don't think that's the right thing to do," for instance, you might say, "Shelly, you've obviously got a strong view on this issue. Take a minute or two and help us see why you're feeling so adamant about it." Or, "Can you take a minute and unpack that idea for me?"

When Someone Smirks or Sighs

Not all communication is verbal. Often a message comes in the form of a wink, a smirk, a roll of the eyes, a slamming down of a pen, a knowing glance, a sigh, a dismissive hand gesture, or a wince. You can treat these *nonverbal forms of communication* like an unexplained *position* and inquire into them:

- *You rolled your eyes at my suggestion. Is there anything about my idea or the way it's being presented that doesn't sit well with you? If there is, I'd be keen to hear about it.*

- *Hey Rick, I notice you just snapped your pencil in half and threw it down on the table. I assume that means there is something about the idea you don't like. If that's the case, help us see what concerns you so much, especially if you think we're missing something important.*

- *I sensed a little hesitation in your response. Did I misread that? And if not, is there something about this decision that concerns you?*

Again, as you can see, getting away with a naked position, a snarky comment, an eye roll, or a belligerent remark is far less likely in a meeting when someone with high conversational capacity is present. This is because they'll hold you accountable for explaining it—not to put you on the spot, or in a "gotcha" way, but in an authentic bid to understand it.

It's a Facilitative Tool

Formally or informally, this underappreciated skill turns you into a powerful facilitator of learning. In my first book, *Conversational Capacity*, the story of Randy in the parent–teacher conference provides a perfect example. When he's accused of grade retribution, rather than acquiesce or argue, he gets curious and asks: "You've said that I'm giving Julia grades as retribution for your wife's relationship with the school. I'm curious, what signals are you seeing from me that lead you to think that's what's happening here?"[4] Asking the parents to account for their claim serves the same two purposes I just outlined above: greater *insight* and *understanding*, and greater *evidence* and *accountability*.

Listening

Both curiosity skills, *testing* and *inquiry*, require genuine listening. This may seem obvious, but it's not standard practice. If you're like most people, "listening" is often little more than just waiting for your turn to talk, formulating your response, or daydreaming about something else entirely. But when you test and inquire in a sincerely curious way, you focus intently on the responses of others because they're the best source of new information and insight.

> *You cannot truly listen to anyone and do anything else at the same time.*
> —M. SCOTT PECK

In *The Road Less Traveled*, in a section titled "The Work of Attention," M. Scott Peck provides an example of the discipline required for genuinely curious listening:

Not long ago I attended a lecture by a famous man on an aspect of the relationship between psychology and religion in which I have long been interested. Because of my interest I had a certain amount of expertise in the subject and immediately recognized the lecturer to be a great sage indeed. I also sensed love in the tremendous effort that he was exerting to communicate, with all manner of examples, highly abstract concepts that were difficult for us, his audience, to comprehend. I therefore listened to him with all the intentness of which I was capable. Throughout the hour and a half he talked, sweat was literally dripping down my face in the air-conditioned auditorium. By the time he was finished I had a throbbing headache, the muscles in my neck were rigid from my effort at concentration, and I felt completely drained and exhausted. Although I estimated that I had understood no more than 50 percent of what this great man had said to us that afternoon, I was amazed by the large number of brilliant insights he had given me. Following the lecture, which was well attended by culture-seeking individuals, I wandered about through the audience during a coffee break listening to their comments. Generally, they were disappointed. Knowing his reputation, they had expected more. They found him hard to follow and his talk confusing. He was not as competent a speaker as they had hoped to hear. One woman proclaimed to nods of agreement, "He really didn't tell us anything."

M. Scott Peck then describes the difference between his experience and that of many in the audience:

In contradistinction to the others, I was able to hear much of what this great man said, precisely because I was willing to do the work of listening to him. I was willing to do this work for two reasons: one, because I recognized his greatness and that what he had to say would likely be of value; second, because of my interest in the field I deeply wanted to absorb what he had to say as to enhance my own understanding and spiritual growth. My listening to him was an act of love. I loved him because I perceived him to be a person of great value worth attending to, and I loved myself because I was willing to work on behalf of my growth. Since he was the teacher and I the pupil, he the giver and I the receiver, my love was primarily self-directed, motivated by what I could get out of our relationship and not what I could give him. Nonetheless, it is entirely possible that he could sense within his audience the intensity of my concentration, my attention, my love, and he may have been thereby rewarded. Love ... is invariably a two-way street, a reciprocal phenomenon whereby the receiver also gives and the giver also receives.[5]

Notice that M. Scott Peck describes listening as a *deliberate, mindful act.* You're focusing your beam of attention on the other person and seeking value in what the person is trying to communicate.

> *By far the most common and important way in which*
> *we can exercise our attention is by listening.*
> —M. SCOTT PECK

Listen Empathically

With a curious mindset, you're not just *listening intellectually,* you're *listening empathically.* You're not just tuned in to the logic of someone's view. You're also listening to how the words are being shared, and to the underlying sentiments, values, and convictions behind the words. You're focusing your attention on the deeper messages being sent, not just the light stuff on the surface.

Steve could sense in Phil, for example, not just his *view* of the situation but the *concern* behind it. Phil seemed sincere in his desire to create an open workspace, and in his view that it was working fairly well. Steve also noticed the frustration behind Phil's attempt to shut down the conversation, and he tried to respond in a way that mirrored the emotional charge: "I'll leave right now if you like. But can you at least tell me how I'm putting you between a rock and a hard spot? That's not what I came in here to do." That brilliant inquiry would not have been possible if Steve had not been listening with an empathetic ear.

Collaborative Design: A Powerful Form of Inquiry

When it comes to making decisions about how to manage people, orchestrate change, deliver feedback, improve the working relationship between people or groups, run effective meetings or any other activity that depends on people working together effectively, you have only two options for making those choices: *guess* or *ask.* That's it. You can either unilaterally *impose* your choices and then cross your fingers and hope you guessed well, or you can collaborate with others to design the smartest way forward.

When you employ *collaborative design*—what I referred to in my first book as *joint control*—you're opting *to ask*. You do this by *inquiring* into the most effective way to work with another person or group to achieve a particular objective. When you adopt this approach, you're in your mental workshop pooling and integrating the relevant perspectives so you can make the most intelligent choices about how to proceed.*

In the second chapter, I provided a short example of how I used this form of inquiry to help Steve, Phil, and their team find a solution to the messy predicament they were facing. "The basic question this team needs to answer is this: 'How can Phil meet his boss's expectations with flying colors, but do it in a way that keeps each one of you coming into his office with all the information he needs to run this business with his eyes wide open?' So, to find an answer to that question let me ask you another one: To help him do a better job of striking that important balance, *what would you like more of and less of from Phil?"*

More Of? Less Of?

As that last example illustrates, when you're working with others to collaboratively design a way to improve a relationship, process, action, or service, the basic question you are asking is: "What do we need more of and less of to achieve X?" Here are a few examples:

- *What do we need more of and less of to make this process far less cumbersome and far more efficient?*

- *As your manager, what do you need more of and less of from me so I'm doing a better job of helping you bring your A-game to this project?*

- *As one of our most valued customers, we're thrilled when you say you're very impressed with our service. But to avoid getting complacent we'd like to ask you a simple question: What do you need more of and less of from us so we can push our customer service to an even higher level?*

- *What does the business need more of and less of from the HR function so we can help you meet your strategic challenges in an even more focused and potent way?*

---

* To review the concept of Joint Control, see pages 71–75 in *Conversational Capacity*.

Additional Points

It's Harder Than It Seems

On the surface, inquiring into the views of others appears to be a simple skill that, when performed well, helps protect you from your *confirmation bias*. But don't let this fool you. It's far harder than it seems. When someone contradicts you, it's tempting to shut down, acquiesce, or jump back to *your* position, often with a little extra heat. "Maybe you didn't grasp what I'm suggesting. Let me run it by you again. Try to keep up this time." But this defensive reaction reinforces your *confirmation bias* and limits learning because it fails to play what's missing—the thinking behind the person's contradiction.

You Might Need to Explain Why

People may misinterpret your motives when you inquire into their point of view, especially if it's a new behavior. They might skeptically assume, for example, that it's just a manipulative strategy, or you're trying to draw their thinking into the open so you can attack it. To guard against such defensive reactions, you can proactively disabuse others of any erroneous interpretations about your motives by explaining *why* you're inquiring into their ideas:

- *I genuinely want to see how you're looking at this issue because you might be seeing things I'm missing. I just wanted to let you know that in case I'm coming across differently. I'm not trying to lawyer you or to set you up for an argument.*

- *I'm asking you these questions because I really want to understand your view. And if I'm sending any signals that suggest otherwise, hit the pause button and point it out.*

It Manifests Authentic Curiosity

This is another point that seems obvious, but it's worth stressing. Inquiry, as I'm describing it here, is far more than just asking questions. *Effective inquiry* is always grounded in curiosity, in a genuine desire to learn. But it's all too easy to ask leading questions that are merely cloaked positions:

- *Do think maybe there's a better way you could do that?*

- *Do you think using an agenda in our meetings might help?*

- *I'm wondering if it would help if you did X . . . ?*

- *Are you wearing that to the dinner?*

Even more destructive are the pugnacious comments and arrogant questions that push people away from the table, block alternative viewpoints, and shut down disagreement. Sadly, these *conversational capacity killers*, which can include everything from a poor test to a lousy inquiry to a dismissive comment, are far too common in the workplace:

- *I've explained how this looks from an intelligent perspective. What does it look like from yours?*

- *I thought you were smarter than that.*

- *If any of you disagree with me, do a little homework, get your facts straight, and then we'll talk again.*

- *Are you stuck on stupid?*

- *"Tell us your thinking and we'll show you where you are mixed up."*[6]

- *You don't really think that, do you?*

- *Really?*

- *"You don't know what to look for—you are not a doctor."*[7]

- *I've forgotten more about this subject than you'll ever know, and here's what I think we should do. You're welcome.*

- *"I love to engage in repartee with people who are stupider than I am."*[8]

- *Look, I'm not trying to be condescending here. (That means I'm not trying to talk down to you.)*

- *"Seriously? How old are you?"*[9]

- *Did your mom drop you as a child?*

- *WTF?*

What the Authentic, Learning-Focused Inquiry Is Not

It should be obvious by now, but for emphasis, here is a short list of things that an inquiry is *not*:

- It is not an *inquisition*.

- It is not *lawyering*.

- It is not a *position* masked with a leading question.

- It is not a setup for a smackdown or a *"gotcha"* moment.

- It is not a *shallow* "going through the motions" activity in which you're inquiring merely because you know you're supposed to, not because your heart is really in it.

Why the Curiosity Skills Matter

"People gain power," says Dacher Keltner, "as a result of small, everyday behaviors: by speaking up first, offering a possible answer to a problem, being first to assert an opinion, freeing up everyone's thinking by throwing out a wild suggestion, question, or humorous observation that gets the creative juices flowing."[10] You can also gain power by sparking a new insight, by starting an effective conversation about an issue that people are avoiding, by bridging a barrier, by pulling a meeting back from the brink of argument, or by helping someone struggling to get their idea into a conversation.

> *Our opportunity for influence increases when we are open and ask great questions, listen to others with receptive minds, and offer playful ideas and novel perspectives.*
> —**DACHER KELTNER**

If your power in a conversation is determined by your influence, the two behaviors we've just explored are potent skills. They give you the ability to spark more insight by shaping conversations in a more constructive and learning-focused direction. Here are a few final points about these skills.

Help Others Speak Up

Both curiosity skills—*testing* your own views and *inquiring* into the views of others—allow you to help other people get their perspective into a conversation. By testing and inquiring you take more active responsibility for helping others be more candid by *inviting* them to share their ideas.

More Engagement

The two curiosity skills are great tools for keeping people *engaged* in a meeting or conversation because they work like conversational glue. When people know that their view may be solicited at any time—either to invite their perspective into a conversation or to test the perspective of another—they're more likely to pay attention and stick with the flow of the dialogue. The skilled use of the curiosity skills, in other words, makes it riskier to disengage from a conversation or meeting because you never know when someone may ask for your view on the matter at hand.

Back and Forth

In a conversation, you'll often bounce back and forth between testing and inquiry. After explaining his concerns to Phil, Steve *tested* his perspective: "Push back on me here," he said, "especially if you think I'm being unfair." Phil responded with a *position*, but he failed to explain it: "I appreciate that you're willing to bring this up, but I think you're making a mountain out of a molehill." Steve then *inquired* to invite more of Phil's thinking into the conversation: "I don't think I'm making a mountain out of a molehill, but maybe I'm missing something. What makes you say that? What are you seeing that I'm not?"

They Cultivate Your Better Angels

These skills also engage many of the characteristics you're trying to cultivate:

- *Candor.* There is no way to test your view if you don't put it out there first.

- *Curiosity.* You are always seeking novel ways of looking at an issue.

- *Courage.* You might be found wrong. You might make someone angry. You might feel "less than fully brilliant" when you recognize that other people have a better grasp of the issue than you do.

- *Humility.* Recognizing the ironic fact that the price you must often pay for getting smarter is feeling dumber (think about it), you refuse to let your ego get in the way of learning.

- *Mental strength.* Keeping your ego in check and maintaining conversational discipline takes focus and grit.

- *Mental agility.* Your eagerness to shift your thinking and double-loop learn requires a degree of cognitive flexibility that more ego-driven people can't muster.

Curiosity Is the Key to Smart Thinking

Bertrand Russell said: "The fundamental cause of the trouble is that in the modern world the stupid are cocksure while the intelligent are full of doubt." But I think that adopting a cocksure stance is what makes people stupid in the first place. Holding your view of "reality" as truth, as if you've got everything all figured out, leaves no space for learning. If you're unable or unwilling to treat a view like a hypothesis and test it, you cripple your ability to think more intelligently. This is the reason rigorous curiosity is so powerful. It dramatically boosts learning. While the cocksure nurse their arrogance and stupidity, those full of doubt—who are curious, asking questions, and constantly seeking new ways of seeing and thinking about the world—grow ever more informed, humble, and wise.

Holding your view of "reality" as truth, as if you've got everything all figured out, leaves no space for learning.

Next Steps

The four basic skills for balancing candor and curiosity, when supported by disciplined awareness and a learning-oriented mindset, provide a powerful framework for seeing what's being played in a conversation and then for playing what's missing. The key is to use them competently in action—in a meeting or in an important conversation—even when someone is screaming obscenities in your face or calling your mother a foul name. That's the focus of the next chapter in which I'll share a range of ways you can build your facility with the skills. Then, in the chapter after that, you'll learn that if you're looking at it through the right lens, your workplace and all its imperfections provides a superb forum for practice.

SHARPENING YOUR SKILLS

Learning to Balance Candor and
Curiosity, One Skill at a Time

You must either modify your dreams or magnify your skills.
—**JIM ROHN**

Earning a black belt in karate. Piloting an aircraft. Driving a car. Performing neurosurgery. Performing a role in a Shakespearean play. Climbing the face of El Capitan in Yosemite National Park. Dancing with the Paris Opera Ballet. Playing tennis, curling, guitar, golf, or piano. Balancing candor and curiosity under stress. What do all these activities have in common? You can't just read a book and pull them off competently—you must first acquire the skills.

This is an important point. As I mentioned earlier, too many books and thought leaders succeed at pushing *concepts*—whether they're about conversation, team building, personal effectiveness, management development, or leadership acumen—while failing to provide the *requisite skills*. They're great at telling you *what* to do and *why* to do it, but they disappoint when it comes to showing you *how* to put that advice into action.

This book is different. It doesn't just provide good ideas; it teaches you practical skills for putting those ideas to work. And because acquiring a skill requires practice, in this chapter I'll share a range of ways you can sharpen your ability to stay in the sweet spot when it counts.*

Reminder: Your Personal Plan

One quick note before we move on. As you review these practices, keep in mind the personal plan I'll help you create—a customized strategy for bringing more focus, discipline, and balance to your conversational style. As you review the practices, reflect on the work you'll need to do to get better at crafting a clear position, putting forward your thinking in a lucid way, carefully testing your hypotheses, and inquiring into the hypotheses of others. Your goal is to *identify* the most valuable activities you can adopt to do that work.

Don't stress out about mastering all the skills at once. Focus on the specific skills that will most enhance your overall conversational balance. In this sense, it's like tennis. A tennis player will improve her overall game by identifying a place she needs to improve—her backhand may be a little sloppy or her serve may be a little soft—and then she'll practice that particular skill. By doing drills to isolate the skill, she increases her overall performance on the court. In the same way, identify the skills that'll bring the most balance to *your* conversational behavior, and then make practicing those skills the focus of your personal plan.

Position Practices

Stating your position—where you currently *stand* on an issue—in one or two sentences is the first step in getting an idea out of your head and into a conversation in a well-structured way. Here are a few practices for improving your ability to do this well.

Ask Yourself Questions

What follows is a list of questions to ask as you craft a position:

- *What is my main point?*

---

* My work is heavily influenced by Chris Argyris, a research-practitioner who placed a superordinate value on conducting *actionable* research. If you can't put the research to use, after all, what's the point?

- *Why does it matter? Why do I think it's important?*

- *How do I feel about this issue?*

- *How can I state all this in the most clear, concise, and compelling way?*

- *If I'm torn between two or more options, how can I clearly communicate that?*

- *What if my position is that I don't have a strong point of view on the matter? How can I convey that, explain why, and see if others feel the same way or have a more focused take on the issue?*

- *If my position is more an intuitive feeling than a clear thought, how can I best express that and then check to see if others have a clearer idea about where those feelings might be coming from?*

Write It Down

Before a conversation or meeting, write down your main point three different ways; be as clear, concise, and compelling as possible. Identify the statement that expresses your overall view most effectively. When you're writing an email, a letter, or a proposal, practice *clear position statements*. Whether you're writing or speaking, clear position statements are a pivotal component of effective communication.

Position Exercise

Another great way to build this skill is to read an article in a magazine or newspaper, or watch a news segment, and to then *summarize the main point* of the piece in one tight sentence. If someone asked you, "What was that article about?" how would you distill the main idea down to its essence? You can also do this when listening to people in meetings, at dinner, anywhere. Condense what others say to the clearest and most succinct point you can.

Active Listening

Inquire into the views of others to make sure that you understand *their position*. To do this, provide a one-sentence summary of what you're hearing and then test your interpretation with them: "It seems to me you're saying X. Do I understand your point correctly?"

Have Someone Rephrase Your Point

Explain your view and then ask a colleague or friend to echo back your main point in just one sentence. Sharing your position with a colleague—and having them help you clean it up—can be particularly useful before a conversation or meeting in which you plan to raise an issue.

Listen Carefully to Others

In meetings, dinner conversations, on TV, podcasts, or radio, listen carefully as people talk and observe how they express their points of view. How clearly do they state their position? How might they have said it more clearly? Jot down how you'd say what you think they're trying to say.

Have a Beer

Whenever people are finding it difficult to nail down their position on an issue, an approach I have found useful is to ask them this question: *How would you frame the basic issue or problem if you were talking casually with a trusted friend over a beer at a bar?* If you can relax and just blurt out your impromptu response to that question, you can then work with that raw observation, perspective, or concern. Starting with that quick, casual, off-the-cuff comment can be a very useful way to identify and craft a clear, succinct position statement.

Steve, for instance, might blurt out to a friend: "You wouldn't believe this guy I'm working for now. He's a piece of work. He tells everyone he wants them to tell it to him like it is, but then when you do, he beats you up for it."

Steve could then clean that up by making sure it's clear, concise, compelling, and contains no unnecessary harshness: "Phil, I've never worked for someone who's more open about his need for timely and accurate information as you, and I applaud that. But despite your good intentions, I think you act in ways that makes it really hard for people to do what you're asking."

Constructive Framing

Remember a good position is as direct as possible with no unnecessary harshness. There is a big difference between "No one wants to work with you because you're an arrogant ass," and "Your behavior is limiting your effectiveness because you often push others away with your aggressive style. Let me give you an example and then tell me if you think I'm off base in some way." Practice reframing your position in the most constructive and compelling way possible.

Thinking Practices

By stating a clear position, you're letting others know *where* you currently stand on an issue. When you explain your thinking, you're explaining *how* you got there. Again, this skill is similar to doing long division in elementary school, where you weren't allowed to simply show your answer—you had to show your work. What follows are a few practices and readings you can use to do this in a sharper and more accessible way.

Think About Your Thinking

Ask yourself questions to reflect on the content and caliber of your thinking:

- *Why do I think what I think?*
- *How did I arrive at this point of view?*
- *How have I "gone up the ladder"?*
- *On how much solid ground does my view sit?*
- *How much evidence do I have for this way of looking at the issue?*
- *What do I think the evidence suggests?*
- *What assumptions am I making?*
- *Are there gaps or blind spots in my way of looking at the situation?*
- *Do other people see it differently, and, if so, how did they go up the ladder?*
- *How can I express all this clearly and succinctly so that others see my train of thought?*

Write It Down

A quick way to get clear on your thinking is to assess how you're making sense of an issue by writing it down:

- What *evidence* do I have for this view?
- How am I *interpreting* this evidence?

Watch Your Own Ladder

Watch your mind at work. How? First, read and review Chapter 6 of my book *Conversational Capacity*, which explores my take on the "ladder of inference," a concept that illustrates how your mind makes sense of the world around you. Then pay attention to how your mind goes up the ladder, where your beam of focus tends to drift, and just as important, how your mind responds. (This activity, by the way, doubles as an *awareness* practice.)

When you walk up the street at lunch, for example, recognize what your mind is up to. What is the sensory input? What judgments, thoughts, interpretations crop up? If you notice a tie someone is wearing, for example, and think, "That purple paisley tie pairs poorly with his brown plaid suit," you should recognize the difference between the directly observable evidence (purple paisley tie and brown plaid suit) and your interpretation of that evidence ("pairs poorly").

This practice, which appears deceptively simple, is actually quite a challenging habit to master. Why? Your mind tends to lump *evidence* and *interpretation* together into a jumbled, fuzzy mess. Learning to distinguish clearly between the two is a prerequisite to thinking and speaking more clearly.

Separate Data from Interpretation

You can perform a similar exercise when you read a short article or listen to a news story. As you read or listen, identify the *evidence* being provided and the *interpretations* being employed to make sense of it. Here are questions you can ask:

- *What data do they share to make their point?*

- *How are they making sense of that data?*

- *Is their point of view well-grounded in evidence? Or are they providing a speck of evidence and then taking you on the equivalent of Mr. Toad's Wild Ride with their speculations?*

Questions to Ask About the Views of Others

Learn to see how others are going up the ladder by paying closer attention to their reasoning. Don't do this to be a judge or to convict them of ignorance or stupidity. Do this to genuinely see how they're making sense of a situation. Here are questions you can ask:

- *Why do they think what they think?*

- *How did they arrive at that point of view?*

- *How much evidence do they have for that way of looking at the issue?*

- *What assumptions are they making?*

Get Help

Seek out partners who can help you work through your "business case" before you have a conversation. Other people can be a valuable resource when it comes to clarifying your thinking, as well as how to best explain it.

Strengthen Your Systems Thinking

Increasing your SysQ, a practice I first shared in Chapter 9, is not just a proven way to sharpen your thinking; it also provides a powerful set of tools for *communicating* it. Below are a few short examples. If you'd like to learn more about the following skills and how they can help you think more clearly and communicate your thinking in a more cogent way, a suite of examples and tools can be found at findinghighleverage.com.

BEHAVIOR-OVER-TIME GRAPHS

"I think our situation is less precarious that it seems. *Let me share with you a behavior-over-time graph that shows a longer-term trend that illustrates my point,* and then I'd love to get your reactions, especially where you see things differently."

CAUSAL-LOOP MAPS

"I think this decision will create some vicious unintended consequences. *Let me share with you a causal-loop map that illustrates how I'm making sense of this problem,* and then I'd love to hear from those of you who see it in a contrasting way."

STOCK-AND-FLOW DIAGRAMS

"I think we're focusing on the wrong place to intervene. *Let me share with you a stock-and-flow diagram that describes a more high-leverage way to take action,* and then get your thoughts and reactions, especially if you think I'm missing something."

Draw a Picture

Another potent way to share your thinking is *graphic facilitation*, the use of images, symbols, metaphors, pictures, and visual descriptions to illustrate your mental model. You can do this yourself, but it's often best to employ a graphic facilitator or visual artist to help you with the imagery.

Graphic facilitation (sometimes referred to as *visual facilitation*) can be an efficient and engaging way to explain your current thinking about an issue in a fresh and creative manner so that you can test, expand, and improve it. For more information, visit www.facilitationgraphics.com/.

Readings

Here is a list of readings, books, and resources that you can use to expand your ability to think well:

- *De Bono's Thinking Course* by Edward De Bono
- *How to Think* by Alan Jacobs
- *Smart Thinking* by Art Markman
- *Surely You are Joking, Mr. Feynman* by Richard Feynman
- *Teaching Thinking* by Edward De Bono
- *The Demon-Haunted World* by Carl Sagan
- *Thinking Critically* by John Chaffee
- *Thinking in Systems* by Donella Meadows
- *Thinking, Fast and Slow* by Daniel Kahneman
- *What Do You Care What Other People Think* by Richard Feynman
- Reread Chapter 6: "Conversational Capacity and the Value of Conflict" in my book *Conversational Capacity*

Testing Practices

Testing your views of "reality" is the first and, in some ways, the most important, curiosity skill. It's a form of mental discipline by which you refuse to thoughtlessly accept the picture of reality that your brain hands you.

Conversational capacity, in fact, can be defined as the ability to hold your perspectives hypothetically under pressure. Your ability to treat your view skeptically is a barometer of your focus on learning; it's the essence of putting your workshop mindset into action. But building the discipline to do this takes practice. Here are several ways you can adopt and strengthen this powerful competence.

Watch for Where You Are Wrong

Pay attention to when a view you hold is proven wrong. Feel it. Notice it. Relish it. It's a gift. That discomfort you feel is the sensation of a closed mind being forced to open. "I wonder where my perspective is wrong?" is a priceless question to ask if you are interested in finding the inevitable disconnects between your worldview and actual events on the ground. Why? Because if you're going to make the goal of expanding and improving your thinking, your North Star, the first step is to get in close touch with the limitations of your mind.

Keep an "Indianapolis Journal"

I was driving to the airport in Los Angeles early one morning, listening to the news, when the traffic report noted two major accidents on the 405 freeway. "I'm going to miss my flight," I thought to myself. Sure enough, when I reached the 405 it was a parking lot. I finally arrived at LAX 90 minutes late, raced to the terminal, and got in the security line. As I approached the agent, I nervously glanced at my watch and thought, "It's going to be close, but I might just make the flight." But my optimism was dashed when, after handing the agent my boarding pass, he looked at me, chuckled, and said, "You're at the wrong airport. You're supposed to be at Burbank."

"Dammit! That's right," I thought. It was yet another "Indianapolis moment."

I've found that keeping an "Indianapolis Journal," a practice I first described in Chapter 9, is one of the most powerful (and humorous) ways to build your ability to hold your views more gingerly. I strongly suggest you not just notice when you're hilariously (or not so hilariously) wrong—write those moments down.

To reinforce the value of this exercise, let me share something a client sent me recently:

Wayne Dyer came home from school one day and asked his mum, "What's a scurvy elephant?" She told him she'd never heard of one and asked where he'd heard it. "From my teacher; he said I was a scurvy elephant." Bewildered, his mother called the teacher and asked what he had meant. The teacher responded, "As usual Wayne got it wrong. I didn't say he was a scurvy elephant; I said he was a disturbing element!"

I love this story because it reminds me of my childhood and the mistakes I used to make. How many times did I mishear something and jumped to a wrong conclusion? Sometimes I have constructed whole alternative explanations for things and incorporated them into my reality, only to learn much later that I have got it wrong, and the misconception has collapsed. It is part of growing up and reevaluating what is happening around you. You learn from your mistakes and grow as a person. However, I wonder how many other things I have misheard or misunderstood and built into a false reality, but not yet learned the error of my ways.[1]

Adopt New Self-Talk

Given the wide range of cognitive biases that distort your views and the natural limitations of your brain, assuming that your view is always wrong to some degree is a very safe assumption. To boost your *anti-confirmation bias*, I again suggest you regularly ask yourself a basic question: "What's wrong with my view?" Being more skeptical of your own thinking not only makes it more likely you'll hold your views hypothetically; it also increases your curiosity and your humility. It's hard to be arrogant when you know your views are off-kilter in ways you can't even see. To that end, here are a few questions you can ask yourself to help maintain a healthy distance from the views of the world that your brain presents to you. (Put them in front of you in meetings or conversations, if you have to.):

- *Where am I wrong?*

- *Is there a better way to look at this?*

- *Who sees things differently and how can I get them to respond to my view?*

- *Do other people see it differently, and if so, how did they go up the ladder?*

- *What are the gaps or blind spots in my way of looking at this situation?*

Use a Different Test Every Time

Too much repetition can be construed as inauthentic. Years ago, I worked with a colleague who would use the same test over and over: "How does that seem to you?" Her heart was in the right place, but her repeated use of the same phrase—which isn't a great test to begin with—came across as forced and fake, and people took her less seriously. So, mix it up by never using the same test twice in a meeting or conversation.

Come Up with a Few of Your Own

To keep it fresh, review the sample tests I provide in this book and in *Conversational Capacity* (pages 87–90), and then come up with a few of your own. (To make this easier, I've compiled a list of these tests at https://www .weberconsultinggroup.net/dojo-item/a-great-big-list-of-tests/.) Better yet, come up with a new test every day for a couple of weeks and keep a record of your expanding list. Be creative, and more important, make sure that the tests are authentic and heartfelt, and that they sound like *you*. A good test not included in my previous samples, for example, is this: "While I am wedded to solving this problem, I'm not wedded to solving it the way I just described. So, if you have better ideas, or see problems with mine, I'd love to explore them with you."

Read A Mind of Its Own

When I coach someone with a strong *"win"* tendency I always suggest they read Cordelia Fine's book *A Mind of Its Own*. It provides an engaging overview of the plethora of reasons we *should not* trust our brains.

Best Test

If you have a full team using the skills, you can adopt this approach. At the end of a meeting, vote on who used the "best test" and explore *why*. Be sure to evaluate not just the caliber of the test, but how well it was employed: the person's tone, demeanor, and sincerity.

Leave the Room

This is especially useful if you're in a position of authority and people are less likely to push back on your thinking rigorously, even when you invite them to do so. The CEO of a small engineering firm in Silicon Valley found that even when he started testing his perspectives in engineering staff meetings, his engineers were averse to challenging his thinking for three big reasons: He owned the company; he was an MIT-trained engineer with an intimidating intellect; and he had a strong *"win"* tendency and didn't like to be wrong.

"I was really excited when I learned about this idea of testing my views, so I was really disappointed when it didn't work at first. I realized that if I was going to convince my engineers I was serious I'd need to start with 'training wheels.'" When I asked what he meant, he said, "I purposefully went to a meeting with a big decision. I explained it to my team in detail, and then said, "Before I make this decision, I want you to help me improve how I'm looking at it. To help you do that, here is what I'm going to do: I'm going to leave the room for 30 minutes. When I come back in half an hour I'd like at least three concerns put up on a flip chart and we'll work through them together." He then got up and left. He gave his engineering team time alone to wrestle with the decision so his presence wouldn't get in the way of their conversation. I thought the flip chart was a particularly good idea. It's more neutral territory.

"When I came back to the meeting," he said, "rather than sit at my customary place at the head of the room, I pulled up a chair at the far corner of the table and said, 'So, what did you come up with?' I listened. I asked questions. I took a ton of notes. I could not believe how valuable that was. My next thought was 'Damn it. Is this what I've been missing?' I was hooked. So, I began doing this as a matter of course. Anytime I had a big decision to make, I'd ask my team for input and leave the room. It was working like a charm," he said. "I actually started looking forward to my weekly engineering staff meetings because I was getting so much more value out of them. I did this for several weeks," he said, "and then something funny happened. I got up to leave the room one day and one of my engineers said out loud, 'Look, we talked about this as a team and you can stay if you want. You don't have to leave the room.'"

That is *culture change*. It's a powerful sign that trust—and the conversational capacity of the team—is going up in a dramatic way. And it happened because the CEO was sending a strong and consistent signal that he not only accepted critical feedback from his engineering team, he *valued* it.

Disinvite Agreement

Ask for counterarguments first. This is especially useful if you're in a position of authority and people are less likely to push back on your thinking rigorously, no matter how strongly you test them. "I already know what I think. So, if you agree with me, I'd like you to hold off for a few minutes. To expand and improve my thinking, I first want to hear from a few people who see this differently than I do." Then, after you've listened to people who disagree with you, go back around to explore what people like about your idea.

Thank People Who Challenge Your Thinking

Thank people who push back on your thinking. "Thanks for challenging me there. That was extremely helpful."

Readings

Here are a few great books that will help you loosen your tight hold on the delusion that the way you "perceive" things is the way things really are. Beyond Cordelia Fine's book, *A Mind of Its Own*, I'd also suggest these:

- *Being Wrong* by Kathryn Schulz
- *Don't Believe Everything You* by Thomas E. Kida
- *Mistakes Were Made (but Not by Me)* by Carol Tavris and Elliot Aronson
- *On Being Certain* by Robert Burton
- *The Demon-Haunted World* by Carl Sagan

Inquiry Practices

Genuine inquiry helps you sharpen your own thinking by leveraging the views of others. Here are a few practices to help you hone this potent but underused skill.

Bring Others Down Their Ladder

An effective inquiry asks people to share their "ladder of inference"—how they've made sense of a situation or issue. When someone makes a claim, states a position, or declares a point of view, imagine people up on the "ladder of inference" and then ask questions to help you see how they got up there.

In a meeting, if a colleague blurts out: "That idea doesn't have a snowball's chance in hell of working," you might bring him down the ladder by asking a question such as: "Can you take a couple of minutes and tell the group what leads you to see it that way?" or "Help me out here. What have you seen or heard that leads you to think that's the case?" If the person you're talking with understands the concept of "the ladder of inference," you can simply inquire into the person's view by saying: "Can you bring that down the ladder for me?"

Inquire in Four Ways

In every conversation or meeting, look for at least one opportunity to use *inquiry* in each of these ways:

1. Listen for someone with an unexplained or only partially explained position, and then inquire into their thinking to help get their full perspective into the discussion.

2. Watch for people not participating and invite them to share their views.

3. Notice colleagues who haven't stated a clear position on an issue and invite them to clarify it.

4. Ask a question that expands the conversation:

   - *What might we all be missing?*

   - *Do we have a collective blind spot?*

   - *What might be an unintended consequence of this decision?*

   - *What person or group would likely see this issue differently than we do and what would be their argument?*

   - *What would our worst critic say about how we're approaching this problem?*

Lean into Frustration

"Behind every frustration," says Robert Kegan, "is something cared about."[2] With this in mind, I encourage you to practice getting curious about behavior that would normally put you off. When people get angry, defensive, aggressive, belligerent, or emotional, ask yourself: "What do they care about here?" Then inquire into their view to help them express what's behind their frustrations or concerns: "Isaac, you just called me a dipstick for stating that I liked the decision. You obviously have some strong feelings about this, and I'd like to understand what's behind them. What about this decision upsets you so much?"

Focus Your Beam on the Ideas of Others

Using your *disciplined awareness*, practice keeping your beam of attention locked onto the views of others. In every meeting, see how long you can stay focused on listening to others without drifting off. Get in the habit of periodically reflecting on how curious you're being in the moment.

In the meeting, periodically ask yourself this question: "Am I actively working to understand how others view things?" If the answer is *yes*, keep it up. If the answer is *no*, deliberately shift gears and listen, in a more disciplined way, to how others are *making sense* of things. Pay attention, in other words, to how *curious* you're being in the moment. The surprising difficulty of doing this well is what makes it such a great practice. (This is also a great example of a multi-solving practice: It helps you build your awareness, humility, patience, curiosity, and mental agility simultaneously.)

Reflect

Reflect on your conversations and meetings. Use your travel time, perhaps, to consider questions such as these:

- *How often did I inquire into the views of others?*

- *How curious was I in the meeting today?*

- *Were there things I put forward without testing?*

- *Why? What triggered me to push my view so hard?*

- *How can I become more aware of this the next time it happens?*

- *What was I feeling?*

- *What were the signs that I was sliding toward the "win" side of the sweet spot and losing my curiosity about the views of others?*

- *Next time I notice this happening, what is a more productive way to respond?*

Keep Score

Measure it. Have a colleague keep score of how many times you inquire into the view of another person during a meeting and track your progress.

Come Up with Your Own

As with the testing practice, come up with one new inquiry per day. This will help you build up a repertoire of ways you can curiously delve into the views of others.

Seek Feedback

When you trigger a reaction in someone that you don't expect (someone gets upset, shuts down, acts nervous, or feigns agreement), inquire into the reaction and how you might have contributed to it:

- *I'm inferring you're uncomfortable about discussing this. (Explain.) Is there something about the issue or how I'm talking about it that's contributing to that? Or am I just misinterpreting things?*

- *Is there anything about the way I raised the issue that triggered your reaction?*

- *How can I bring up an issue like this again and NOT trigger the same defensive reaction?*

Readings

Here are a few readings that reinforce this important skill:

- *Appreciative Inquiry* by David Cooperrider and Diana Whitney

- *Humble Inquiry* by Edgar H. Schein

- Reread Chapter 6 in *Conversational Capacity*, "Conversational Capacity and the Value of Conflict," which explores the value of conflicting perspectives.

Want to Learn More?

For a regularly updated list of practices, readings, and other resources, visit conversationalcapacity.com.

PART IV

MOVING FORWARD

*Here is a test to find whether your mission on
earth is finished: If you are alive, it isn't.*

—RICHARD BACH

PUTTING IT ALL TOGETHER

Building Your Skills While Doing Meaningful Work

> *We can change the world and make it a better place.*
> *It is in our hands to make a difference.*
> —NELSON MANDELA

onversational capacity is a skill-based competence and building it requires practice. (If you don't need practice to acquire an ability, then it isn't a skill.) To that end, it's now time to put what you've learned to work.

As I said in the Introduction, the purpose of this book is twofold:

- First, to help you build your *personal* conversational capacity.

- Second, to build a healthier and more productive workplace by doing work that makes a difference.

The first step is to start looking for *opportunities* to do this. Is there a relationship, process, or activity that is pivotal to your team's performance but isn't working as well as it could? There you go. Is there a problem in need of attention or a conflict to be resolved? If so, there's another opportunity.

Your goal is to find a place you can initiate a conversation that sparks an improvement in your team, workplace, or community and to use that work as practice to build your conversational discipline. Then, once you've identified an issue you'd like to address, the next step is to plan for how to engage it effectively. What follows are a few suggestions for how to do just that. (You may have already identified opportunities for practice, but if not, don't fret. In the next chapter, we'll go into even more detail about places to look.)

Three Options

I'm asking you to identify places where there's a gap between how things are currently working and the potential for greater performance. When you find such a gap—like Steve did in Chapter 1—you're immediately faced with a question: "What will I *do* about it?"

You have three basic choices:

1. **Put up with it.** Live with it. Suffer it. Complain about it, perhaps, but don't take action to address it. Maybe you'll get lucky and someone else will take care of the problem, or it'll just magically disappear on its own.

2. **Walk away from it.** Quit. Bail. Move on. "I'm sick of all this nonsense. I'm outta here."

3. **Do something about it.** Adopt a constructive and responsible orientation and engage the problem, and use that work to expand your conversational competence.

When you choose the third option, in the pages that follow I'll share four ways to dramatically increase your odds for success:

1. Collaboratively designing a way forward.

2. Putting together a "Conversational Game Plan."

3. Following the "Basic Discipline" of Conversational Capacity.

4. Facilitating conversations.

What I like to do is try to make a difference with the work I do.
—DAVID BOWIE

Collaboratively Designing a Way Forward

To help you get started, let's revisit a simple approach I've helped many clients employ to improve a wide range of issues: from meetings, decision-making, strategy, and change, to customer service, interpersonal relationships, team dynamics, and management behavior. *Collaborative design*, the form of *inquiry* I first introduced in Chapter 13, is the process of cooperatively working through a problem and mutually designing a way to address it. It's a simple way to structure a conversation about almost any sort of constructive change. I encourage you to consider it as you take what you've learned in this book and start applying it to issues that matter.

Guess or Ask

As I pointed out earlier, when you're making important choices you have two basic options: *guess* or *ask*. When you *guess*, you take unilateral control of the choice, making it based solely on your perspective. When you *ask*, however, you're deliberately designing the best way to achieve the goal by allowing the perspectives of others to influence and shape your ideas and decisions. If your mind is a workshop in which you're producing smart, intelligent, well-informed choices, then *collaborative design* is a powerful part of your *process*.

If you decide to improve the working relationship between your team and another team in the organization, for example, you can either *guess* how to improve the relationship and unilaterally impose your solution, or you can *ask* others for their ideas, input, suggestions, and concerns and then collaboratively design a way forward. This basic choice is true for all sorts of decisions:

- When deciding how to provide useful feedback to someone, you can either *guess* or *ask*.

- When trying to improve your working relationship with a colleague, you can either *guess* or *ask*.

- When deciding how to manage your people so they consistently bring their best work to your team, you can either *guess* or *ask*.

- When trying to figure out how to provide outstanding customer service, run better meetings, orchestrate change, resolve conflicts, bolster innovation, improve a "baton pass" between people or groups, or generate more trust, you can either *guess* or *ask*.

More Of? Less Of?

If you adopt a *collaborative approach*, you can start by stating the problem you're facing and a basic goal, and then pursue the best ways to bridge the gap between the two. A *simple inquiry* you can use to start off the conversation is this: "What do we need *more of* and *less of* to get from point A to point B?"

One team, for example, engaged a challenge this way: "Our meetings receive a steady stream of harsh complaints in our monthly employee survey. They're seen as a big waste of time. So here is what I'd like to explore as a team: What do we need *more of* and *less of* in our meetings so they're half as long and twice as effective?"

They then used the discussion about that question to practice the skills. They started with a conversation focused on the first part of the issue: "What about our current meetings limits their effectiveness?" before moving on to a conversation that focused on solutions: "What changes would help us meet our goal of meetings that are half as long, yet twice as impactful?"

You can adopt the same approach when you raise an issue. Start with the *"more of* and *less of"* frame. Then make suggestions if you have them, taking care to explain and test the thinking behind your suggestions. If others disagree or have different views, *inquire* to learn more about how they're viewing the situation.

The collaborative approach can be challenging. There are often conflicting perspectives, messy conversations, and hard feedback to digest. But if you're driven by the need to make the smartest choices possible, asking is the obvious way to go. As one client once put it: "You can either collaboratively design the solution with the people that matter or you can just dumbass it."

Remember, it's *not* about consensus decision-making, or accepting every idea or opinion. It's about helping make decisions that involve others with more than just your limited perspective as the guide. You're seeking input, not taking directions.

It's Not as Obvious as It Seems

You may think this approach is obvious, but it's far less common than you'd think. Managers often define what makes a good manager—based on the books they've read, the classes they've taken, or the way they've been managed in the past—and then, with good intentions, they impose their definition of a "good manager" on their team. But while their management approach might make perfect sense to them, it may not make sense to the people they're managing. The managers are then baffled when they receive critical remarks about their management style in their 360-degree feedback. One manager complained to herself: "This ungrateful team wouldn't know good management if it fell from the sky and hit them on the head."

Phil provides another example. After receiving feedback that he was too soft on the business, he unilaterally imposed his solution on his team. With the best of intentions, and in a way that made perfect sense to him, he guessed how to solve the problem. It wasn't until after Steve helped him see how his unilateral approach was creating more problems than it solved that they were able to *collaboratively design* a more integrated approach to their predicament.

What Are We Doing to Drive You Nuts?

To give you a better feel for what this looks like in practice, here's an example of the approach being employed in an exceptional way. A program director for an aerospace contractor put together a two-day offsite with their customer, the U.S. Air Force, to improve a strained working relationship. For years, the program had enjoyed a banner relationship between the contractor and their customer, which was held up as a shining example for other programs to emulate. But due to management changes on both sides, things had devolved to the point that the relationship was artificially polite on good days, and acrimonious and argumentative on bad ones. "Both sides are using the contract as a weapon," the program director told me. He wanted this two-day workshop to help turn the situation around.

Ten people from the aerospace firm and an equal number of officers from the Air Force attended the session. On the morning of the first day, after brief introductions and opening remarks, the program director began the hard work: "As we've noted, we're really hoping to use these two days to improve our working relationship. We know we're frustrating you. We don't mean to do it. It's not part of our strategy. We don't start every day by trying to figure out how to make our relationship worse. But we know we're doing it just the same. So to kick-start the process of improvement, we'd like to ask the Air Force a simple question: '*What are we doing to drive you nuts*?' "

There was silence at first, but slowly the officers began to share their concerns. The aerospace team followed up with clarifying questions, such as *"Can you explain how that plays out on your side of the fence?"* The aerospace team captured key details on flip charts. When the officers realized the executives were genuinely interested in their feedback, the momentum grew, and soon they had several pages of issues to address. After categorizing the topics, they broke into smaller groups to address the details, while working hard to stay in the sweet spot.

On the morning of the second day, a colonel asked if he could have the floor. "We were taken aback by what happened yesterday," he said. "We came to this event prepared for a fight. We expected you to throw complaints in our face, and we came armed with a big list to throw right back at you. When you went to the board and asked us, 'What are we doing to drive you nuts?' that really surprised us. We talked in the bar last night and decided we'd like to ask you the same question: 'What's the Air Force doing to drive *you* nuts?'" The Air Force officers captured key responses on flip charts, and then broke into smaller groups, repeating the same process from the previous day.

At the end of the two days, we conducted an evaluation to see how people felt about the offsite. The biggest complaint? There was not enough time to work through all the issues. There was such low defensiveness and such open and constructive dialogue that they scheduled an additional day the following month to work through the remaining issues. This simple but powerful process—coming together to *collaboratively design* a way to move forward in a more healthy and concerted way—became a regular part of their program management best practices, and it helped to restore some of the old shine to their working relationship.

Creating a Conversational Game Plan

Okay, you've identified an issue you'd like to address, and you want to collaboratively design a solution. The next step is to put together your *conversational game plan*—how you'll use the concepts and skills you've been learning to structure and facilitate your conversations. To do that, I encourage you to work through the same five-step process that Steve and his partners used to prepare for his conversation with Phil:

1. **Identify your conversation.** *What is the conversation I need to have to address this issue? And with whom do I need to have it?*

2. **Identify your objectives.** *What are my goals for this conversation? What's the problem I'm trying to solve? What is the ideal outcome I'd like to achieve? What do I want to accomplish?*

3. **Identify your intentional conflicts.** *What intentional conflicts, or "binds," will I experience in the conversation? How, for example, might my need to minimize (min) or "win" (or both) make it difficult for me to stay in the sweet spot? What are the potential triggers I need to watch*

out for? In conversations like this in the past, what has led me to be less effective than I intended to be? (Here are two examples: *"I want to be candid in my discussion with my boss, but I'm worried that she'll react defensively and I'll back down."* Or, *"I want to bring up this issue and work it through with my colleague, but I'm concerned that I'll trigger my need to 'win' and spark an argument."*)

4. **Plan out the conversation.** Given your responses above, think through the structure of the conversation by considering these questions:

    a. *What is my position on the issue? How can I explain it in one or two clear, concise, compelling sentences?*

    b. *How can I explain my thinking so that the other person (or persons) can see how I'm making sense of the issue? Why do I think what I think? What examples can I provide to illustrate my position? What evidence do I have? How am I interpreting that evidence? Why do I feel so strongly about this issue? What is at stake?*

    c. *How will I test my view so that others see I'm holding it like a* hypothesis *rather than a* truth? *How hard will it be for this person to challenge me, to openly disagree, or to share another way of looking at the problem, and how can I test in a way that makes it more likely they'll do it?*

    d. *What are possible reactions to my test, and how will I use inquiry to help others get their views on the table? How will I lean into their reactions, especially where they differ from mine, or are not what I expect? What might be two or three realistic responses I can expect from the person, and how will I use inquiry to respond productively?*

5. **Role-play the conversation.** Practice it. Take it for a test-drive. Like astronauts who prepare for a spacewalk by practicing their moves in a neutral buoyancy simulator (or as President Franklin Roosevelt would probably call it, "a big swimming pool"), you can prepare for your conversation by practicing your moves in a role-play. Ideally you do this with a partner or two. But if that's not possible, mentally simulate the conversation in your head. Imagine the back and forth. Picture yourself enacting your game plan in a focused, disciplined way.

6. **Reflect and assess.** *What did I learn by working through the previous five steps?*

- *"I keep forgetting to inquire when the other person disagrees with my assessment."*

- *"My mind tends to go blank when someone asks me a question that I'm not ready for, so I probably need to keep some notes about my basic view in case I get lost."*

- *"What did I learn? I need more freaking practice. That's what I learned!"*

Priming the Conversation

Before you jump into the conversation by stating your position, it's often helpful to provide a little context so you don't catch other people by surprise, and perhaps make them unnecessarily defensive in the process. To do this you can prime the conversation by describing the issue you'd like to discuss, what you hope to get out of the conversation, and whether or not they're is *interested* in having the conversation. If they're willing to have the conversation, you can next describe any bind you're experiencing. In this way, you're setting a clear context for the discussion and making it far less likely others will misinterpret your intentions. You're *collaboratively designing* how you'll address the issue in the most constructive way possible.

Here's an example:

- *I'd like to talk about the meeting yesterday and provide a little feedback about how you handled it. Is that something you're interested in talking about? If so, is this a good time?*

If the answer is *yes*, respond with this response:

- *My goal here is to be honest and provide some useful feedback so you can make some informed choices about how to move forward. If I come across in a way that's not helpful, please hit the pause button. That's not my intention.*

If the answer is *no*, respond with this question:

- *Would you be willing to talk about this issue at a later time? If not, is there something about the issue, or about me, that makes you reticent to discuss the matter?*

To help you think about how you might set up a specific conversation by providing some *context*, here's a simple template:

- *To start things off, I have a perspective I'd like to share with you and then get your reaction, especially if you see things differently. Does that work for you?*

- *I would like a conversation with you about _____. I think it is important because _____.*

- *My intention is to spend a little time exploring our views around this issue so we can make some smart choices about how to address it.*

- *I do feel like I'm in a bit of a bind. On the one hand, I'm eager to explore how we each see this issue, especially where our views differ. On the other hand, I'm concerned about _____.*

Once you've decided on a way to monitor and manage the concern, kick off the conversation with your position and follow the basic discipline. If at any point the conversation starts to move in an unproductive direction, you can harken back to the primer:

- *I feel like we're falling into the trap we discussed before we started. We're starting to argue and lose curiosity. Let's hit the pause button like we agreed and talk about where we are, how we got here, and how we can get back on a productive track.*

Having the Conversation:
The Basic Discipline of Conversational Capacity

The key now is to stay in the sweet spot as you engage in the conversation, or if you leave it, catch it and quickly regain balance. To do this, here is what the basic discipline looks like when it all comes together.

Catch It, Name It, and Tame It

- *Catch it.* Having cultivated your personal awareness, you're monitoring your emotional and mental reactions in the conversation. You quickly notice when your *min* and *"win"* reactions threaten to separate your behavior and your good intentions.

- *Name and tame it.* Labeling the emotion helps to "brake" the reaction and gives you more control, so as soon as you catch it, name it and tame it: "There's my *minimizing tendency* tugging at me again." Or "There's my *'win'* tendency telling me to argue the point. That didn't take long." Remember, just labeling your emotional reaction has a dampening effect that makes it easier to manage.

Refocus and Replace

- *Refocus. Naming* and *taming* the reaction gives you the ability to refocus on what matters in the conversation: *learning.* So, *mindset forward*, you stay in your mental workshop with your *beam of attention* focused on making the smartest choices possible. To help you do this, you ask yourself three questions:

  - *What am I seeing that others are missing?*

  - *What are others seeing that I'm missing?*

  - *What are we all missing?*

- *Replace.* To keep your behaviors in line with your mindset, you replace your habitual *min* or *"win"* reactions with the appropriate skills for staying balanced. When your need to *minimize* is being triggered, for instance, *the candor skills*—stating your *position* and explaining your *thinking*—will help you retain balance. When your need to *"win"* is being triggered, *the curiosity skills*—*testing* your view and *inquiring* into the views of others—help you stay in the sweet spot. It's not that you ever stop being triggered, it's that when you're triggered, rather than reacting in your habitually defensive way, you choose a more constructive and balanced response.

Reflect and Repeat

- *Reflect.* Once the conversation is over, reflect on your performance

  - *How consistent was my behavior with my game plan?*

  - *How well did I stay in the sweet spot?*

  - *Where did I surprise myself by responding well under pressure?*

  - *In what ways did I respond differently than I used to?*

  - *Where did I drop the ball?*

- *What triggers did I identify?*

- *I notice I triggered to minimize when* _____. *Next time that happens, how will I respond in a more balanced way?*

- *I notice I triggered to "win" when* _____. *Next time that happens, how will I respond in a more balanced way?*

- *What did I learn about myself?*

- *What did I learn about the other people with whom I was talking?*

- *What did I learn about the situation or problem we're facing?*

- *What can I do to be more effective in a similar situation in the future?*

Here's an important point: When you fail, don't get upset, disappointed, or despondent, get curious. View it as an opportunity to break out your *trigger journal* and reflect, learn, plan, and grow.

- *Repeat.* This is the last step in the basic discipline. You don't do this once and stop; you look for another conversation about an important issue to take on. In this way you're *repeatedly practicing* conversation-by-conversation, meeting-by-meeting, day-by-day.

Ed Harris

You never fully rid yourself of the defensive reactions that threaten your competence. That's not the goal. The fight-or-flight tendencies that knock you out of the sweet spot never completely disappear, but you can lessen the power they exercise over your behavior. You can learn to notice them without giving in to them. And by refusing to exercise them, the mental muscles behind them will atrophy from lack of use.

In this sense, you're like John Nash in Ron Howard's film *A Beautiful Mind.*[1] In the first part of the film, Nash, a schizophrenic—played by Russell Crowe—has a tendency to establish close relationships with people who aren't really there. They're figments of his imagination. They're delusions.

As Nash comes to term with his illness, he slowly extracts himself from those relationships. They never fully go away; they still loiter around, waiting for Nash to let them back into his life. Ed Harris's character, the government agent, for example, still lurks around, trying to goad Nash. But while Nash sees him, he refuses to interact with the delusion. By the end of the film, which takes place many years later, Nash is still plagued by his tendency to see people who aren't really there, but his relationship to his predilection is transformed. He manages his delusional tendencies; they no longer manage him.

Your *min* and *"win"* tendencies are like that. They'll never disappear. You can't exorcise them. (Nor would you want to, actually. They're very useful in many circumstances.) No, your "Ed Harris" tendencies will never fully go away, but just like John Nash, with discipline and practice, you can get better at recognizing and managing them.

In this way you're creating an upward spiral of competence, in which thoughtful and disciplined action is followed by reflection and learning, which in turn leads to even more thoughtful and disciplined action. That's the practice, the basic discipline of conversational capacity: Find a problem, an issue, or a place to make a constructive difference. Do your homework and engage it. Reflect on the experience to absorb what you've learned, both about yourself and about the situation you're striving to improve. Then, taking into account your new learning, dive back in and repeat the process.

The "Heads-Up Display"

A helpful way to visualize and share the basic discipline is with what I now refer to as the "heads-up display"—or HUD, an idea suggested by a test pilot who attended one of my workshops. This simple diagram, which I put up on a flip chart when I present, covers all three domains of the discipline:

- *Awareness.* You're monitoring the reactions—yours and others—that threaten to pull a conversation out of the sweet spot so you can *catch it, name it,* and *tame it.*

- *Mindset.* After you *catch it, name it,* and *tame it,* you next *refocus* on learning by intentionally heading into your "workshop."

- *Skill set.* You *replace* your habitual defensive reactions with the behaviors that keep you in the sweet spot. When you notice someone else has left the sweet spot, you respond in a way that helps keep the overall conversation in balance.

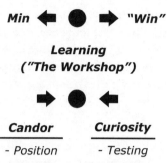

Informal Facilitation

The HUD provides a way to informally facilitate a meeting or conversation, even if no one else in the room is aware of the skills. The test pilot put it this way: "I find that when I'm sitting in a meeting, this simple framework serves as a HUD, or a 'heads-up display.' Because I'm 'looking through' this framework, I'm now picking up on things I didn't used to catch, and as a result I have a range of new choices for how to respond."

The basic idea is to remember Airto Moreira's description of jazz performance: Listen to what's being played and then play what's missing.

- If someone blurts out a strong opinion but doesn't explain it, for example, invite their thinking into the conversation with *inquiry*: *"You've obviously got a strong view on this matter. Take a couple of minutes and explain to the team how you're looking at the situation."* (One person asking a few great questions in this way can alter the course of an entire meeting.)

- If you notice that someone states a view and explains it, but then fails to test it, just jump in and *test* it for them: *"Leilani put a strong view on the table. I'd be interested to hear from others, especially those who have an alternative view."*

- If you have a concern about an idea someone is proposing, put your concern on the table by stating your *position*, explaining your *thinking*, and *testing* your hypothesis. *"I've explained my concern and my thinking, so now I'm interested in hearing from those of you who see a flaw in my analysis."*

- If someone isn't participating in the dialogue, invite him or her in: *"Jose, we've been bouncing this issue around for a while now. I'd be interested in hearing your take on the decision."*

- If someone is heating up and taking more than their fair share of the meeting, you can help bring more balance to the dialogue: *"Rodney's done a good job of sharing how he's looking at this predicament in a clear and passionate way. Let's get a few other perspectives on the table to expand and improve how we're looking at this situation."*

Formal Facilitation

This heads-up display can also help you to formally facilitate better meetings and conversations. You can use the basic framework, for example, to establish a "Conversational Code of Conduct" for the encounter by providing a few ground rules:

> We have several important issues to address here today, and there are strongly differing views about how to address them. We're not going to get much done if people are shutting down and not participating, and we're not going to get much done if we're butting heads and arguing. So that we're using our time as effectively as possible, I'd like to share with you a simple framework for how we can work together in something called "the sweet spot."

You can then write the HUD up on the flip chart, explaining the ideas and skills as you go along, and then use them to facilitate the discussion. By using this simple "heads-up display," either formally or informally, every meeting is smarter because you're in the room.

Where We Go from Here

I try to practice with my life.
—HERBIE HANCOCK

You've now learned a few ways you can turn your workplace into your personal dojo, a space where you can practice and learn every day. I hope you're feeling more empowered to create a team, workplace, organization, or community that is smarter, healthier, and stronger.

As with any practice it takes a lot of effort at first, but as you build your strength and discipline, it'll get easier and easier. To that end, it's now time to take all that you've learned and put together a personal plan for how you will build your conversational capacity while doing something *challenging* and *meaningful*. In the next chapter, *Influence in Action* will become more your book than mine.

YOUR ROAD MAP TO COMPETENCE

Crafting a Powerful Personal Plan

Life is complex. Each one of us must make his own path through life.
There are no self-help manuals, no formulas, no easy answers.
The right road for one is the wrong road for another . . . The
journey of life is not paved in blacktop; it is not brightly lit, and it
has no road signs. It is a rocky path through the wilderness.

—M. SCOTT PECK

Thanks for sticking with me this far. In this chapter, all the learning and reflection you've done up to this point will get personal—literally. I'm going to help you create a *personal plan* for deepening, expanding, and sustaining your conversational capacity. Your personal plan turns this book into a catalyst for continual learning rather than a "read it one time and set it on the shelf" experience.

What Is Your Personal Plan?

Simply put, a *personal plan* is your road map to competence. It's a blueprint for how to bring more intentionality and self-control to how you behave under pressure. This is important. Without a deliberate strategy, your *min* and *"win"* tendencies will continue to get the best of you, no matter how proper and principled your intentions. Think of your personal plan, therefore, *as an ongoing investment in yourself*, in your ability to keep your behavior and your good intentions aligned when it matters, in your emotional and social intelligence, your grit and gumption, and your leadership effectiveness. It's an investment, in other words, in your *conversational capacity*.

What You'll Do

In this chapter, you'll put together a personal plan by doing the following things:

1. Generate "structural tension" by assessing your current state (where you're now in terms of your ability to stay in the sweet spot when it counts), and a vision of where you want to go (the conversational capacity you want to achieve).

2. Identify a meaningful place to practice in what I call the "leadership and learning zone (LLZ)."

3. Select specific practices you'll use to bridge the gap between your current conversational capacity and the capacity you'd like to achieve.

4. Create a progress and accountability strategy to help you stick with the practice.

5. Review an example of a Personal Plan.

Structural Tension

As I mentioned in the Introduction, to create a path forward, you want to be clear about two things: where you are now (your current state) and where you want to be (your desired state).[1] "I call the relationship between the vision and current reality *structural tension*. During the creative process, you have an eye on where you want to go, and you also have an eye on where you currently are," says Robert Fritz, the author of *The Path of Least Resistance*. "There will always be structural tension in the beginning of the creative process, for there will always be a discrepancy between what you want and what you have . . . In fact, part of your job as a creator is to form this tension."[2]

Your personal plan will help generate this creative gap and outline the ways you're going to bridge it.

Your Current State

To assess where you are now, reflect on these questions. I've included space below in case you want to take a few notes:

- *Where do I need to shore up my ability to remain balanced under pressure?*

- *What are the situations in which I'd like to be more conversationally effective?*

- *In what situations do I tend to see daylight between my intentions and my behavior?*

- *Where would I like to wield more influence, or respond more deliberately and less defensively?*

- *Where do I find my effectiveness hijacked by my need to "win"? What are typical triggers?*

- *Where do I find my effectiveness compromised by my need to* minimize? *What are common triggers?*

_____

_____

_____

Your Vision

To generate *structural tension,* you also need to create a compelling vision of your future state. To do this, ask yourself: *"Where do I want to go? What is the level of competence I want to achieve?"* To find answers to these questions, imagine it is six months from now and you're celebrating your progress:

- *What is different about your conversational capacity?*

- *How do you see yourself thinking and behaving differently?*

- *What is the competence you can now demonstrate?*

- *How do other people describe the differences they see in your behavior, especially how you react under pressure? (Your colleagues? The people who report to you? Your boss? Your family and friends?)*

_____

_____

_____

The Leadership and Learning Zone

You now have a view of your current state and your future vision. Your goal now is to close the gap, and that will require practice. To find a spot to perform that practice, I encourage you to look for a place where your personal development goals and the needs of your team or organization intersect. This is your *leadership and learning zone (LLZ)*—the place where your personal goals and the challenges facing your team, organization, or community meet. Your objective is to identify an issue in the LLZ that meets three criteria:

- You care about it.

- It'll make a constructive difference.

- You are in a position to influence it.

220

Organizational Needs and Challenges

If you want to build your competence while exercising leadership, the issues in your leadership and learning zone (LLZ) provide the best place to practice. (If you're going to practice while addressing an issue, after all, it might as well be something significant.) Steve's a great example. He increased his competence while addressing a destructive dynamic in his management team. With the same work, he elevated his own performance and that of his organization. Not bad.

To help you identify a similar opportunity, let me reiterate this idea from the Introduction. Your workplace is full of places to practice:

- *Do you see policies that subvert your organization's strategy or decrease the effectiveness of the workplace?*

- *Do you see management behavior that undermines the goals of the organization?*

- *Are your meetings less than stellar?*

- *Is there an opportunity for improvement that is being missed or ignored?*

- *Are there "baton passes" between people and groups during which people keep dropping the baton?*

- *Are there interpersonal or intergroup relationships in need of repair?*

- *Is the decision-making in your team unclear and inconsistent? Are major problems continually downplayed or avoided?*

- *Is your organization facing hard new realities that people refuse to take on and tackle?*

- *Are people clinging to the status quo when major change is required?*

- *Are there festering conflicts that generate lots of heat and dysfunction but little light and progress?*

If you answered *yes* to any of these questions, you've just identified a place you can practice, learn, and grow.

With all of this in mind, here are a few additional questions to help you identify opportunities in your leadership and learning zone (LLZ). I've included a little space below so you can jot down your ideas:

- *What do I see as the major challenges facing my team or organization?*

- *How adaptive are these issues?*

- *What do others see as the main challenges? Are people on the same page, or do they see things differently? If they do see things differently, why?*

- *Is there a lack of fit between our conversational culture and our organizational strategy?*

- *Are there gaps between what is espoused in the organization and how people actually behave?*

- *Is there a problem with how information flows up and down the chain of command, or between people or groups?*

- *Are there important issues that trigger more arguing and bickering than learning or progress?*

- *Are there important, but undiscussable, issues lurking in the hallways?*

- *Are there festering conflicts eroding morale, trust, and performance?*

- *Are there issues that aren't getting the traction they deserve because there is not enough curiosity in the conversations?*

- *Is there a gap between our strategy and organizational capabilities required to make the strategy work?*

- *Are there places where critical factors such as engagement, trust, or alignment are lacking?*

- *Are there cultural, functional, or other boundaries across which people need to work more effectively?*

- *Where do teamwork, essential work relationships, or organizational performance need improving?*

- *Are there critical processes, important meetings, pivotal decisions, strategic changes, or other important activities that aren't functioning as well as they should?*

Use this list of questions to prime the pump, and consider what opportunities you see in your team, organization, or community.

_____

_____

_____

Your Personal Plan

The measure of intelligence is the ability to change.
—**ALBERT EINSTEIN**

You've been thinking about your current state, your goals, and places for practice. Before moving on, take a few minutes and answer the following questions:

What are your personal conversational capacity development goals in these three areas?

Awareness: _____

Mindset: _____

Skills: _____

What are one or two significant issues in your LLZ that you plan to address?

Okay. You're now ready to pick the practices you'll use to close the gap between where you are and where you want to be. I encourage you to revisit Chapters 5, 9, and 14 to review your options. Your choices should include the following practices:

One practice to start strengthening your awareness: _____

_____

One practice to adopt and strengthen the conversational

capacity mindset: _____

_____

One practice to build a skill that will bring more balance to

your behavior: _____

_____

Don't Overdo It

You might be tempted to do more than just one practice in each area, but I strongly suggest you balance patience with persistence and stick with just one. This is going to be harder than it seems, so don't overdo it. And remember, you're going to be revisiting this process periodically to assess your progress and begin new practices, so you'll have plenty of time to do all the work you'd like.

Progress and Accountability

Don't view this as a simple four-step process: (1) Assess (2) Plan (3) Practice (4) Re-assess. Done. View it instead as an ongoing process of learning. It's an iterative, adaptive development process, not a routine, one-time, check-the-box activity. You don't go through the process once and receive a diploma. You don't ever really graduate. If you're serious about building your conversational capacity, you'll repeat the process over and over.

Take time every three to four weeks to get off the dance floor of your busy office and practice to climb back up to the balcony and ask yourself reflective questions: *How am I doing? Do I need more time on these practices, or is it time to expand my practice and try something new?* Revisit your goals after you've made progress and continue to set higher goals and adopt new practices.

Again, it's like a jazz performance. Rather than having every note in your personal learning plan all scripted out in advance, begin with a set of ideas, start practicing, and then improvise and learn as you go along. Improvisational learning, as Frank Barrett puts it, is "the art of adjusting, flexibly adapting, learning through trial-and-error initiatives, inventing ad hoc responses, and discovering as you go."[3]

Yes, let's see where this leads.
—**FRANK BARRETT**

The idea is to create a feedback loop of learning in which your practice sparks more growth and competence, which in turn leads you to adjust your plan in order to push yourself to even higher levels of performance. The basic process looks like this:

- *Plan.* Identify a practice in each domain to help you move toward your goals.

- *Practice.* Conduct that practice for a specific amount of time as you address an issue in your leadership and learning zone.

- *Assess* your progress. From time to time reflect on these questions:
  - *Where am I now?*
  - *What have I learned?*
  - *How far have I progressed?*

- *Adjust* your plan.
  - *Given my progress, do I need to adjust my goals?*
  - *What practices do I now need to adopt to further close the gap between my current state and future vision on the awareness, mindset, and skill set fronts?*

- *Continue* to practice. Onward and upward you go.

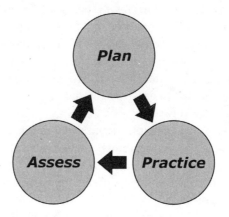

Think of your personal plan as you would an exercise plan. Consider distance running. You don't just get up one day and run a marathon. You start with shorter runs and slowly build up your fitness. In the same way, you don't just read my books, complete my eCourse, or attend a workshop, and immediately master your ability to stay in the sweet spot under pressure. You slowly build up your capacity with regular practice. If you want to join the ranks of elite runners or people with high conversational capacity, you must put in the miles.

The trick is to create a plan and then follow it through. Here are three things that will help you get traction and build momentum:

- Create a "Daily Question List."

- Work with learning partners.

- Schedule your review.

Create a "Daily Question List"

In his book *Triggers*, Marshall Goldsmith outlines a strategy for establishing a new habit called a "Daily Question List" (DQL).[4] A DQL is a list of questions you ask yourself each day to check in about your goals and the work you're doing to meet them. Because you track your answers, a DQL is a great way to hold yourself accountable for your effort and progress. The trick is to ask the right kind of questions. Goldsmith explains that you should avoid *passive questions*:

> When people are asked passive questions they almost invariably provide "environmental" answers. Thus, if an employee answers "no" when asked, "Do you have clear goals?" the reasons are attributed to external factors such as, "My manager can't make up his mind" or "The company changes strategy every month." The employee seldom looks to take responsibility and say, "It's my fault." Blame is assigned elsewhere. The passive construction of "Do you have clear goals" begets a passive explanation.

Goldsmith then nails the point, ". . . passive questions can be the natural enemy of taking personal responsibility and demonstrating accountability. They can give people the unearned permission to pass the buck to anyone and anything but themselves." Put differently, *passive questions* produce *victim-oriented responses*.

He then explains the power of using *active questions* in your DQL: "There's a difference between 'Do you have clear goals' and 'Did you do your best to set clear goals for yourself?' " he says. *Active questions*, in other words, encourage us to take *responsibility*, to hold ourselves accountable, to take stock of our actions relative to our goals, and train our beam of focus on the fit between our goals and our efforts. "Adding the words 'did I do my best?' " Goldsmith explains, injects "an element of *trying* into the equation." *Active questions* produce *responsibility-oriented answers*.

Here is a list of questions you might consider for your DQL. I've also included a question that focuses on *upcoming* learning opportunities:

- *Did I do my best to notice and journal situations in which I was triggered today?*

- *Did I do my best to remain focused in situations where focus was key to my effectiveness today?*

- *Did I do my best to notice a situation in which patterns of behavior, mine or others, and the purpose of the conversation, were out of sync today?*

- *What opportunities for practice will I experience tomorrow, or in the next few days, and how can I take the greatest advantage of those situations?*

Work with Learning Partners

Another practice that Marshall Goldsmith and I both advocate is to select and work with a learning partner. (Goldsmith uses the term *coach*.) A learning partner can be a colleague, friend, professional coach, or even a boss. Your partner can play a variety of roles to help you build your skills and stick with your plan, from more casual conversations about your progress, to daily check-ins and regular feedback. The point is to share with your learning partner all your goals and DQLs, and to invite them to provide as much support as needed to help you along your learning path.

Schedule Your Review

Schedule a regular time on your calendar (every few weeks, perhaps) to review your progress and adjust your plan. If you don't schedule it, you'll likely forget to do it and your progress will grind to a halt. It doesn't matter if you have a membership if you never visit the gym, and it doesn't matter if you have a personal plan if you don't continually use it and revise it.

Example: The Flamethrower's Personal Plan

Imagine that the Flamethrower, the colorful character you met in my first book, created his own personal plan. It might look something like this:

- *Goal and description.* "I want to be more genuinely curious, less stuck in my own views and more open to seeing things through the eyes of others. I'm not doing this to agree with everyone but to learn, and to earn a reputation as someone genuinely collaborative and trustworthy."

- *Awareness practice.* "I need to get better at catching, naming, and taming my reactions, so I'm going to keep a trigger journal."

- *Mindset practice.* "I'll start an 'Indianapolis Journal,' which will have the added benefit of increasing my awareness, and I'll keep the three questions in front of me on a small laminated card."

- *Skill practice.* "Testing my views will make the biggest difference in how I come across to my team, so it's the logical place to start. To get better at doing this, I'm going to create a master list of tests, starting with those Craig has provided, and then add to the list by coming up with new tests of my own. I'll then use these tests every time I put forward a view."

- *My DQL:*

  - "Did I do my best to monitor and document my triggers today?"

  - "Did I do my best to notice and document any 'Indianapolis moments' "?

  - "Did I do my best to test my views today?"

  - "What opportunities for practice and learning will I have tomorrow?"

- *Learning partners.* "I'll share my plan with my entire team and ask them for patience and help. I'll also ask one colleague, Camila, to check in with me every other day, watch me in meetings, and provide feedback on how well or how poorly I'm doing with my goals."

- *Scheduled check-in.* "I've scheduled a review every third Friday of the month for the next six months. This will give me a chance to assess my progress and adjust my practices accordingly."

Short Wrap

"Ambition is the path to success," said Bill Bradley. "Persistence is the vehicle you arrive in."[5] As you practice be persistent and serious-minded, but also remember to be patient and lighthearted, especially when you stumble. Your quest is for ongoing learning and expanded competence, not comfort-seeking or ego-strokes. View the inevitable surprises, frustrations, and slipups as a valuable part of the learning process—as encouraging signs that you're making progress.

If you can muster the discipline to stick with this process, you'll see remarkable growth in your conversational capacity. You'll be better next week than you are this week, better next month than the month before, and better next year than you are this year.

THE ILLUSION OF CONCLUSION

Why Your Leadership Journey Never Really Ends

The purpose of life is to contribute in some way to making things better.
—ROBERT F. KENNEDY

When faced with messy problems in their teams, organizations, and communities, people respond in a variety of ways. At one end of the spectrum sit those, who, when they see a problem, shrink back and say, in essence: "Yes, it's a big problem, but there's nothing I can do. It's not my job. I'm not responsible. I'm not in charge. I'm no expert. I can't make a difference." People in this group often complain about problems, pontificating ad nauseam about what ought to be done, but they rarely stand up, get involved, or do something constructive to address them.

At the other end of the spectrum, there is a smaller but far more influential group of people. When people in this group see a problem, they take responsibility for addressing the issue. They say to themselves: "This won't do. I may not be perfect for the role, and it may not be in my job description, but I'm unwilling to just stand by and do nothing. So, I'm going to roll up my sleeves and engage this problem. Who's with me?"

Little progress comes from the first crowd. It's the largest faction, but it's the least influential. People in this group drift along with the status quo, feeling justified in their inaction because, in their view, nothing will change, improvement is unlikely, and the risks aren't worth the potential for progress. This feeble response spurs no change or improvement because it fails to challenge the existing state of affairs.

All *intentional* progress comes from the people in the second group. It's a much smaller faction, but it's the most powerful. Acting as agents of change, they choose to engage the status quo because the potential for progress justifies the risk of taking action. Motivated by this responsible and constructive orientation, they're willing to put themselves on the line to make a difference.

Take the Lead

My mission in life is to *convert* people in the first group and to *empower* people in the second one. This is important because, as Peter Drucker observed, "the only things that evolve by themselves in an organization are disorder, friction, and malperformance."[1] Meaningful progress is only possible, in other words, when someone takes purposeful action and wields productive influence.

We face a raging onslaught of tough, messy, adaptive challenges in our organizations and communities, and we desperately need more people willing to lead. But we don't just need people *willing* to blunder into difficult situations, armed with little more than good intentions. We need individuals who can do so *skillfully*—people who can engage tough, adaptive issues in a way that provokes more discovery than defensiveness, more collaboration than conflict, and more progress than problems. We need people with the discipline to stay in the sweet spot, and to keep their intentions and their behavior aligned under pressure. We need people with an *affirmative bias*, who say "yes to the mess," people willing to jump in and learn as they go, who lean into difference to spark more learning, and who refuse to shy away from tough issues because they choose progress over feeling comfortable or right.

Imagine it. There'd be far less inhumanity, double-dealing, and underhanded nonsense if more people would speak up in its presence. People, organizations, and communities would be less likely to suffer from injustice, unfairness, incompetence, and malfeasance if there was a larger group of people willing to competently confront these problems.

You Have More Power Than You Think

An *organization* is a community of discourse. Leadership is about shaping the nature of the discourse. And someone exercising real leadership is shaping the discourse in the direction of openness, learning, and constructive progress. My hope is that you now have more power to do this.

⸻ ● ⸻

An organization *is a community of discourse. Leadership is about shaping the nature of the discourse. And someone exercising real leadership is shaping the discourse in the direction of openness, learning, and constructive progress.*

⸻ ● ⸻

"Our power is found in simple acts that bind people together and yield the greatest benefits for the group," says Dacher Keltner. "The difference we make in the world depends on the quotidian: on raising the right question, offering encouragement, connecting people who don't know one another, suggesting a new ideas."[2] No matter your status or station, you can play a leading role in building healthier work relationships, teams, organizations, and communities. *You* can take action and have an impact. *You* can wield greater influence. *You* have more power than you think.

Four Ways You Can Lead

There are four ways you can do this:

1. **Leading UP.** You can exercise leadership up the chain of command by candidly raising issues so that the people upstairs have a clearer view of what's really going on and are in a better position to make wise decisions.

2. **Leading DOWN.** If you're in a position of authority, your challenge is to lead *down* by creating an environment in which people can speak up under pressure and put their best ideas to work.

3. **Leading ACROSS.** You can assume responsibility for leading *across* by reaching out and building bridges to other people and groups.

4. **Leading OUT.** You can lead *out* by working to improve relationships with partner organizations, customers, clients, suppliers, and other vital external entities.

What we need now are heroes and heroines, about a million of them.
—EDWARD ABBEY

It Doesn't End Here

Before I wrap up, I want to highlight a couple of thoughts: First, this is the conclusion of the book, but you shouldn't confuse that with the conclusion of your work and practice. If you're serious about building your ability to work in the sweet spot under pressure, your practice never really ends.

Second, you're not alone. Even if you're the only person in your organization working to build your skills, you don't have to do it by yourself. You can connect with a growing community of people determined to build their conversational capacity by working to make their teams, workplaces, and communities a better place. Visit conversationalcapacity.com to engage with other smart and committed people from around the globe to ask questions, seek help, share best practices, introduce new ones, and provide counsel and encouragement to other like-minded souls.

So here you are, at the end of the book. The question before you now is this: When you see inefficiencies, ineffectiveness, injustices, or other problems, will you just go along with the status quo or will you try and make constructive change? I'm hoping that you're more inclined to do the latter. I'm hoping that you're more likely to point out a better idea, help a team avoid a bad decision, push back against destructive behavior, confront inhumane or inefficient conditions, and support others who are engaged in noble work. I sincerely hope you view leadership and learning as a way of life, that you'll strive to make the world a better place, and, in the process, become a better person.

In short, I hope you're more willing—and more able—to stand up, speak out, and make a difference.

NOTES

INTRODUCTION

1. Dean Williams, *Leadership for a Fractured World: How to Cross Boundaries, Build Bridges, and Lead Change*, San Francisco: Berrett-Koehler Publishers, 2015, p. 3.

CHAPTER 2

1. Leah Weiss, "Mindfulness & Business." CNBC. March 16, 2018, at https://www.cnbc.com/video/2018/03/16/mindfulness-business.html.
2. I'm echoing the idea of Cordelia Fine and her book, *A Mind of Its Own: How Your Brain Distorts and Deceives*, New York: W.W. Norton, 2006.
3. Daniel Goleman and Richard J. Davidson, *Altered Traits: Science Reveals How Meditation Changes Your Mind, Brain, and Body*, New York: Avery. 2017, pp. 76–77.
4. See Sakyong Mipham, *Running with the Mind of Meditation: Lessons for Training Body and Mind, New York: Harmony, 2013*. Also also see Sakyong Mipham, "5 Tips for Running with the Mind of Meditation," *Huffington Post*. April 12, 2012, https://www.huffingtonpost.com/sakyong-mipham-rinpoche/running-with-the-mind-of-meditation_b_1418102.html.
5. Jeffrey Schwartz and Sharon Begley, *The Mind and the Brain*, New York: HarperCollins, 2002, p. 11.
6. Daniel Goleman, *Working with Emotional Intelligence*, New York: Bantam, 2000, p. 22.

CHAPTER 3

1. Dan Siegel, "About Mindsight: An Introduction to Mindsight," dansiegel.com, https://www.drdansiegel.com/about/mindsight/.
2. Daniel Goleman, "Emotional Intelligence," October 4, 2015, http://www.danielgoleman.info/daniel-goleman-how-self-awareness-impacts-your-work/.
3. Daniel Siegel, *Mindsight: The New Science of Personal Transformation*, New York: Bantam, 2010, p. ix.
4. Tasha Eurich, *Insight: The Surprising Truth About How Others See Us, How We See Ourselves, and Why the Answers Matter More Than We Think*, New York: Crown Business, 2018, p. 41.
5. Stephen R. Covey, *The 7 Habits of Highly Effective People: Powerful Lessons in Personal Change*, New York: Free Press, 1989, pp. 30–31.
6. Daniel Siegel, *Mindsight: The New Science of Personal Transformation*, New York: Bantam, 2010, p. xi.
7. Tasha Eurich, *Insight: The Surprising Truth About How Others See Us, How We See Ourselves, and Why the Answers Matter More Than We Think*, New York: Crown Business, 2018, p. 5.

8. Ellie Lisitsa, "Making Sure Emotional Flooding Doesn't Capsize Your Relationship." August 3, 2013, https://www.gottman.com/blog/making-sure-emotional-flooding-doesnt-capsize-your-relationship/.

9. Chris Argyris, *Overcoming Organizational Defenses: Facilitating Organizational Learning*, Boston: Allyn & Bacon, 1990, pp. 12–23.

10. Matthew D. Lieberman, "The Brain's Braking System: And How to 'Use Your Words' to Tap Into It," *Neuroleadership*, University of California, Los Angeles, http://www.scn.ucla.edu/pdf/Lieberman%28InPress%29Neuroleadership.pdf.

11. David Rock, "Leadership on the Brain," *Harvard Business Review*, April 28, 2010, https://hbr.org/2010/04/leadership-on-the-brain.

12. Matthew D. Lieberman, "The Brain's Braking System: And How to 'Use Your Words' to Tap Into It," Neuroleadership, University of California, Los Angeles, http://www.scn.ucla.edu/pdf/Lieberman%28InPress%29Neuroleadership.pdf.

13. Daniel Goleman, *Emotional Intelligence: Why It Can Matter More Than IQ*, New York: Bantam, 1995, p. 10.

14. Tasha Eurich, *Insight: The Surprising Truth About How Others See Us, How We See Ourselves, and Why the Answers Matter More Than We Think*, New York: Crown Business, 2018, pp. 4–5.

CHAPTER 4

1. Airto Moreira, Personal Interview, April 8, 2011. I approached Airto Moreira based on a previous conversation with Paul Cicco, who originally called my attention to the quote.

2. Jeff Bacon, "Lt Col Hughes—'Take a knee,'" The Broadside Blog, *Navy Times*, April 11, 2007, http://broadside.navytimes.com/2007/04/11/ltcol-hughes-take-a-knee/.

3. Daniel Goleman, *Focus: The Hidden Driver of Excellence*, New York: Harper, 2013, p. 99.

4. For a more thorough exploration of cognitive and emotional empathy, I'd suggest reading Chapter 10, "The Empathy Triad," in Daniel Goleman, *Focus: The Hidden Driver of Excellence*, New York: Harper, 2013.

5. Edward L. Thorndike, "Intelligence and Its Uses," *The Harpers Monthly*, January 1920, https://harpers.org/archive/1920/01/intelligence-and-its-uses/.

6. For a rigorous exploration of the concept of "asshole" see Aaron James, *Assholes: A Theory*, New York: Doubleday, 2012, or Robert I. Sutton, *The Asshole Survival Guide: How to Deal with People Who Treat You Like Dirt*, Boston: Houghton Mifflin Harcourt, 2017.

CHAPTER 5

1. Chade-Meng Tan, "Just 6 Seconds of Mindfulness Can Make You More Effective," *Harvard Business Review*, December 30, 2015, https://hbr.org/2015/12/just-6-seconds-of-mindfulness-can-make-you-more-effective.

2. Sue Shellenbarger, "Tuning In: Improving Your Listening Skills: How to Get the Most Out of a Conversation." *The Wall Street Journal*. Updated July 22, 2014, https://www.wsj.com/articles/tuning-in-how-to-listen-better-1406070727.

3. Ellen Langer, "Mindfulness in the Age of Complexity," *Harvard Business Review*, March 2014, https://hbr.org/2014/03/mindfulness-in-the-age-of-complexity.

4. Gretchen Reynolds, "How Walking in Nature Changes the Brain," *New York Times*, July 22, 2015, https://well.blogs.nytimes.com/.

5. Gregory N. Bratmana, Gretchen C. Daily, Benjamin J. Levy, and James J. Gross, "The benefits of nature experience: Improved affect and cognition," https://www.sciencedirect.com/science/article/pii/S0169204615000286.

6. Alex Hutchinson, "How Trees Calm Us Down," *The New Yorker*, July 23, 2015, https://www.newyorker.com/tech/annals-of-technology/what-is-a-tree-worth.

7. Nora Isaacs, "Bring More Mindfulness onto the Mat," *Yoga Journal*, Oct 21, 2008https://www.yogajournal.com/practice/peace-of-mind.

8. Srini Pillay, "Your Brain Can Only Take So Much Focus," *Harvard Business Review*, May 12, 2017, https://hbr.org/2017/05/your-brain-can-only-take-so-much-focus.

9. Robert Wright, *Why Buddhism Is True: The Science and Philosophy of Meditation and Enlightenment*, New York: Simon & Schuster, 2017, p. 20.

CHAPTER 6

1. Cordelia Fine, *A Mind of Its Own: How Your Brain Distorts and Deceives*, New York: W.W. Norton, 2006, p. 202.

2. Madeleine L. Van Hecke, *Blind Spots: Why Smart People Do Dumb Things*, New York: Prometheus Books, 2007, p. 19.

3. Nate Silver, *The Signal and The Noise*, New York: The Penguin Press, 2012, pp. 232–261.

4. Roger Martin, *The Opposable Mind: How Successful Leaders Win Through Integrative Thinking*, Boston: Harvard Business Review Press, 2007, pp. 123–124.

5. Ibid., 125

6. Margaret Heffernan, "Dare To Disagree," Ted Talk, https://www.ted.com/talks/margaret_heffernan_dare_to_disagree?

7. Martin, 15.

8. Martin, 9–13.

9. Martin, 6.

10. Gordon Pennycook, James Allan Cheyne, Nathaniel Barr, Derek J. Koehler, and Jonathan A. Fugelsang, "On the reception and detection of pseudo-profound bullshit," *Judgment and Decision Making*, Vol. 10, No. 6, November 2015, pp. 549–563, http://journal.sjdm.org/15/15923a/jdm15923a.pdf.

11. Ibid., 549

12. Emily Willingham, "Why Do Some People Find Deepak Chopra Quotes Deep and Not Dung?" *Forbes*, Nov 30, 2015, https://www.forbes.com/sites/emilywillingham/2015/11/30/why-do-some-people-find-deepak-chopra-quotes-deep-and-not-dung/#3a8689c91f02.

13. Richard Feynman, *What Do You Care What Other People Think? Further Adventures of a Curious Character*, New York: W. W. Norton & Company, 1988, pp. 163–164.
14. Amy Gallo, "How to Deliver Bad News to Your Employees," *Harvard Business Review*, March 30, 2015, https://hbr.org/2015/03/how-to-deliver-bad-news-to-your-employees.

CHAPTER 7

1. Again, for a more rigorous exploration of the concept of "asshole" see Aaron James, *Assholes: A Theory*, New York: Doubleday, 2012, or Robert I. Sutton, *The Asshole Survival Guide: How to Deal with People Who Treat You Like Dirt*, Boston: Houghton Mifflin Harcourt, 2017.
2. Frank Barrett, *Yes to the Mess: Surprising Leadership Lessons from Jazz*, Boston: Harvard Business Review Press, 2012.
3. Jim Collins, *Good to Great: Why Some Companies Make the Leap and Others Don't*, New York: Harper Business, 2001, p. 84 (italics mine).
4. Richard Bach, *Illusions* (mass paperback), New York: Dell, 1989, p. 100.
5. Alex Lifeson, as quoted in Josh Dehaas, "Advice for students from the rock band Rush," Macleans, June 13, 2014, https://www.macleans.ca/education/uniandcollege/advice-for-students-from-the-rock-band-rush/.
6. Emile Lahti, "What Is Sisu?" https://www.emilialahti.com/what-is-sisu.
7. Barrett, 12
8. Barrett, 41–65.
9. Dean Williams, *Leadership for a Fractured World: How to Cross Boundaries, Build Bridges, and Lead Change*, Oakland, CA: Berrett-Koehler Publishers, 2015, pp. 173–174.
10. Barrett, 112.
11. Williams, 173–176.
12. Barrett, 110.

CHAPTER 8

1. Brian Tracy, "This Personal Power Formula Will Change Your Life," https://www.briantracy.com/blog/personal-success/this-personal-power-formula-will-change-your-life/.
2. Carol Dweck, "What Having a 'Growth Mindset' Actually Means," *Harvard Business Review*, January 13, 2016, https://hbr.org/2016/01/what-having-a-growth-mindset-actually-means.
3. Constitutional Rights Foundation, "Slavery in the American South," http://www.crf-usa.org/black-history-month/slavery-in-the-american-south.
4. Edward A. Miller, Jr., *Gullah Statesman*. Columbia, SC: University of South Carolina Press, 1995, pp. 1–8.
5. Henry Louis Gates, Jr., "The African Americans: Which Slave Sailed Himself to Freedom?," PBS.org, http://www.pbs.org/wnet/african-americans-many-rivers-to-cross/history/which-slave-sailed-himself-to-freedom/.

6. Miller, Jr., 3.

7. M. Scott Peck, *The Road Less Traveled: A New Psychology of Love, Traditional Values, and Spiritual Growth*, New York: Simon and Schuster, 1978, p. 37.

8. Erich Fromm, *The Heart of Man: It's Genius for Good and Evil*, New York: Harper & Row, 1964, pp. 37–61.

9. Michael Lewis, "The Wolf Hunters of Wall Street," *New York Times Magazine*, March 31, 2014, https://www.nytimes.com/2014/04/06/magazine/flash-boys -michael-lewis.html.

10. First People: American Indian Legends, https://www.firstpeople.us/FP-Html -Legends/TwoWolves-Cherokee.html.

CHAPTER 9

1. Cordelia Fine, *A Mind of Its Own: How Your Brain Distorts and Deceives*, New York: W.W. Norton, 2006. p. 23.

2. Kathryn Schulz, *Being Wrong: Adventures in the Margin of Error*, New York: HarperCollins, 2010, p. 20.

3. I paraphrased this line from Roger Martin, *The Opposable Mind: How Successful Leaders Win Through Integrative Thinking*, Boston: Harvard Business Review Press, 2007, p. 16.

4. Martin, 9–13.

5. Madeleine L. Van Hecke, *Blind Spots: Why Smart People Do Dumb Things*, New York: Prometheus Books, 2007, pp. 239–240.

6. Dean Williams, *Real Leadership*. San Francisco: Berrett-Koehler, 2001, p. 256.

7. Peter Economy, "This Navy SEAL Says Your Lack of Motivation Does Not Matter (but This 1 Thing Does Big Time)," Inc.com, September 6, 2017, https:// www.inc.com/peter-economy/good-news-a-navy-seal-says-your-lack-of -motivation.html.

8. Nathan DeWall, "I Went From Sedentary Academic To 100-Mile Marathon Runner—thanks to the science of self-control," *Quartz*, July 2, 2017, https:// qz.com/1019928/i-went-from-sedentary-academic-to-100-mile-marathon -runner-thanks-to-the-science-of-self-control/?utm_source=atlfb.

9. Loretta Breuning, "How to Train Your Brain to Go Positive Instead of Negative," Forbes.com, December 21, 2016, https://www.forbes.com/sites /womensmedia/2016/12/21/how-to-train-your-brain-to-go-positive-instead -of-negative/2/#14ed35025e55.

10. I'm echoing the work of Albert Ellis with this list. For a thorough overview of his ideas about contesting the negative and "nutty" thinking that warps our decision-making and creates a range of psychological and emotional disturbances, see Albert Ellis and Robert Allan Harper, *A New Guide to Rational Living*, North Hollywood, CA: Wilshire Book Company, 1975.

11. Fred Rogers, "Look for the Helpers," https://www.youtube.com/watch?v= -LGHtc_D328.

12. Frank Barrett, *Yes to the Mess: Surprising Leadership Lessons from Jazz*, Boston: Harvard Business Review Press, 2012, p. 49.

13. Emma Seppala and Adam Rifkin, "The Surprising Science of Why You'll Get More Done by Having Fun," December 10, 2014, http://www.fulfillmentdaily .com/surprising-science-youll-get-done-fun/.

14. The Association for Psychological Science, "The Energizing Effect of Humor," January 19, 2016, https://www.psychologicalscience.org/news/minds -business/the-energizing-effect-of-humor.html.

CHAPTER 10

1. Chris Argyris, *Flawed Advice and The Management Trap*, New York: Oxford University Press, 2000.

2. Dacher Keltner, *The Power Paradox*, New York: Penguin, 2016, p. 11.

3. Elizabeth Abrams, "Topic Sentences and Signposting," Harvard College Writing Center, 2000, https://writingcenter.fas.harvard.edu/pages/topic -sentences-and-signposting.

4. Topic Sentence, http://www2.actden.com/writ_den/tips/paragrap/topic .htm.

5. Dorothy Turner, "Writing Topic Sentences," The Writing Center, University of Ottawa, http://www.writingcentre.uottawa.ca/hypergrammar/partopic .html.

6. "Essay Writing Skills: Topic Sentences," RMIT University. https://www.dlsweb .rmit.edu.au/lsu/content/2_assessmenttasks/assess_tuts/essay_LL/structure /topic.html.

7. Turner.

8. Turner.

9. Turner.

10. William Zinsser, *On Writing Well: An Informal Guide to Writing Nonfiction*, New York: Wildside Press, 1996, p. 23. [Parenthetical comment is my own.]

11. Zinsser, pp. 8–9.

12. Thomas Kane, *The New Oxford Guide to Writing*, New York: Oxford University Press, 1988, p. 140.

13. William Strunk and E.B. White, *The Elements of Style*, (fourth edition), New York: Longman, 1999, p. 23.

14. Strunk and White, p. 21.

CHAPTER 11

1. Craig Weber, *Conversational Capacity: The Secret to Building Successful Teams that Perform When the Pressure Is On*, New York: McGraw-Hill Education, 2013, pp. 121–140.

2. I cannot use the phrase "mental maps" without giving credit to M. Scott Peck, *The Road Less Traveled: A New Psychology of Love, Traditional Values, and Spiritual Growth*, New York: Simon and Schuster, 1978, pp. 25–27.

3. Francis Flaherty, *Elements of Story*: *Field Notes on Nonfiction Writing*, New York: HarperCollins, 2009, p. 59.

4. Antonio Damasio, *Descartes Error: Emotions, Reason, and the Human Brain*, New York: Penguin Books, 1994, pp. 52–79.

5. Remmers, C., Topolinski, S., and Michalak, J. (2015). Mindful(l) intuition: Does mindfulness influence the access to intuitive processes?, *The Journal of Positive Psychology*, 10(3), 282–292. doi:10.1080/17439760.2014.950179.

6. Carl Sagan, *The Demon-Haunted World: Science as a Candle in the Dark*, New York: Random House, 1995.

7. Sagan, p. 10.

CHAPTER 12

1. The Online Etymological Dictionary, "Test," https://www.etymonline.com /word/test.

2. Kathryn Schulz, *Being Wrong: Adventures in the Margin of Error*, New York: HarperCollins, 2010, p. 5.

3. Harry Frankfurt, *On Bullshit*, Princeton: Princeton University Press. 2005.

4. Edward De Bono, *Six Thinking Hats: An Essential Approach to Business Management*, Boston: Little, Brown, 1985.

5. Nick Hornby, *A Long Way Down*, New York: Riverhead Books, 2005, pp. 304–307.

6. Cordelia Fine, *A Mind of Its Own: How Your Brain Distorts and Deceives*, New York: W.W. Norton, 2006, p. 208.

CHAPTER 13

1. Online Etymological Dictionary, "Inquire," https://www.etymonline.com /word/inquire.

2. Frank Barrett and Ronald Fry, *Appreciative Inquiry: A Positive Approach to Building Cooperative Capacity*, Taos, NM: Taos Institute Publications, 2005, p. 36.

3. Edgar H. Schein, *Humble Inquiry: The Gentle Art of Asking Instead of Telling*, San Francisco: Berrett-Koehler, 2013, p. 2.

4. Craig Weber, *Conversational Capacity: The Secret to Building Successful Teams That Perform When the Pressure Is On*, New York: McGraw-Hill Education 2013, pp. 94–97.

5. M. Scott Peck, *The Road Less Traveled: A New Psychology of Love, Traditional Values, and Spiritual Growth*, New York: Simon and Schuster, 1978, pp. 86–87.

6. This is a line from the jury member, played by Edward James Begley Sr, in the film *12 Angry Men*. Directed by Sidney Lumet, Westinghouse Studio One. 1957. Film.

7. Laurie Tarkandec, "Arrogant, Abusive and Disruptive—and a Doctor," *New York Times*, December 1, 2008, https://www.nytimes.com/2008/12/02/health /02rage.html.

8. Ann Coulter, "Protests Force Columnist Coulter to Stop Speech." NBCnews .com, December 8, 2005, http://www.nbcnews.com/id/10379693/ns/us_news -life/t/protests-force-columnist-coulter-stop-speech/.

9. I borrowed this phrase from my energetic young neighbor, five-year-old Cali Sosebee.

10. Dacher Keltner, *The Power Paradox*, New York: Penguin, 2016, p. 34.

CHAPTER 14

1. Bruce Thompson, "Scurvy Elephants and Childhood Misconceptions," December 6, 2010, http://brucethompsoncoaching.com/main/scurvy -elephants-and-childhood-misconceptions/.
2. Robert Kegan, from the personal lecture notes of the author, Workplace Learning Institute, Teachers College, Columbia University, 1996.

CHAPTER 15

1. *A Beautiful Mind*. Directed by Ron Howard, Universal Pictures, 2001. Film.

CHAPTER 16

1. For more on this concept, see Robert Fritz, *Path of Least Resistance: Learning to Become the Creative Force in Your Own Life*, New York: Ballantine Books, 1989.
2. Robert Fritz, *"Tensions Seeks Resolution,"* Robertfritz.com, http://www .robertfritz.com/wp/principles/tension-seeks-resolution/.
3. Frank Barrett, *Yes to the Mess: Surprising Leadership Lessons from Jazz*, Boston: Harvard Business Review Press, 2012, p. 12.
4. Marshall Goldsmith, *Triggers: Creating Behavior That Lasts—Becoming the Person You Want to Be*, New York: Crown Business, 2015, pp. 101–124.
5. Bill Bradley, AZ Quotes. https://www.azquotes.com/author/1780-Bill _Bradley.

CHAPTER 17

1. Peter Drucker, quoted in Joan Magretta, *What Management Is*, New York: The Free Press, 2002, p. 132.
2. Dacher Keltner, *The Power Paradox*, New York: Penguin, 2016, p. 34.

INDEX

ABOUT THE AUTHOR

CRAIG WEBER is the founder of The Weber Consulting Group, an alliance of experts committed to helping people build healthy, engaged, and adaptive organizations. He shows people and teams how to improve their performance by treating dialogue as a discipline. An award-winning consultant, advisor, and speaker, he has worked with leaders and teams from 40 different countries and from such diverse organizations as: Boeing, Kaiser Permanente, Royal Bank of Canada (RBC), Ingram Micro, Pfizer, SAP, Pancreatic Cancer Action Network (PanCAN), The Medical University of South Carolina, Clif Bar, PricewaterhouseCoopers (PwC), NASA, Los Alamos National Laboratory, Centers for Disease Control and Prevention (CDC), the U.S. Air Force, and Vistage International, among others. He is the author of *Conversational Capacity: The Secret to Building Successful Teams That Perform When the Pressure Is On*.

To learn more about Craig's unique work, visit
www.conversationalcapacity.com

Open, Balanced Dialogue—
The Key to Peak Team Performance

Print ISBN: 978-0071807128
Ebook ISBN: 978-0071807135